Gз

Er

Critical Dance Studies

edited by Gabriele Bra   me 21

D0234677

Gabriele Klein, Sandra Noeth (eds.)

Emerging Bodies

The Performance of Worldmaking in Dance and Choreography

[transcript]

The publication was kindly supported by the Department for Human Movement Studies/University of Hamburg

Bibliographic information published by the Deutsche Nationalbibliothek
The Deutsche Nationalbibliothek lists this publication in the Deutsche Nationalbibliografie; detailed bibliographic data are available in the Internet at http://dnb.d-nb.de

© 2011 transcript Verlag, Bielefeld

Cover concept: Kordula Röckenhaus, Bielefeld
Proofread by Gabriele Klein, Lejla Mehanovic, Sandra Noeth
Translated by ehrliche arbeit – freelance office for culture/Berlin
Typeset by Lejla Mehanovic
Printed by Majuskel Medienproduktion GmbH, Wetzlar
ISBN 978-3-8376-1596-8

Global distribution outside Germany, Austria and Switzerland:

Transaction Publishers
New Brunswick (U.S.A.) and London (U.K.)

Transaction Publishers
Rutgers University
35 Berrue Circle
Piscataway, NJ 08854

Tel.: (732) 445-2280
Fax: (732) 445-3138
for orders (U.S. only):
toll free 888-999-6778

Contents

DIGITAL WORLDS – PROCESSING BODIES

WORKING PRINCIPLES

Introduction

GABRIELE KLEIN, SANDRA NOETH

In Europe, dance has brought forth a multitude of new 'worlds' over the last few decades, especially in Germany against the backdrop of *Tanzplan Deutschland*[1]: dance houses, dance centers, dance forums, dedicated completely or in the context of other arts to dance and choreography; mobile self-organized, often temporary artist collectives, which are not limited to a certain region; new education programs at art academies and universities; academic and artistic research, not only in dance theory and as a result newly generated discourses; professional journals on dance and choreography, some of them residing in the digital realm; artistic work in dance projects at schools, in other educational and cultural institutions or in urban areas and public spaces. These examples demonstrate that contemporary dance has visibly gained importance in the fields of culture, education, art and academia in spite of its often precarious financial situation and meager lobby in educational and cultural policy. This new public attention for contemporary dance is connected to a number of changes within the dance scene: the differentiation and diversification of the European experimental dance scene and its audiences, a reflection of former historical, as well as contemporary fundamental assumptions about and categorizations of dance, new experiments with forms of collaboration, changing approaches to the concepts of practice and theory, a shift in the understanding of working and research processes.

---

1   *Tanzplan Deutschland* (Dance Plan Germany) was an initiative of the German Federal Cultural Foundation. From 2005 until 2010, the project acted as a catalyst for the German dance scene. Equipped with a budget of 12.5 million Euros, its goal was to provide dance in Germany. In 2006 and 2009 the German Federal Cultural Foundation hosted two Dance Congresses in Berlin and Hamburg which also came within the ambit of *Tanzplan Deutschland* (cf. Tanzkongress.de; Tanzplan-Deutschland.de).

Since the 1990s, the 'world of dance', so it seems, is (once again) in a productive crisis.

In this historical situation, all players in the dance field, be they dancer, choreographer, dance theorist, curator or scholar are faced with the challenge of handling a diversity of resources, processes, concepts, discourses and aesthetics. The concurrence of various differing frameworks of reference, discursive paradigms and institutional forms, the hybridity of dance identities and the simultaneous necessity of permanent (self)positioning create problems and para-doxes, which in turn are framed by the 'new globalized world' of post-Fordian modes of production, the globalized economy and the neo-liberal state. It is therefore no coincidence that contemporary dance is (again) directing its focus towards the processes that creating the world(s) in which we live, our 'being-in-time' – between affiliation and detachment, presence and absence, immediacy and mediation, particularity and the demand for universality, temporality and contingence. *How* are 'dance worlds' created? Is there an intrinsic logic to these 'dance worlds'? *How* can 'we' speak and write about them? And how does the knowledge of these worlds become socially effective?

In his book *Ways of Worldmaking*, Nelson Goodman succinctly states: "If attempts to answer the question 'What is art?' characteristically end in frustrati-on and confusion perhaps – as so often in philosophy – the question is the wrong one." (Goodman 1978: 57) Goodman avoids the ontologization of the question "What is art?" by asking "When is art?". This volume of essays also seeks to answer the question of 'dance worlds' by doing more than inquiring into their properties, but by instead examining their operative logic and the strategies of their production in specific historical and cultural contexts. In doing so, questions concerning the 'nature' of 'dance worlds' fade from the spotlight in favor of an interest in how – and if – the performative production of 'dance worlds' is different from other ways of worldmaking.

The idea underlying Goodman's concept of "worldmaking" is that 'world' is not given, but a process of creation: 'world' is thus, according to the basic epistemological premise, made when actions and language bring forth meanings. Worldmaking is therefore always social, cultural, religious, framed, historically in flux and reliant on scientific and philosophical discourses and experiences. It does not only relate to one 'world' and cannot be comprehended in totality: dif-ferent ways of worldmaking provoke different, interlocking worlds. World, originally a singular word, which only came into use in the plural sense end of the 16th century, here disintegrates into multifarious and yet structured concepts of world. In his symbol-theoretical approach, inspired by Ernst Cassirer's philo-sophy of symbolic forms, Goodman concludes that we live in as many worlds as symbolic ways of worldmaking, i.e. linguistic or figuratively conveyed ways permit. However, which worlds are created with corporeal and dance-aesthetic methods? This question is not primarily directed at interpreting productions and dance pieces in the traditional academic sense, but instead seeks to focus on performative processes of the generation of meaning and, in doing so, concentrate on processes that organize the – possibly dance specific – creation of (social) meaning.

Over the course of the 20th century, dance in the modern age has addressed such relationships as fundamentally discussed in the topos of "worldmaking" – nature and culture, reality and the image, objectivity and subjectivity – in various ways. Parts of German Expressionist Dance and American Postmodern Dance at the beginning of the 20th century presumed that the way the body dealt with inner, as well as outer nature contained an incontestable certainty of being and thus regarded 'world' as given in an act of dance that was felt to be natural. Meanwhile, other dancers and choreographers – such as Oskar Schlemmer, who was active at Bauhaus – searched for formal and structural principles of constructing the body and choreography. In the 1960s, first in so-called postmodern dance and in computer animated dance, which developed in close connection with cybernetics, and also in other ways in the dance theater of the 1970s, the art of dance reflected prior aesthetic strategies of worldmaking as dance is capable of creating as a specific practice of movement and choreography and a specific way of organizing of movement, as well as arranging space and time. In doing so, new aesthetic positions of dance emerged, which interpreted the questions of accessing and creating world differently: less as phenomenally given or anthropological fixed points, but rather as subjective positions or as political-aesthetic strategies and transcultural practice. Since the 1990s, the question of "worldmaking" has gained new meaning in the face of globalization and trans-nationalization, which finds its expression in the humanities e.g. in the discussion on the concept of "global history" (cf. Foster 2009) or the establishment of *postcolonial studies* in international dance research. It has found expression in those styles, which have been written into dance history as post-structural dance or conceptual dance.

This volume is based on the assumption that dance reveals its effectivity not in the representation of existing structures and systems, but unfolds its potentiality precisely in the offering of alternatives, of utopias, developed with the help of the body and through the organization of movement. It therefore focuses on the challenges and the possibilities that lie in "ways of worldmaking" in dance. It asks how dance creates 'world' as a medium bound to the body and whether and how these processes and strategies differ from those of other arts and sciences. A central motif that pervades the history of modernity and has been supported by the performative-theoretical approaches of the last few years is especially up for critical debate: that dance is an ephemeral, elusive medium, which creates 'world' in contrast with other media via the body and its ambiguous 'languages' and forms of expression; a world that has aspects of instantaneity. Critical involvement with the motif of the 'ephemeral' and of elusiveness is of central importance for dance research when inquiring into the 'how' of worldmaking. But it is also of epistemological urgency, considering that dance, as a medium of the body and presence, can be seen as a field of knowledge par excellence for research into how certainty about the world is created between the poles of perception, imagination, action and cognition.

The contributions inquire into how 'worlds' are made in dance. In doing so, they discuss specific worlds of production, perception and experience in dance and choreography and examine them from an interdisciplinary perspective. Against the backdrop of current theoretical approaches in the fields of social, cultural and media studies, aesthetic theory and philosophy, the specific worldmaking of dance and choreography is compared to other art forms and the research methods. In addition, forms of knowledge as practiced in the sciences are brought into relationship with those forms of knowledge, which can be found in artistic forms of working.

The subsection *social realms* brings together articles by Gabriele Klein, Randy Martin and Bojana Kunst. These are complemented by a conversation with the artist group LIGNA.

Gabriele Klein discusses various forms of worldmaking in dance and choreography. She focuses on the relationship of politics and aesthetics in contemporary dance and its historical genesis, as she inquires into the political and social significance of dance and the articulation of the political in artistic processes, dance aesthetics and discourses.

Randy Martin describes how dance moves between the poles of intervening practice and a conceptual definition of the future and how multiple notions and forms of the political become visible in dance. He defines the dance ensemble as a form of ideal community, the dance performance as a place in which artists and audience assemble, thus making it also, much like a political demonstration, ephemeral.

Bojana Kunst's contribution focuses on the organization of movement and work in the 20th century. Her argument is that due to changing production conditions, dance formulated concepts of freedom and future, which, because of the way that movement engages time and space, not only allowed an aesthetic, but also the social and political potential of transgression to become recognizable.

In the performative audio play *Der Neue Mensch* (*The New Human*), which was performed during the Dance Congress 2009, the artist group LIGNA employed movement instructions and multiple shifts of perspective and roles. In a conversation with Sandra Noeth, they describe the choreographic processes involved in producing a collective body by questioning the relationship of audience and action, as well as the construction of subjectivity and community through the body.

The subsection *hybrid spheres* contains essays by Susan Leigh Foster, Sabine Sörgel and Anette Rein, which all discuss the construction of identity. They are framed by an interview with German theater director Monika Gintersdorfer.

Susan Leigh Foster analyses the presence and representation of the category gender in intercultural collaboration from a postcolonial perspective. Her text is an imagined and staged dialogue with French choreographer Jérôme Bel, in which she critically reflects his artistic work with the traditional Khon dancer Pichet Klunchun regarding individual and collective processes of identity formation.

The postcolonial gaze also plays a role in Sabine Sörgel's essay, in which she shows how dancing bodies produce spaces of identity and imagined communities, in which transnational politics are negotiated. Based on the example of Congolese choreographer Faustin Linyekula she traces the ambivalence of contemporary dance, which is political, while simultaneously attempting to evade political exploitation and representation.

Anette Rein writes about 'world' as cultural memory. Based on her research into Balinese dances, she demonstrates the challenges faced by museums as places of collective memory in the collection and preservation of tangible/intangible dance cultures. By identifying the special ephemeral quality of dance, she formulates a perspective, which aims at introducing new terms of action for museums, but also at redefining their educational mandate.

Monika Gintersdorfer speaks in a conversation with Gabriele Klein about her experiences working as a theater director with dance and choreography. Based on the series *Logobi*, she reflects on the conditions and possibilities of intercultural artistic work and gives a detailed account of her collaborations with dancers from the Ivory Coast. According to Gintersdorfer, political work and artistic work cannot be separated from one another.

Gabriele Brandstetter, Julie Townsend, Knut Hickethier and Michael Diers address the particularities of dance in the subsection *art worlds* by reflecting them in the context of other art forms.

Gabriele Brandstetter discusses the ambivalent relationship of dance and *Schrift* (writing as a material trace, i.e. text), dancing and writing (as an action) and emphasizes the similarities between these two media of worldmaking. Manifestations, materiality and signature are the perspectives under which Brandstetter argues convergence and resistance in dancing and writing, both of which she regards as movement phenomena.

Julie Townsend focuses on desire and concentrates on the production of desire in the body and in texts, based on examples from the so-called literature of the *coulisses* and the figure of the *danseuse* in the 19th century.

As moving images, respectively pictorial movements, dance and film are movement phenomena, which create worlds in different ways. Knut Hickethier examines the relationship between dance and film by discussing theoretical and analytical strategies and concepts of creating, visualizing, repeating and recording movement in film based on selected dance scenes from popular mainstream films.

The relationship of dance, music and the filmic image are the main focus of Michael Diers' essay. Here, Michelangelo Antonioni's film *Blow Up*, which not only concisely captures the mood of the 1960s, but is also a contemplation on the nature of the image itself, here serves as an object of research for questions of media differentiation.

The subsection *digital worlds – processing bodies* gathers contributions by Frédéric Bevilacqua, Norbert Schnell and Sarah Fdili Alaoui, Stephen Turk and Norah Zuniga Shaw. By looking at various artistic-digital projects, they inquire into the medial quality of dance based on various processes of notation, digitalization and storage.

Frédéric Bevilacqua, Norbert Schnell and Sarah Fdili Alaoui work at IRCAM (Institute for Research and Coordination Acoustic/Music, Paris) at the interface of movement and music. Their research on *Gesture Capturing* aims towards a paradigm shift. Their work goes beyond mere experimentation with technology and digital interactive systems in dance to instead pursue more fundamental issues concerning the description, notation and transmission of gestures and movement.

Stephen Turk focuses on the relationship of choreography and architecture and its rendering in digital space. He presents and reflects the research project *Synchronous Objects*, which translates the choreography of William Forsysthe's *One Flat Thing, reproduced* into digital space. With recourse to concepts and figures of thought such as environment, entanglement and the frame, he draws attention both to the 'architectonic affinity' of choreography as well as to the performativity of architecture, to which he ascribes dynamic potential for the perception and the occupation of choreographic space.

Norah Zuniga Shaw's research takes as its starting point the interface of dance and digital media. Based on the project *Synchronous Object for One Flat Thing, reproduced*, she analyzes in her interdisciplinary theory and practice the relationship of movement and media and the translation of one medium into another. Using these processes of transmission and translation as examples, she demonstrates the potential of dance knowledge for dancers and dance researchers alike, but also for theorists of other disciplines.

Working principles is the broad title of the last subsection with contributions by Sabine Gehm and Katharina von Wilcke, Gesa Ziemer and Sandra Noeth, all dedicated to the discussion of curatorial, artistic and dramaturgic working processes.

Sabine Gehm and Katharina von Wilcke inquire with Elisabeth Nehring into suitable formats for an artistic and academic occupation with dance. Based on their experiences with the Dance Congress 2009 in Hamburg, they describe curatorial strategies for developing topics and formats that facilitate a 'dance congress world' as a temporary choreographic construct.

Gesa Ziemer focuses on the situational potential of artistic working processes in dance and performance art in her discussion of complicity as a specific form of collaboration. By differentiating it from other social and organizational models such as teamwork, the forming of alliances, networking or friendship, she inquires into the creation of collectivity and collaboration in the context of instable and temporary 'dance worlds'.

Finally, Sandra Noeth's essay addresses current attempts at redefining dramaturgy in the context of contemporary choreography as a place for negotiating coexistence and community. In this sense, dramaturgy also gives room to discuss the body's capacity for action and questions choreography's mechanisms of effect as critical practice.

This volume took its beginning at the international conference supported by the German Research Foundation on the subject of *Performing Reality. 'Making Worlds' in Dance and Choreography*. It took place in November 2009 at the International Kulturfabrik Kampnagel in Hamburg in cooperation with the Dance Congress 2009, which was attended by ca. 3000 people. The organizers of the Dance Congress and thus also cooperating partners of the conference were the Federal Cultural Foundation, together with the Department for Culture of the City of Hamburg, Internationale Kulturfabrik Kampnagel and K3 – Centre for Choreography Hamburg/Tanzplan Hamburg. The cooperation sought to facilitate encounters between different fields of science and art, theory and practice, academic and artistic research and encourage the transfer of knowledge between them. The topics introduced in the lectures at the conference found their continuation in various artistic and practical formats (panel discussions, lecture demonstrations, workshops, open spaces) during the Congress.

An edited volume is a collaborative process and a joint effort. We would therefore like to sincerely thank all who had a part in it: first of all the contributors, who we thank for allowing us to use their essays and their excellent and collegial cooperation. We thank ehrliche arbeit/Elena Polzer for the translation of the German texts into English, as well as proofreading the English texts. Our thanks also go to Lejla Mehanović for her dedicated, editorial assistance and the design of the layout and to Gitta Barthel, who also proofread the manuscripts. To Jennifer Niediek, we are indebted for the professional and helpful support on behalf of the publishing house.

Last but not least, our thanks go to all colleagues, who helped to prepare and organize the international conference and the Dance Congress 2009. We thank the German Research Foundation for its financial support of the conference and the Department of Human Movement Studies at the University of Hamburg for its generous support of this publication.

Hamburg, June 2011

REFERENCES

Foster, Susan Leigh (ed.) (2009): Worlding Dance, Basingstoke: Palgrave Macmillan.

Goodman, Nelson (1978): Ways of Worldmaking, Hassocks, Sussex: The Harvester Press.

SOCIAL REALMS

Dancing Politics:
Worldmaking in Dance and Choreography

GABRIELE KLEIN

I.

Dance is a world in itself – this is a central figure of discourse since the beginning of the 20th century, i.e. the period in which modern industrial society was established.[1]

As a world of the body and the senses, of movement and feelings, as a world of metaphors, for which words fail us, dance in the modern age, according to the modern dance discourse, constitutes an alternate world, namely a world beyond language and rationality. In the 20th century, dance, regardless of what kind, whether artistic dance, popular dance, religious ritual or therapeutic setting, represented a contrast to rationality, mechanization, technology and geometry. It was seen as an alternative realm to industrial work (cf. Klein 1992). Dance in the modern age drew its aesthetic legitimacy and its social justification for existence from this pattern of discourse, which allotted dance the social position of 'Outsider' and defined it as the 'Other'. Dance was considered an expression of feelings and understood as honest, authentic, organic or holistic: and this pattern of discourse formed the basis for asserting its subversive power and socio-critical and emancipatory potential, from which dance has derived and still derives its avant-garde claims as well as its educational mandate.

---

1   The text is a revised version of the opening lecture held at the Dance Congress Germany by the author on November 6, 2009 at the International Cultural Factory Kampnagel in Hamburg, Germany.

However, this self-perception of dance has met with little response from the political field. Quite the contrary: dance was – and this is still the case with many politicians – and is considered non-political. Conservatives have appreciated this fact, as for example, the Bavarian state parliamentarian, who justified the lifting of a war-time ban on dancing in the period of the 'Red Revolution' in Munich in November 1918 with the words: "People should dance rather than demonstrate." (Eichstedt/Polster 1985: 44) The leftist wing, on the other hand, has bemoaned mindless dancing: Theodor W. Adorno, for example, believed himself to behold "the coordinated battalions of mechanical collectivity" (Adorno 1941: 312) in the dance craze. The student movement as well sought to stir up society and set new social structures in motion, but this largely remained a metaphor. Ultimately, it meant that people should take to the streets, instead of dancing their heart out, mindlessly and half-naked, caught up in the simultaneously occurring boisterous disco trend of the 1970s – or later in the 1990s, the techno craze. To the same effect as Adorno, the social-democratic oriented German daily newspaper *Frankfurter Rundschau* described the discos in the 1970s as "uniform centers of enforced conformity" and after the Berlin Love Parade in 1996, the liberal German weekly newspaper *Die Zeit* wrote:

"We see hundreds of thousands of people semi-naked, laughing, while coercing their bodies to produce seemingly epileptic movements ('dancing'). Is this a mass of invalids meeting in the city for a demonstration of happy madness? The answer is short and sweet: yes." (Klein 1999: 18)

II.

In the 1960s, the pattern of discourse that assumed dance and politics to be opposites began to be challenged parallel to the social transformations and political movements of the age. This occurred on two levels: on the level of general developments in society and on the level of forms of thought.

The rapid social, political and economic changes since the 1960s produced a society, which today has been diagnosed and labeled as the media society, information society or knowledge society, as globalized, post-colonial or neoliberal. In this new world, societal and political contexts have themselves also changed; they have liquefied, their boundaries dissolved. As Richard Sennett vividly demonstrates in his book *Flesh and Stone* (cf. Sennett 1994), the metaphor of 'flow' first manifested itself in the end of the 19th century in, what were at that time, new concepts of the modern and mobile city, the flow of traffic and arterial roads. It also manifested itself in concepts of physiology, such as blood circulation and neural pathways. In the 20th century, this found its expression in a specific understanding of the organization of the body, e.g. as an energetic body and society or as an (auto)mobile society. Movement, dynamics, flow – these terms form the kinetic basis of the modern age. It has often been neglected in theories of modernity, but Randy Martin and André Lepecki have shown that this is extremely important for the discussion of dance and politics (cf. Lepecki 2006; Martin 1998). The modern topos of endless movement marks the topographic fantasy and the colonial principle of modernity: the positing of movement as an ontological principle and its abstraction from specific cultures, bodies and lifestyles. The modern fantasy of endless movement also carries within it the notion of a colonialization of space, of subjects and bodies. The fact that this movement may not be interrupted by catastrophes, suffering and personal tragedy, that these should be considered natural catastrophes and fate, also points to the "kinetic reality of the modern age as mobilization" (Sloterdijk 1989: 27) as Peter Sloterdijk calls it. From this perspective, suffering, death and lamentation, the central topics of German Expressionist Dance in the 1920s, can be interpreted as resistance, as exposing the subsurface history of modernity.

With the advent of the globalized society, this basic kinetic principle of modernity was staged as a "spectacle of innocence" (cf. Lepecki 2006): the free movement of data-streams, the unlimited flow of capital, new waves of migration, the fall of political walls and symbolic borders permitted the emergence of a philosophical idea of openness. With it the spotlight of aesthetic discourse fell on contingency, a term that in sociology addresses the principle openness of possible life forms, and on potentiality, a concept in philosophy intended to overcome the dualism of possibility and reality. However, from a pragmatic point of view, it was the promising set phrase 'everything is possible', which became the ideology of a society that had lost its political perspective on the future and had pilloried the fundamental possibility of a political utopia with the fall of the Berlin wall and the disbanding of confrontational social systems. On the other hand, this society also began to suffer amnesia and a loss of history as part of its growing medialization.

The concept of limitless opportunities in the here and now became more than just the motto of a neo-liberal, so-called free world market, with the devastating consequences of its uncontrolled financial markets. It also transformed into the paradigm of a governmental politics of self-sufficiency that – whether in healthcare, education or pension systems, even in public funding for the arts – increasingly shifted responsibility onto the individual and made self care and self-formation of one's own optionalized body its credo.

The so-called "liberation of people from traditional obligations" (cf. Beck 1992), sociology's unpleasant description of this process since the 1980s, also provoked the fiction of the limitless possibilities available to organize the conditions of one's own life. The figure of the 'global player' appeared as a fictional role model on the horizon of a society based on the imaginary circulation of money. Behind this figure lies a subject type, which is 'kinetic', following an endless, self-motivated desire for unlimited movement. It is a type of subject that colonizes, because in subtle ways, it is defined as male, heterosexual and white.

This type of subject is not just a type of global economic activity. Even a group quite important to the globalized economy, the so-called creative class, represent distinct areas of competence that matter to the *modus operandi* of the 'global player' – creativity, virtuosity and intellectualism (cf. Virno 2004). Artists are its main representatives – albeit under precarious living conditions and the 'new poverty'. And so the new societal model of the flexible, geographically unattached and vagabond kinetic self-recursive subject has found its prototype in the 'freelance dancer'. The dancer: unattached, nomadic, an eternal migrant passing by.

In this historic moment, dance steps forth from its long confinement in the shadows and becomes the main focus of societal, philosophical and educational interest. It has become a symbol of a globalized and medialized society, which has promoted the ephemeral, fluid, momentary and placeless as its guiding metaphor. But the ephemeral, which was until recently always a characteristic feature of dance as an alternative corporeal world that made it distinguishable from a modern society that valued calculated reason, has become a fundamental societal problem in a globalized society. This is because ephemerality and liquidity here not only mean boundless movement and infinite possibilities, but also a fundamental change in the topology of social perception: social security, the welfare state, sedentism, social integration and a mutual sense of responsibility have disappeared in favor of a lack of obligations, loss of emotional ties, nomadic lifestyles and social disintegration. How can dance – given this social topos of 'ephemerality' – be critical and political?

III.

At the same time as these societal changes are hollowing out the basis of the welfare state (and its grande dames – social democracy and the trade union movement – along with it) and the so-called creative class is appointed a pioneering role in future society after the end of the welfare state, the foundations of modern thinking are also radically being called into question: born forward by French philosophy, post-structuralism has attacked the binary logic of modern thought in particular. The image, language, writing and art have become the focus of many philosophical discussions attempting to define one or several of these semantic systems as a binding framework for humanity's understanding of reality or rather as the foundation for "ways of worldmaking" (cf. Goodman 1978) in Western culture – as Nelson Goodman would formulate it.

Largely unnoticed by philosophy and aesthetic theory, post-structuralist thought left its traces in the aesthetic practice of contemporary dance. The dancer's own medium, the body, was intensely scrutinized, new movement techniques invented, expanded or modified. Body techniques such as Alexander Technique or BMC, movement techniques such as contact improvisation and various Asian martial arts were mixed with new (post)modern dance techniques (e.g. Cunningham, Limón) and the deconstruction of classical vocabulary (e.g. by Forsythe) broadened not only the technical basics of dance, but also its aesthetic approach. *Tanztheater* ('dance theater') used everyday gestures to bridge the realms of art and everyday life. The narrative disappeared in favor of fragmented montage-like choreography: the linearity of narration literally broke apart into 'dance pieces'. Contemporary dance questioned and defeated existing concepts concerning the nature of movement in breaks, stills, stumbles and falls. Not movement as flow, but interruption, not presence (as in the omnipresent media landscape), but rather absence (cf. Siegmund 2006) now became the focus of attention. Choreography increasingly became a matter of dramaturgy; whereas the once close link between dance and choreography gradually loosened. Choreography as an arrangement of movement, as work and as notation was in itself challenged and the previous dualisms of composition and improvisation, work and process were called into question. This development occurred analog to the rise of various new paradigms in the cultural sciences: whereas, in the 'linguistic turn', dance was considered text and choreography an order of language, after the 'performative turn' and its critique of representation, concepts such as liveness, presence/absence, instantaneousness, authenticity, identity or authorship took center stage in contemporary choreography. Whether in philosophical-theoretical references or in forms of aesthetic criticism or even in the presentation of illness, marginalization or ugliness, all these pieces addressed the un-portrayable, non-treatable, invisible in the portrayal of physical existence, physical 'truth' and physical difference.

Post-structuralist thinking did not only influence dance and choreographic practice. Although only rarely applied to dance, it also instituted a reversal in the discourse surrounding the art of dance in modernity by calling into question Adorno's dictum of the autonomy of art – in part underpinned by a glorification of carnival or the search for hybrid forms of art and everyday life, art and pop – and furthermore challenging the respective 'specificity' of the arts, but also by gradually relieving dance of avant-garde aspirations. Thanks to post-structural thought, a paradox was thus revealed in the relationship between politics and dance, which is typical for modernity making it difficult for some to provide answers to questions concerning the political dimensions of dance and for others making these questions itself seem redundant. In other cases still, this paradox leads to the opinion that an affinity of dance and politics may even be damaging for dance itself. So what really constitutes this paradox?

IV.

According to the considerations of French philosopher Jacques Rancière (cf. Rancière 2006), it is a paradox that is deeply ingrained in the modern age: on the one hand, there is the emphasis on the freedom and autonomy of art, as well as the specific natures of the individual arts (in the case of dance as a physical art, transient art, etc.) and on the other, the aspiration of the avant-garde to play its part in the fulfillment of the principles of modernity.

This paradox is based on two antagonistic positions. First, we have a position that postulates the autonomy of dance and identifies it as pure art. According to this position, dance has special powers, because it produces poetry via abstract language liberated from the everyday functions of the body. Accordingly, dance in the modern age is comparable to pure movement, which is free from any analogy to language, as well as from any form of representation. Its relationship with the societal modern age is detached and analogical. Depending on the respective historic tide of events, this dance aesthetic is either considered sober and free of magic or radical and revolutionary. A prominent example of this dance aesthetic is the work of Merce Cunningham.

The other position is one that defines dance as a way of life and sees its task as that of fulfilling the claims of modernity to equality, self-fulfillment and emancipation. This position can be traced back e.g. to Friedrich Schiller's concept of the "aesthetic education of man". It can be found in the philosophy behind expressionist dance, in the importance that was ascribed to dance theatre in the past and the importance that is ascribed to dance today in current debates about cultural education. Dance is therein a specific physical-sensual way of accessing worlds and by providing people with this specific form of 'aesthetic education', they are given the chance to live in a free and equal political community based on self-development. The societal modern age is thus faced with the challenge to implement the 'anthropogeny of humanity' in and through sensual forms and practices. Art – and especially dance as a corporeal art – is considered societal avant-garde and the ideal media capable of fulfilling this task.

Both positions provoke various aesthetic paradigms. The first position, which maintains the relative autonomy of dance and sees the revolutionary and emancipatory potential of dance in precisely this aspect, avoids associating dance with societal work, improving the world or the reintegration of alienated life. Adorno succintly formulated the paradox inherent in this position: "Insofar as a social function may be predicated of works of art, it is the function of having no function." (Adorno 1997: 336)

The other position, which seeks to bridge dance and life, inevitably has to depart from the concept of aesthetic experience – generally defined as a sensual experience distinct from everyday experience – in order to overcome the presumed difference between art and life. Instead its aim is to create forms of aesthetic experience everywhere: in art and politics, in sports and commerce, in work and leisure. It defines dance not as an alternative world, but as a meta-world that strives to do what politics – here meaning political institutional work – claims to do, but only indirectly realizes through laws and regulations, if at all: to change specific lifestyles. The paradox of this position consists in the fact that it ultimately makes art superfluous, namely when art merges with politics. How can this paradox of dance and politics as inscribed in modernity be resolved?

V.

One line of thought is not to understand dance and politics as two separate worlds, as autopoetic systems with their own rules, norms and values, but, in keeping with the words of philosopher Jacques Rancière, to see them as two forms of "dividing the sensual". Accordingly, dance and politics are interwoven strategies of a "politics of the kinaesthetic" and a "kinaesthetic policy". Politics is thus less to be understood as a form of power or institutional strategy and dance not as a field subsidized by politics or as a purely aesthetic practice. Instead, the political is here formulated normatively and focuses on only one aspect: political activity, which according to Rancière is "whatever shifts a body from the place assigned to it or changes a place's destination. It makes visible what had no business being seen, and makes heard a discourse where once there was only

place for noise; it makes understood as discourse what was only heard as noise."
(Rancière 1991: 30)

Analog to linking the concept of the political to specific practices, aesthetics
is therefore not simply art theory and the aesthetic not just a form of perception.
Instead, the aesthetic is inscribed in political practice – precisely because these
practices with their norms, rules and habits already determine sensual perception
by socially positioning people, allocating social and political space for them to
maneuver in and thus framing social perception. Exactly therein also lies the political dimension of the physical-sensual, of movement perception, in other
words, the dimension of "kinaesthetic politics": a concept of political activity as
the sensual practice of making cultural and social codes visible and shifting them
– in such a way that they contradict the "police order" as Rancière calls it.

VI.

From this perspective, the relationship of dance and politics does not allow itself
to be reduced to representative, interventionist or documentary aspects. In other
words: the simple fact that there is and should be a lobby for dance, the fact that
dance should become a fix element of cultural and educational policy and that
dance must be documented better as knowledge culture, is self-evident. Intervention into the "police order" of the fabric of artistic, cultural and educational
policy is an important and indispensable step.[2] However, political activity as a
concrete-sensual practice, as a "politics of the aesthetic" is then only just beginning.

If cultural and educational politics are political intervention, then the "politics of the kinaesthetic" has consisted and consists of micro-politics in how "the
practices and forms of the visibility of *dance* itself intervene in the division and
rearrangement of the sensual" (Rancière 2006: 8).

---

2   On this level, *Tanzplan Deutschland* (Dance Plan Germany), an initiative of the Ger-
    man Federal Cultural Foundation, has attempted the exceptional, shown courage and
    achieved something extraordinary and unique. Tanzplan Deutschland provided the
    framework for the potentiality of political practice. It has changed the topology of
    how contemporary dance is perceived: Hamburg – with K3, the Centre for
    Choreography and improved support for contemporary dance from the cultural
    authorities and other institutions in Hamburg in cooperation with Performance Studies
    University of Hamburg – is a good example of this.

From this perspective dance is not political per se, because it is a physical-sensual medium. For the same reason, it is also not non-political per se. It is rather, as I argue, political when the aesthetic practice grates against the reigning order, norms, habits and conventions – and not only grates against them, but also changes them.

So-called conceptual dance, as it emerged in Europe in the 1990s, mainly sought these micropolitics within the artistic process – and here also saw itself as an experiment with the social. There are traditions underlying this work – in Germany, too; we need only to think back on Gerhard Bohner's attempts at collective work (in Darmstadt) at the end of the 1960s. Contrary to the theories of many recent academic dance publications, contemporary dance, as an artistic practice, did not simply become political in the 1990s by focusing on collectives, on collaborations, on networks. These forms were neither new nor are they 'a field of experimentation' with the social, a 'model' of a reality to come. They are social, but as such not political per se. In my understanding, they are political when they attack the societal division of the sensual, i.e. transform norms and conventions, namely those that are always also distinctive and which include and exclude. And they are political when they produce a critical difference to the "kinaesthetic reality of the modern age" (Sloterdijk 1989: 25), but this also occurs via a critical theory and practice of gender, of the body (the dancing body and body concepts), of class and of post-colonial politics. And finally, they are political when they exist not only as functional networks, but also develop a sense of community: a feeling that does not declare community to be the goal, but assumes it as a precondition for the practices themselves. Politics as a concrete sensuous activity requires the creation of collective identities – and therefore these cannot be created solely through transient and non-binding networks and politics, however important these may be for dance.

VII.

Consensus is a favorite catchword of present-day politicians on the left, as well as the right, or better said: all those coming from right or left, who want to occupy the centre. But politics, as political theorists from Carl Schmitt to Karl Marx, i.e. right as well as left, agree, is created out of difference. It emerges where sensual perception and experience rub up against the traditional order. Many social movements – women's lib, the peace movement, gay and black rights – have proved this in practice. Because the political activity of these social movements – and this, too, is little noted by political theory – were and are above all grounded in corporeal practices. Activists chaining themselves to radioactive containers, African-American women remaining seated on a bus, homosexual couples kissing in public, but also the choreo(graphic) politics of demonstrations, sit-ins or smart mobs – these and many other examples in the recent history show that political practices can change the order and perception of these "police orders" when above all expressed in the form of corporeal activity. Dance can be a medium for training corporeal perception. But – as Randy Martin (cf. Martin 1998) has shown: Dance is much more. Dance is a key area of the political and by questioning central categories, such as rhythm, force, space, time, energy, dynamics and flow, it sheds light on the kinetic foundations of modern society.

Seen from this perspective, the customary separation of dance from other areas of society, but above all the demarcations within the dance field itself – for example between dance as art, dance studies and dance education – are irrelevant. The political dissent of dance does not consist of the fact that artists, politicians, academics or teachers are so terribly different as to misunderstand one another and to (have to) distance themselves or their thoughts from one another. Instead it always occurs where the concrete practice of dance is confronted with an order that wishes to codify. This is an experience equally shared by academics, dance teachers and choreographers – although in different cultures, as well as in different ways in the context of hegemonic cultural policy.

To conclude: dance as politics is dissent, understood in the ancient Greek sense as *agon*, as an intellectual and sensual competition over the specific sensual conditions and possibilities of dance in the future.

REFERENCES

Adorno, Theodor W. (1941): "On Popular Music", in: Simon Frith/Andrew Goodwin (eds.) (1990), On Record: Rock, Pop and the Written Word, London: Routledge, pp. 301-314.
_____ (1997): Aesthetic Theory, Minneapolis: University of Minnesota Press.
Beck, Ulrich (1992): Risk Society. Towards a New Modernity, New Delhi: Sage.
Eichstedt, Astrid/Polster, Bernd (1985): Wie die Wilden. Tänze auf der Höhe ihrer Zeit, Berlin: Rotbuch.
Goodman, Nelson (1978): Ways of Worldmaking, Indianapolis: Hackett Publishing Company.

Klein, Gabriele (1992): FrauenKörperTanz. Eine Zivilisationsgeschichte des Tanzes, Weinheim/Berlin: Heyne.

_____ (1999): Electronic Vibration. Pop Kultur Theorie, Hamburg: VS Verlag für Sozialwissenschaften.

Lepecki, André (2006): Exhausting Dance. Performance and the Politics of Movement, New York/London: Routledge.

Martin, Randy (1998): Critical Moves. Dance Studies in Theory and Politics, Durham/London: Duke University Press.

Rancière, Jacques (1991): Disagreement: Politics And Philosophy, Minneapolis: University of Minnesota Press.

_____ (2006): The Politics of Aesthetics: The Distribution of the Sensible, London: Continuum.

Sennett, Richard (1994): Flesh and Stone. The Body and the City in Western Civilization, New York: W.W. Norton.

Siegmund, Gerald (2006): Abwesenheit. Eine performative Ästhetik des Tanzes, Bielefeld: transcript.

Sloterdijk, Peter (1989): Eurotaoismus. Zur Kritik der politischen Kinetik, Frankfurt am Main: Suhrkamp.

Virno, Paolo (2004): A Grammar of the Multitude. For an Analysis of Contemporary Forms of Life, Cambridge: MIT Press.

Between Intervention and Utopia: Dance Politics

RANDY MARTIN

SOCIALIST ENSEMBLES

Myriad are the intersections that locate dance in the realm of the political. The conceptions of who can move for what, the conventions by which people gather, the spaces made available, the training and preparation, notions of embodiment – all bear upon dance, and constitute the field of forces and constraints through which it is borne into being. Yet dance also makes its own politics, crafts its own pathways and agency in the world, moves us toward what we imagine to be possible and desirable. Dance tangibly if momentarily materializes bodies assembled on their own behalf, a social ensemble made by its own means towards its immediate ends. It gathers its public then disperses them suddenly, leaving a sensible residue of what has been and what can only be desired, namely the will to create more. An offering of what we can have together now, a promise manifest immediately of what we might be, dance sets in motion is and ought, it moves into the world pressing our surround to be otherwise, while it figures a taste of what world we might have if it were left to our own creative designs. Against the facile dismissal of political aspirations as forever insufficient to what they face, dance offers a surfeit of possibility, it makes legible the very means by which action is joined, measures taken, steps carried through. An ensemble that manufactures a social body that releases its own excess, that orients practical accomplishment toward itself, this expansive sense of the social that exists in and for itself, grounds a socialism that issues from the loins and beads of sweat made in movement together.

While dance is no one thing as much as it is all around, it is hardly sufficient to the world it would seek to render onto our public stages. Rather than insist that all stay in line, keep in step, for politics, it must be insisted, dance is good to think with. To the expectation that a solitary performance make all the difference, can be the change it wants to see in the world, admittedly dance and protest share a certain predicament (cf. Foster 2003). Both organize ephemerality, stage disappearance, leave a sense of lack (if only more had been done to get people to come, if only some more, a few, a few hundred, the event would have made its mark). All the work of planning, rehearsing, propagandizing, arranging the space, coordinating the moment, meeting and meeting again, vanishes within moments of its consummation in the live act of inhabiting the appointed space. When the curtain closes, the march is done, the crowd disperses – where do all those people go? What do they bring with them of that fragile collectivity? How is the prowess of possibility traced when the ensemble in its unique condition of ensemble has been undone? What might give that glorious critical presence a longer run? The organizers, presenters, performers all know that their fate lies near, that the show cannot go on forever, that there will be a return. Surely the experience will have delivered its change, which now morphs into the fractured bodies and quotidian pathways still bristling with the achievement of the newly departed performance, but unsure of how to recognize its durable impression. A critique, a news notice passes judgment. It was good or bad, successful or not. But these cards of evaluation are stacked against the deck of this lone event.

Perhaps in both performance and protest, the lack lies not in what was put on display, but in how to notice the ways that an assemblage invited to take a different course, to move otherwise, now lives on. The movement for change and the changeful movement are most commonly viewed through the lens of arrest, the critical act of judgment fixes what it looks at, creates a theater for theory by stripping out the very motion that would take the event beyond itself. This regard of critical evaluation is tempted to freeze motion and fix the present, unmoor the ongoing movement that makes history from its animating ideas, in short to provoke a crisis of seeing that it ascribes to the thing it sees. To this sense that what we create is forever insufficient to what needs doing – a disposition that joins activism and art-making that compels further creativity but also dismisses the efficacy of what has been made – we need a corrective. To think, to see, to sense from within dance, is to take motion not stasis as our posture of evaluation.

To privilege dance analytically, as a critical method, invites thought from within its own conditions of movement, from the means through which bodies are assembled and not by the terms through which their impact is brought to an end. To find ourselves in dance is to locate our repertoires of engagement as already in motion. And these self-making bodies move variously, interdependently, multiply. Even in unison, difference is legible. Choreography discloses multiplicity under an artistic signature. What seems to issue from one body rests upon the coordinated and interdependent effort of so many and occasions a self-expansive sociality. Dance is an ensemble of ensembles, an accomplishment of its own surplus that bequeaths a fateful remainder, an unabsorbable promise to all in attendance.

MOBILIZATION

In conventional politics, to characterize something as a dance is to see it as evasive, afield of authenticity, swirling around its object, somehow caught out of time unable to affect the progress it seeks. According to the Oxford English Dictionary, this figurative invocation of dance suggests, "to lead, rarely give (a person) a dance; fig. to lead (him) in a wearying, perplexing, or disappointing course; to cause him to undergo exertion or worry with no adequate result" (cf. OED.com). A casual scan across the digital horizon would yield such phrases as "The Reconciliation Dance" (on politics and crime); "Wild Finance: Where Money and Politics Dance" (on the financial bailout); "The Dance of the Apologists" (on the persistence of racism in response to Obama's election) (cf. Google.com, December 2, 2009). Dance, in these examples, is a prelude to real decisions taken, more, it is a distraction side-stepping what really needs to get done if only a more muscular encounter could plant antagonists firmly before one another. The political stage is already set, its props familiar, the characteristics, motives, and methods of its dramatis personae already known. The actors take their places, ready to make history once the music stops and the distracting dance comes to an end.

Despite this script for heroic narrative, the agency therein, is thoroughly diminished. Actions unfold in a time and space that have been preordained, the parameters of difference, the staging of conflict, the drama of decision already determined by conditions fixed in advance. For dance to exert its politics, it must be demetaphorized, reliteralized, its body must be entered and effects felt as conditions of perception. Lived from within, dance is not locked in time and space, not an apostle at the Cartesian altar, but an apostate of containment. Dance allows it achievements to appear to precede it, its compelling capacity to inhabit time and space, to make of these its art, rests upon its own artifice, its internal devices for generating the very environment in which it takes place.

The shift in perspective from movement to mobilization names this salient distinction. It forces our attention on how space and time are accomplished, on how agency (the forces that bear a critical idea) and history (the material embodiment of possibility) are intertwined. By this reckoning within the terms of dance, choreography and performance constitute precisely this fragile dialectic between political becoming and being, a desire for difference and a capacity for realization. Choreographic agency proceeds from training and conception to rehearsal and staging to enunciate the occasion by which we gather ourselves, while performance is a moment of realization whereby the immediate public, the unstable audience (cf. Blau 1990) constitutes the reception through which further mediation, efficacy and impact will transpire.

The double temporality by which the dance moves towards its performative ends and the public is assembled out of its own diffuse corporality marks this fleeting co-production of a tangible space and time. This ongoing mobilization, is made legible in performance but also seemingly brought to an end by it, the critical presence thereby assembled passes from history as a constitutive to its own historical trace of the event past. That the dance unleashes its physicality as a practical capacity to assemble, also speaks to the movements elsewhere, the mediations, or social-corporal media through which a danced idea percolates through the world. The dance of politics is not a prelude to its becoming reality, but rather, a realization of its operations, its play of script and inscription, the images that form on its bodily materializations. Yet the conventional language for politics is all about stop and go, failure and success, loss and gain. Steps are recorded without the movement that would allow us to see what made it possible for these measures to be taken, what other forces still move in our midst, what multiplicities were unleashed when the ultimate decree was rendered. Without mobilization, politics is only crisis, an arrest of its own conditions of possibility without hope of how these might be superceded. The omnipotent theoretical gaze fixes what it regards, deprives its object of the motion internal to thought, brings what it sees into crisis. Mobilization is the perspective of that which is already in motion, that whose turning point invariably turns into something else, which provides its means to continue past arrested conditions. Thinking through dance, keeps its object in sight as it continues to move with what animates reflection, the incessant assembly and dissolution of what and how we move. To address how movement may sidestep its compulsions, affect its own counterpoints, drive itself into unacknowledged registers, even surpass its own initiatives and impulses, dance delivers amplitude of understanding.

SOCIAL KINESTHETIC

Dance is an art that is not one. Neither singular in where it comes from nor fixed in where its goes, it can be found anywhere, at any time. Too often regulated by definition, boundaries policed by formal preference, it is more generatively understood and put to work through its operations, methods and effects. It is no less possible to imagine a language of dance's critical techniques than to catalog its esthetic registers and to classify preferences for what gets to be called (and who is allowed to hail) that moveable feast devoured as dance. A few gestures toward that critical analytic grammar can be offered, but certainly dance will not be exhausted through such exercises. Dance is at once a vast and immeasurable inventory of concepts and practices. But it is also a promissory note by which we can give value to movement in our midst. Such a gambit requires a constant shuttling between abstract and concrete, elaborate flights and sticky encumbrances. Dance will be invoked and inscribed in exercising and discharging this double duty.

Past and present share a moment in dance, as reconstructions display as much about movement that once was as it does about steps that have never left us. Dance gathers what is temporally durable and ephemeral, the deep knowledge of how bodies are mutually enabling and how pregnant each moment can be. The body is a movable archeology, it layers the long duree of bipedalism, the composite of what is mediated from elsewhere and what presses flesh-to-flesh, the hammered rhythms of urban density and global migrations, the restless appropriations, the ceaseless citations, the unauthored innovations. Dancing articulates this time of times, it crafts a passageway for difference to converge – albeit fragilely, momentarily. While dance traverses a multiple temporality, its spatial arrays are no less complex. Moving together anywhere encumbers a debt to others elsewhere. Performance is but one currency of repayment. Theft is but one instance of damage, but permission to give what has already been taken typically proves elusive. Dance bears all the traces of where people have been forced to move and where they have forced movement, of how the body has been shackled and what might constitute its emancipation, of ways around its detractors and novel applications of its cooperation.

If dance's specificity is a reflexive mobilization, an assemblage of how we move together to disclose where we might get to, a material inscription of the time and space that assembles social bodies making their world, its idioms, methods, occasions, and effects cannot be readily regulated by aesthetic fiat. Restricted to the genealogy of the western proscenium, the concert stage, dance is as a consequence considered a minor art form. But as a minority discourse, a condensation of the unspoken and unthought repertory of embodied practice, dance is a crucial analytic method that makes legible a larger sweep of how we move together. Of course in the expanded field of cultural and corporal practice, there is plenty of dance to go around, and few steps need to be taken to run into it. While dance can be affiliated with its global manifestations and articulated with popular and professional body techniques like sport, its principles of operation and affinity, its means of appropriation and innovation, suggest a broader corporal mapping of society as ongoing movement. Yet before there is movement, enunciation or inscription, there needs to be some shared sensibility, some array of physical pressures and agglutinations that orient and dispose what may get produced as bodily practice and what might get concatenated in dance practices. This predicate of movement, this disposition to assemble, adhere, pass through, align and locomote, the physical grounds and motional loam of a particular social and historical conjuncture, can be called a social kinesthetic.

Hence, it is not enough to say that the lineaments of embodied practice have a history, it is also important to ascertain the ways in which they make history. As such, social kinesthetics emerge and recede in relation to other societal formations, constitutions of population, aggregations of collective capacity and wealth. The combined histories of capitalist development and underdevelopment, the colonial trick of civilizational subjugation, the imperial displacements of periphery to metropole, the great sorting of population by race, the gendered differentiation of space into public and private, the normalization of libidinal economies into straight and queer, the rendering of nature into a salvageable and manageable environment, the parsing of belief into reason and faith, the cleavage of knowledge by metrics of expertise – compel the world to be wrought in terms of a global body, a mighty and unrealized corporal humanity. Efficiency, rationalization, integration, individuation, universalism, progress, freedom, enlightenment, modernization are the watchwords of this grand social kinesthetic.

But just as these forces are marshaled to make the body, a body, the human body cohere at the center of its universe, consummating the value of the upright, the balanced, the gyroscopic momentum freeing and gravity defying energies of transcendence as a centering kinesthetic calling all to get in line, much more was slipping out and away, reorienting itself and redirecting its flows. The vivid and manifold movements of decolonization would voice themselves in a thousand chants that collide and collude in an irrepressible polyrhythm. The contest between the forces that center and decenter bodies in movement is no less resolved than that between colonization and decolonization as such. The efforts to liberate nations from the stronghold of their colonial formation, which led in the 1950s to the declaration of a third world, one out of alignment with the polarizing grip of Cold War geo-politics are still being played out in what is now more commonly referred to as the global south (cf. Ahmad 1992). And just as the networked movements of the 1960s would render political whole realms of endeavor once consigned to the unactionable grounds of unconscious desire, the private, the spaces of reproduction, consumption and domesticity, new technologies of enclosure, control, data-mining and intellectual property, commodification of affect and traffic in bodily material would devise all manner of capture media.

In the friction between social kinesthetics, in the myriad combinations of movement, bodily practices emerge that craft disparate principles of congregation, alignment, affiliation, routes of passage and historical locomotion. While the decolonization of the mind yields vast archives of writing, voicing, critique, that of the body produces manifold repertories of motional expression, bodily stylistics, physical resonance (cf. Wa Thiongo 1986). More than a struggle of control and refusal, of domination and resistance, of appropriation and escape, the politics and practices that issue from a given social kinesthetic make tangible the resources of mobilization, the aesthetics of difference, the mediations of social ensembles, the deepening techniques of mutuality that forge their ways in the world. Hence decolonization breaches that seal that had governed movement verticality, much dance emerges in the break and in turn, the physicalization of movement breaks open what is taken to be dancing. Certainly, one instance of this break is referred to as the postmodern, a valorization of the pedestrian over the exalted, of ensemble composition and improvisation over a possessive choreographic authority, of a participative community over a proscenium-divided audience, of a spatial diffusion of where dance might occur against a hierarchy of specialized theatrical venues.

No doubt, the break or periodization scheme is easy to overstate, as those artists clustered as modern where the contemporaries of those designated as postmodern, and the larger narrative of succession through formal innovation so fundamental to the ethos of modernism was carried forward. Yet if we widen our critical optic beyond esthetic evaluation and stylistic innovation, the genealogies that lead from Judson Church to contact improvisation, to the urban dance scenes of San Francisco, Seattle, Minneapolis, Boston, New York, as well as Montreal, Paris, Berlin, Havana, Mexico City, Buenos Aires, Tokyo, a different principle of association will hove into view – one already hinted at when the fable of an originary location for an avant-garde is subject to greater scrutiny (cf. Burt 2006). At issue here are not some ultimate bragging rights as to where it all began, but a re-valuation of how movement moves, of diasporic dispersions of style, of a certain corporal globalization.

The decentered social kinesthetic sets many practices into global circulation, and by so doing spreads a different means by which mobilization takes place.

Capoeira, for example, which shares with contact improvisation the re-orientation of upward alignment, spends a century under construction in Brazil before becoming part of an international attention to traveling movement practices (cf. Browning 1995; Lewis 1992). Break-dance too elaborates upon the released hips of black popular dance, incorporates call-and-response forms grounded in practices such as the ring-shout, and inverts the cosmology of up and down, front and back (cf. Gottschild 2003; Banes 1979; Stuckey 1987). Boarding culture, from its appropriation of a centuries-old Hawaiian practice in the desuburbanized beachfront of Los Angeles, and translation from surfing ocean waves to skating the edges of empty swimming pools, to shattering the pristine moguls of ski slopes, is branded as extreme (sport) even as it continues its street routes (cf. Borden 2001).

While these practices span diverse geographies and populations, and evoke disparate performance protocols and ensemble ethos, they also share dimensions of lateral affiliation, an expansive valorization of quotidian spaces, a commitment to flying low when high flying mobility has visited such ruin, and perhaps above all, an engagement with the production of risk as a promise of self-appreciation and unexpected gain (cf. Feher 2009). Surely these practices share the ambiguous legacy of appropriation and commercialization, of sponsors and celebrity, but it is safe to say that none are exhausted by these conventions of market culture. While individual risks may be captured as exemplary, the expanded capacities for what bodies do together, for what ground they break, for the desires they unleash, the debts they place in circulation, and the demands they place upon one another in a sustainable sociality, all point to a more ambitious realization of this potential for moving otherwise. The social kinesthetic is the loam from which emerges this ceaseless stream of possibility.

RISK

An inventory of the movement capacities unleashed by the decentered social kinesthetic of decolonization lends itself to a veritable visceral exuberance. By the 1980s, dance typed as experimental, to say nothing of sport labeled extreme, would be celebrated for its embrace and elaboration of risk (cf. McNamee 2007). There is certainly dance that courts danger, that demands sustained exertion, relishes speed, and subjects bodies to an edgy precarity, foregrounding risk also pursued the arts of surprise, violation of expectation, trespass of norm that might more readily place established cultural norms in danger of being disturbed. Risk in this regard, fueled dance's gift economy. By enjoining participants to rely so highly upon one another for making and sustaining art, the cultural discount of free labor (cf. Ross 2000) crafted an intimacy of social engagement that made the immediacy of an idealized community an offering for what could be conceived as society. But this affirmative conception of risk, the generous grasp of what could be ventured to make the most of creative excesses, quickly met its evil twin.

The dance world was under assault by a series of forces that also fell under the rubric of risk. Certainly there was acquired immune deficiency syndrome (AIDS), which made its epidemiological debut identified as Gay Related Complex by the government body for public health, the Centers For Disease Control (cf. Altman 1986). That risky dance was in many ways queer to normal habits of movement, that it distressed notions of monogamous non-touching intimacy, that it rendered movement itself promiscuous, unbounded, voracious, seemed a condition destined to draw dance into the victimology by which the Human Immuno-deficiency Virus (HIV) was initially called to account. The anxiety that some category of subject carries baleful qualities that can quickly infect others with the purported failure of being is known as a moral panic (cf. Hall et al. 1978). The notion of a racially encoded crime wave is modeled on one such instance of contagion. Queer sexuality certainly qualifies as well. Art that produces a state of risk not readily reabsorbed into standard metrics of worth would also stand for an unbearable risk. No doubt such reasoning was in evidence when four of eighty-thousand grants conferred by the National Endowment for the Arts in the United States were deemed indecent to some imagined community's standards of propriety (cf. Yudice 2003). And yet to stop the spread of such bad risk, the Endowment itself would need to be defunded. At stake, of course, were not huge sums – or even monies commensurate with the expansive impact of the arts in question, let alone sufficient to either arrest or enable an arts economy. Rather, the excessive attention given to public funding of the arts stood in for the question of what the social body itself might be entitled to as a condition of its further development.

Within this constellation, dance met its own public controversy in the form of the accusation of victim art that critic Arlene Croce directed at choreographer Bill T. Jones. The manifest claim was that a work entitled *Still/Here*, placed dying bodies onstage and transgressed the line between life and artistic representation, and justified a criticism based on a refusal of the critic to actually view the piece. Underneath lay an accusation that Jones had deigned to speak back to the critic from his privileged place onstage. By so doing, he usurped her role, making criticism itself a victim of dance's newfound powers of representation (cf. Croce 1994; Martin 1996). This displacement of expertise, the loss of the specialist's authority, already anticipated in dance's own decolonizing pedestrian turn, was now directed at the object over which it once claimed mastery. Clearly, dance was not alone in this predicament of seeing its very expansion or democratization, its expanded access and energized publics, now turning back on its ability to govern its own practices, reception, and valuation. In this, dance shared a circumstance with the larger condition known as the postmodern (cf. Lyotard 1984). But what was then viewed as an undermining of the sweeping narrative by which all peoples would be given a history, now in the context of what came to be called the culture wars, looks more like a skepticism toward the authority of specialized knowledge, the very petit recit whose decentring triumph the postmodern was said to celebrate.

Dance – at least as referenced here – stood at the crossroads of a much larger conjuncture. Its exploration of risk looked as though it might have been drowned in the din of something called the risk society (cf. Beck 1992). Its expanded valorization of movement seemed to suffer the same menacing disorientation as the more general mistrust of expertise. Its commitment to the experimental, the speculative, the detour from security, came face to face with a generalized logic of accountability, hyper-productivity driven investment, and loss of a social compact dedicated to securing the domestic population (cf. Klein 1997; Power 1997; Harvey 2005). This is not to say that the traps known as neoliberalism, neoconservatism, globalization, privatization, deregulation, re-engineering, shock therapy, and the like where lying in wait to take up dance's every move. Rather, it is to remember that what we take as a ruling notion has its roots elsewhere and lives with the likes of which it cannot abide and that suggest what else is already available.

Yet by dismantling what once had been a material commitment to security on the basis of citizenship was now shifting from a public good to a presumably private initiative. A basic cleavage became legible, a sorting of population between those who could bear risk, who can manage it for their own pecuniary and existential gain, and those who failed to meet the demands of these various metrics, those who passed into this failed state would be termed the at risk. The line between the risk capable and the at-risk could be crossed at any time, as the recent subprime meltdown in the United States made abundantly clear. Removing the means of security from a population treats them as an enemy within, one best dealt with through the framework of war. A series of such domestic wars ensued, signaled by a study commissioned in 1983 by then President Ronald Reagan to eliminate the department of education and pave the way for private and religious primary and secondary schooling where public education with its reliance on progressive tax revenues, once stood. The report, *A Nation At Risk* analogized low tests scores of students when compared to those in other countries as a threat to national security tantamount to a condition of war (National Commission on Excellence in Education). A war metaphor was also central to the *No Child Left Behind Legislation* implemented two decades later under George W. Bush, which treated kids as casualties who would be rescued by raising their test scores. This war on education, was joined by a war on crime, drugs, welfare, culture and the arts, each designed to evacuate local autonomy in the name of nationally enforced remedial measures. The notion that some small portion of the population might detonate a failure for the rest also became the basis for the preemptive logic of the war on terror (cf. Martin 2007).

The future was not for the waiting, but needed to be anticipated and acted upon in the present. As such, the affirmative management of risk, the realization of excessive gain through a speculative venture, shared a temporal sensibility with the negative condition of risk. The focus of economic policy shifted from maximizing growth to minimizing inflation, from planning for the future through public investments to controlling monetary flows through interest-rate adjustments. The presumption that lay behind the policy shift was that few would undertake financial risks if their gains would be eroded through inflation, and indeed the double-digit inflation of the seventies left stock market participation to but one in ten U.S. households. By the time of the Internet bubble in the late 1990s, more than half of households held some kind of financial portfolio (cf. Martin 2007). Unlike savings, or earlier logics of home ownership based on the adage, "buy-and-hold" liquidity, the ability to set money into motion became the order of the day (cf. Bryan/Rafferty 2006). The failure of the risk management models to maintain liquidity was the proximate cause of the financial meltdown that erupted in 2007. The shock and awe promised by the brilliant formulae quickly turned to disappointment and disbelief. Over and over again we heard incredulity toward the inability of financial knowledge to control its domain. "They were the smartest guys in the room. How could they have so completely misunderstood what they were doing?" (cf. McLean/Elkind 2003) If this faith in small numbers and a few brilliant minds turned out to be misplaced, if the obscure ideas rehearsed in small rooms proved incapable of delivering on there promise of risk, might there be some other quarter for risk making to which we might want to again direct our attentions. Perhaps the standard polarity of smart minds and dumb bodies would need to be reversed if risk would again seem to be a gambit worth undertaking.

UTOPIA AND INTERVENTION

The regime of risk just described was not simply an ideology, a mode of cognition, or a way of knowing – though surely it was all these things. The appeal of risk was to a new kind of being, one that eschewed security for self-appreciation, unexpected gain – above all risk would be subject to somatization, embodied, borne peripatetically. The vendors of risk management when asked how to ascertain whether an investment portfolio had an appropriate load for the individual in question would typically reply, "can you sleep at night". Risk thus became a kind of dream, a delivery from the future to the present. But this rush of what was to come into the realm of what now is offers a very different time sense than the conventional formulation of modernist utopia as a space from elsewhere in a time still to come. The dreamscape that claimed a life of hard work and labor would lead to emancipation from work in the form of retirement and a better life to the generations to come was capital's utopia that rested on an allochronic sense of time, one securely set-off from the present. If the protocols of risk reconfigure time, they also reconstitute spatial sensibilities. While the old forms of consumer credit and debt dating to the days of Henry Ford assuming life-long employment in a firm or occupation, a career, and a stable home where one could repair from the exhausting demands of the work-day, the drive to flexibility usurped continuous employment and the home joined other forms of consumer credit as a liquid asset to be bundled with other debts, such as mortgages and securities (cf. Allon 2008). Lost were the anchoring relations of work and home to location, community, neighborhood as a spatial heartland. Drawing together debts from disparate sources and far-flung locations, slicing these financial assets according to their risk attributes, rendering local experience a function of widely dispersed affiliations and associations, a vertiginous series of effects was in evidence in both the subprime meltdown and the war on terror. Intervention – the sense of being able to act anywhere without proximate cause – shifted from a realm of necessity to one of discretion, from a fixed space to a spatial fix.

At this point, the production of time and space, the embodiment of risk, the tangible offering of what can be and what is – all of which form such potent aspects of the present moment – find an immediate and coherent articulation in dance. Understandably, dance that is considered both experimental and speculative draws upon some of the very metrics of risk association with the expansion of rampant managerialism and burgeoning financial investment. The movement in question would share a social kinesthetic whose political effects it could not fully master. Dance work in these newly blossoming urban scenes would be flexible in ways that managerial humanism with its focus on quality circles, teams, and other intimate ensembles would come to celebrate (cf. Gordon/Newfield 1996). The pick-up company could be taken as a kind of prototype for the self-managed, project-based, occasion-generated collaboration that was a celebrated feature of the new managerial approaches to conventional organizations (cf. de Monthoux 2004). But if dance would join other artistic profiles as the poster-children for a gentrifying, neo-liberal fantasy of economic renewal dubbed the creative class, dancers would also get caught, resist, and redirect the naïve bait-and-switch promises of these schemes. Here the formalism of risk management mirrors the esthetically-empty paeans of the creative class; to wit, gather artists in de-industrialized and blighted urban cores, add cafes, bars, theaters, mix and stir (cf. Pasquinelli 2008). The facile measures used to justify such programs definitively lacked a utopian aspect. Nor did they see in aggregations of artists' squats, collectives, self-organization and auto-production an intervention that might challenge the assimilation, appropriation and cooptation of artistic energies (cf. Sholette/Thompson 2004).

Surely, resolving dance's utopian energies and interventionist capacities into a single esthetic, a unitary organizational form, or a typical mode of dissemination would be equally problematic as the esthetic indifference common to much policy discussion in the arts. Symptomatic here is the rise of community-based arts as a funding rubric that would replace critical operations with promised delivery of social services in the name of authentic non-specialist ties (cf. Kwon 2002; Kester 2004). For dance, the move to community in this respect, whether popular-front inspired works of the 1930s, or the turn to the pedestrian associated with the postmodern, the professionalization of dance education and dance therapy, all represented multiple possibilities for affiliation that preceded the constitution of community-based work as a funding rubric that could soften the threatening aspects of work considered avant-garde. Croce's invocation of victim art slyly performs an esthetic essentialism for what she takes to be the literal transcription of real dying bodies into the protected sanctuary of artistic representation. Here, the irony of the criticism (lost to the critic) for this particular dance was that far from a spectacle of night-of-the-living-dead shuffling, *Still/Here* exhibited an excessive exuberance for dance in the face of death, an extensive inventory of dance styles, pyrotechnic abilities that precisely assembled a power to keep going when confronted with the threat to arrest movement and silence consideration of the work it should be permitted to do.

That dance has a capacity to stage such a close and productive encounter between what are often treated as discreet and incompatible temperaments, the vision of what could be and the move into what is, needs to be taken as testimony to how critical attentions could be effectively organized. In one way the break in the visual arts between utopian and interventionist dispositions is redolent of the periodizing associations of the modern and postmodern as such (cf. Jameson 1984). Accordingly, the utopian belongs to an older avant-gardist metaphysic by which the artist, freed by their very marginality from society, offers a vision of the future that those ground by numbing normalizations cannot perceive. The interventionist sensibility would thereby provide a needed corrective, wherein artistic initiatives would issue from the pragmatic ground, take the long march through institutions as its canvas or medium, install, occupy, parody, reappropriate in order to demonstrate that direct action is possible and can, even if momentarily, disclose what the world can be (cf. Rossiter 2006). Notice that this last aspect, the coercive, corrective function's association with the tragic form is quickly turned comedic in a way that suggests something no less utopian, namely the cry that the world can be different and the confidence to state what this difference might entail. The art work does not substitute for the social service, but provides a spatial portrait and a temporal proxy, a momentary timeshift that seizes the imagined future.

Certainly there is exciting dance work that shares an interventionist sensibility. It is in-your-face, or in-the-streets, or extensively-online, or amidst-a-demonstration, or none-or-all of these things (cf. Gere 2004; Chatterjee 2004; Albright 1997). That is to say, dance is both caught up in a range of esthetic and political currents of which it cannot claim authorship, and a meshing ground where ensembles, mobilizations, kinesthetics, affiliations and associations can be composed and mixed. Dance does inscribe visions of how we can move together. It does array and concentrate forces and differences in manners both demonstrable and sustainable. It does report on what a very few can accomplish together, that can be passed on and enable passing, open passages. It can recalibrate time, detail its shifts, manufacture its assemblies. All of this is very tangible material of which life – as we know it and might want it – could be assembled. Dance moves into a space but also makes room out of what it inhabits, invites gatherings of publics and enhances their capacities to pay attention, give audition, conduct kinesthetic effects and affects elsewhere (cf. Savigliano 1995).

Surely the complexity and scale of what makes life and what ails it can seem incomprehensible, unmovable, impermeable. Yet attention is repeatedly paid to those small rooms where such generalized harm was meted out, the meetings where decisions were made to war, to expropriate, to enclose. Dance offers a different intimacy of attention, an alternative somatization of risk, a sustainability of difference, a mutuality of debt that can also be shared, leveraged, embraced. We are living an excess that breeds so much scarcity. There is time to turn to what registers an excess in small spaces, tiny movements, unexpectedly expansive reliance that begins to assemble how else we might move together and how we might continue where these fleeting yet persistent performances leave off. Therein lays dance's promise beyond any singular incarnation, to amplify its means and methods toward a social that exceeds itself, a danced socialism from each accordingly toward all that find need in realizing what they want.

REFERENCES

Ahmad, Aijaz (1992): In Theory: Classes, Nations, Literatures, New York: Verso.

Albright, Ann Cooper (1997): Choreographing Difference: The Body and Identity in Contemporary Dance, Middletown, CT: Wesleyan University Press.

Allon, Fiona (2008): Renovation Nation: Our Obsession With Home, Sydney: New South.

Altman, Dennis (1986): AIDS in the Mind of America, Garden City, NY: Anchor Press.

Banes, Sally (1979): Terpsichore in Sneakers: Postmodern Dance, Middletown, CT: Wesleyan University Press.

Beck, Ulrich (1992): Risk Society: Towards a New Modernity, Newbury Park, CA: Sage.

Blau, Herbert (1990): The Audience, Baltimore: John Hopkins University Press.

Borden, Iain (2001): Skateboarding, Space and the City: Architecture, the Body and Performative Critique, New York: Berg.

Browning, Barbara (1995): Samba: Resistance in Motion, Bloomington: Indiana University Press.

Bryan, Dick/Rafferty, Mike (2006): Capitalism with Derivatives: A Political Economy of Financial Derivatives, Capital and Class, Basingstoke: Palgrave MacMillan.

Burt, Ramsay (2006): Judson Dance Theater: Performative Traces, London: Routledge.

Chatterjee, Ananya (2004): Butting Out: Reading Resistive Choreographies Through Works by Jawole Jo Zollar and Chandralekha, Middletown, CT: Wesleyan University Press.

Croce, Arlene (1994): "A Critic at Bay: Discussing the Undiscussable", in: The New Yorker, December 26, 1994, pp. 54-60.

de Monthoux, Pierre Guillet (2004): The Art Firm: Aesthetic Management and Metaphysical Marketing, Stanford, CA: Stanford University Press.

Feher, Michel (2009): "Self-Appreciation, or the Aspirations of Human Capital", in: Public Culture, Volume 21, Number 1, pp. 21-41.

Foster, Susan Leigh (2003): "Choreographies of Protest", in: Theatre Journal, Volume 55, Number 3, October 2003, pp. 395-412.

Gere, David (2004): How To Make Dances in An Epidemic: Tracking Choreography in an Age of AIDS, Madison, WI: University of Wisconsin Press.

Gordon, Avery/Newfield, Christopher (1996): Mapping Multiculturalism, Minneapolis: University of Minnesota Press.

Gottschild, Brenda Dixon (2003): The Black Dancing Body: A Geography from Coon to Cool, New York: Palgrave.

Hall, Stuart et al. (1978): Policing the Crisis: Mugging, the State, and Law and Order, New York: Holmes and Meier.

Harvey, David (2005): A Brief History of Neoliberalism, New York: Oxford University Press.

Jameson, Fredric (1984): "Periodizing The Sixties", in: Sohnya Sayres et al., The Sixties Without Apology, Minneapolis: University of Minnesota Press, pp. 178-209.

Kester, Grant (2004): Conversation Pieces: Community and Communication in Modern Art, Berkeley: University of California.

Klein, Naomi (1997): The Shock Doctrine: The Rise of Disaster Capitalism, New York: Metropolitan Books.

Kwon, Miwon (2002): One Place After Another: Site Specific Art and Locational Identity, Cambridge, MA: MIT Press.

Lewis, J. Lowell (1992): Ring of Liberation: Deceptive Discourse in Brazilian Capoeira, Chicago: University of Chicago.

Lyotard, Jean-Francois (1984): The Postmodern Condition: A Report on Knowledge, Minneapolis: University of Minnesota Press.

Martin, Carol (1996): "High Critics/Low Arts", in: Gay Morris (ed.), Moving Words: Re-writing Dance, New York: Routledge, pp. 320-333.

Martin, Randy (1998): Critical Moves: Dance Studies in Theory and Politics, Durham, NC: Duke University Press.

_____ (2007): An Empire of Indifference: American War and the Financial Logic of Risk Management, Durham, NC: Duke University Press.

McLean, Bethany/Elkind, Peter (2003): The Smartest Guys in the Room: The Amazing Rise and Scandalous Fall of Enron, New York: Portfolio.

McNamee, M.J. (2007): Philosophy, Risk, and Adventure in Sports, London: Routledge.

National Commission on Excellence in Education (1983): A Nation At Risk: The Imperative for Educational Reform, Washington, D.C.: Department of Education.

Pasquinelli, Matteo (2008): Animal Spirits: A Bestiary of the Commons, Amsterdam: NAI Press.

Power, Michael (1997): The Audit Society: Rituals of Verification, New York: Oxford University Press.

Ross, Andrew (2000): "The Mental Labor Problem", in: Social Text, 63 Summer 2000, pp. 1-32.

Rossiter, Ned (2006): Organized Networks: Media Theory, Creative Labour, New Institutions, Amsterdam: NAI Press.

Savigliano, Marta (1995): Tango and the Political Economy of Passion, Boulder, Co.: Westview Books.

Sholette, Gregory/Thompson, Nato (2004): The Interventionists: User's Manual for Creative Disruption of Everyday Life, Cambridge, MA: MIT.

Stuckey, Sterling (1987): Slave Culture: Nationalist Theory and the Foundations of Black America, New York: Oxford University Press.

Wa Thiongo, Ngugi (1986): Decolonising the Mind: The Politics of Language in African Literature, London: J. Currey.

Yudice, George (2003): The Expediency of Culture: Uses of Culture in the Global Era, Durham, NC: Duke University Press.

WEBSITE

Oxford English Dictionary, http://www.oed.com (September 13, 2010).

Dance and Work:
The Aesthetic and Political Potential of Dance

BOJANA KUNST

MOVEMENT BURSTING ON THE DIVIDING LINE

The first film ever made captured the movements of the workers of the Lumière factory collectively surging through the factory gates upon leaving their workplace at the end of the day (1895). This same film also opened the performance *1 poor and one 0* by BADco., a Zagreb-based performance group[1]. This mass exodus from the factory not only marks the beginning of cinematic history, but also the problematic relation between cinema and labor, which is also explored in Harun Farocki's documentary and text of the same title *Arbeiter Verlassen die Fabrik* (1995). In his commentary of the documentary, Farocki states that the primary aim of the movie was to represent motion, using the mass exodus of the workers. According to Farocki, there may also have been signposts helping the workers coordinate their movements when exiting the factory. Interestingly, this invisible movement takes place along specific lines, those marking the difference between labor and leisure time, between the industrial process and the factory, on the one hand, and the private lives of the workers, on the other. The movements of the workers, their simultaneously organized and spontaneous dispersal into different directions is choreographically organized as movement and filmically framed by the line separating the enclosed industrial space from

---

1 BADco. is a collaborative performance collective based in Zagreb, Croatia (from 2000). The artistic core of the collective are Pravdan Devlahović, Ivana Ivković, Ana Kreitmeyer, Tomislav Medak, Goran Sergej Pristaš, Nikolina Pristaš and Zrinka Užbinec.

private life, strictly rationalized procedures and so-called flexible leisure time. This is a line dividing dull work organization from leisure, when the workers can enjoy themselves, the mass organization of work and the atomized private lives of the workers. The dispersal of the workers renders their place of work invisible: the door to the factory is closed after their departure and the space, in which labor occurs, is left in darkness. Farocki mentions, that in the history of the cinema, the insides of factories were highlighted only when somebody wanted to leave, break it down or organize a strike. It was thus only featured when it became a space of conflict and was not only a dull, repetitive space to work in (cf. Farocki 2008: 1).

The whole performance *1 poor and one 0* revolves around that dividing line, always re-entering through that door, which is marked on stage by a simple crossbar. The performers repeatedly come through the gate, copying the movements of the workers in Lumière's movie. It almost seems as if they are in a motion picture experiment by Edward Muybridge, combining many short sequences of movement to give an impression of timing. In between these scenes, they discuss work-related issues: "What happens when you get tired? What happens when you leave work behind? When is the work we devote ourselves to exhausted? What comes after work? More work? What happens when there is no more work?" In the performance, these discussions clearly refer back to historical aspects of labor in the 20th century, especially to the gradual disappearance of that aforementioned dividing line. In this sense, they add another aspect to Farocki's observations. The place of work is no longer in darkness, but dispersed all over. It is not only a constituent part of leisure time, but intrinsically connected with its creative and transformative potential. By constantly repeating the movements from the 'first ever choreographed' movie, the performance becomes a collection of fragments and memories of movements, revealing that the first movie ever made arrived through a door, which today seems to have been taken off its hinges.

The movement of the workers is captured on a doorstep, which no longer exists; today there is no longer a dividing line between the movements of bodies subject to the rational organization of work and the dispersed atomization of society. Not only is the division between work and life being erased in post-industrial society; the essential qualities of life after work (imagination, autonomy, sociality, communication) have actually turned out to be at the core of contemporary labor.

FREEDOM OF SINGULAR MOVEMENT

How is the disappearance of the dividing line between labor and leisure time related to contemporary dance and the conceptualization of movement? To answer this question, I would first like to briefly reflect on the appearance of contemporary forms of dance in the 20th century and in particular how their aesthetical and political potential is continuously being formed in a complex relationship with existing production modes. There are many issues where the organization of labor production and the conceptualization of movement converge in the history of contemporary dance (like scientific management, movement reforms, return to the natural body, etc.), however, these aspects are especially intriguing where they are intertwined with the political and aesthetical potential of dance.

It is a well-known fact that, from the beginning of the 20th century, new dance forms were experienced as something strongly connected to the potentials of the contemporary human being. Autonomous movement of the body opened new potentials of human experience and relationships, and had strong emancipatorial effects on the understanding of the future. To put it simply, the new, modern forms of dance (Isadora Duncan, Martha Graham, Mary Wigman, etc.) were perceived as breaking with old modes of perception. They provided the possibility of a new aesthetic experience, because of their intrinsic relationship between movement and freedom, which was presupposed in almost every attempt at movement reform. Even today, as Bojana Cvejić writes, "dance still works as a metaphor for going beyond contracts, systems, structures, as models of theorizing subjectivity, art, society, and politics" (Cvejić 2004: n.p.). According to her, this might be because "movement operates from the middle of things. Makes us step outside the pre-determination of points and positions. Expresses the potential of moving relations." (Id.) It thus seems that movement itself is intrinsically political, in the sense that it tackles relationality and the dynamics of expression, the potentiality of what it could or could not be. However, in that 'middle of things', movement also operates in the introductory image of the text, in the image where we see the workers exiting the factory. Movement is captured to disappear into the unknown future; nevertheless it came from a particular threshold, which frames the potential of moving relations in a very specific way. This potential is then developed outside the rationalized organization of labor; outside the Fordist structure of production, it is the potential of movement that springs from life without work. Alliances, relations, divisions exist outside the factory, in the space which not only becomes a political space, but also a field of autonomous aesthetic experience in which the crisis of the subject, new methods of kinaesthetic perception were developed and institutionalized through the history of art in the 20th century. Therefore, it is no coincidence that the dance reforms of the early 20th century appeared at the same point in time as the movement of the working body was being heavily rationalized in the Fordist factory: as the organization of production was based on a scientifically researched kinaesthetic experience, which instrumentalized the movements of the body to increase the efficiency of production. The (largely female) dance pioneers (Isadora Duncan, Loïe Fuller, Ruth St. Denis, Mary Wigman, Valentine du Saint Point, etc.) entered the stage at a time when the organizational model of labor had become omnipresent, when all forms of false, expressive, slow, still, unexpected, wrong, clumsy, personal, lazy, ineffective, imaginative, additional movement was eliminated from physical labor. The utopian relationship between movement and freedom in the early stages of contemporary dance and dance reform was therefore associated with a notion of abstract freedom, but expressed the potential of moving relationships outside the factory door. This was the freedom of another kinaesthetic experience, which would not yield to instrumentalization or be subject to work, but discover the inner potential of the body.

One of the ways of describing this experience is the discovery of the 'natural body', which had less to do with resistance to the mechanization of contemporary life (whereby the term 'natural' wrongly implies that it is only about the difference between natural and artificial) and more with the discovery of a new universality, the natural sympathy of one body for another, as, for example, described by John Martin (cf. Martin 1990). The moving relations are no longer subordinated to dull routine and rationalization, but oscillate between the newly atomized society of capitalism and the new kinaesthetic subjects of industrialized western society.

I would like to argue that the appearance of dance reform and modern dance provided a movement and moving alternative to the kinaesthetic experience behind the factory door, which demanded the kinaesthetic sympathy of one body for another (and of course between body and machine) in order to create an efficient work process. We can even say that the feeling of modernity, contemporaneity of dancing, this disclosure of the kinaesthetic potentiality of body, was connected to the new kinaesthetic experience of leisure time, to this unknown and dynamic transversal outside work that is no longer subject to rational organization and the instrumentalization of movement. This is where we come to the core of the freedom implied in the emancipatory potential of dance. The conceptualization of movement in dance reform concerned the freedom of time without work, the discovery of the potential of leisure time, as opposed to the dull routine of movement during work. Movement expresses the potential of moving relationships within the creative time of the non-laboring subject. This can also be connected to the emerging consuming class, where movement reveals the unexpected, imagination, privacy, chance, flexibility, and discloses its expressive power. Here, time without work also becomes time for new aesthetic experiences. Contemporary dance had to develop new techniques, which could transform this freedom into language, develop the open virtuosity of the moving body rather than that of the instrumentalized product, and unleash spontaneity of movement as an aesthetic language rather then the scientific naturalization of movement. In this sense, the political and aesthetical potential of dance in the 20th century was strongly intertwined with the exit from the factory.

MOVEMENT OF GENERALITY

From this perspective, it is also interesting how popular imagination dealt with the work processes in the factory. Fordist production was often represented as synchronized group dancing, whereas dancing together functioned as an ornamental or critical representation of the subjugation of the worker's body to the industrialized and mechanistic processes in the factory. However, the only way to disturb this collective process came from the intervention of a singular body, from a body, which couldn't follow, was to clumsy, slow, dreamy, lazy or expressive, a body which took to much freedom to move, to express, or to achieve something.[2] Exactly these physical qualities, which prevented the body from dancing with others, were understood as expressions of humanism, or even better – of uncontrollable and undisciplinable human nature. The singular kinaesthetic experience continuously resisted the tuning of the group and its subjugation to the rationalized social machine.

However – what, in 20th century capitalist societies, was an expression of freedom, became, in other ideological constellations, the sabotage of society in general, the representation of an obsolete individualism, which is not able to adjust itself to the new transformations of society. I especially have in mind here the communist countries of Europe, where the image of dancing together functions as a depiction of societies where the dividing line between factory and private life is ideologically erased. Communist systems adopted all movement reforms in the production and work process, but did so with a different underlying concept. The socialist defenders of Taylorism (which included Lenin himself) understood the scientific management of work as a tool for the management of a

---

2   A famous example is Charlie Chaplin as working at a conveyor belt in the movie *Modern Times* (1936).

new society, where there would be no door between the factory and private life. In fact, there was a lot of discussion among Soviet communists and Russian avant-gardists on the hidden potentials of Taylorism and Fordism, which, in their opinion, went unnoticed by the Western capitalists, who had invented both. Lenin wrote that the Western (capitalist) implementation of Fordism, so it was believed, alienated the workers and developed an authoritarian method of organizing work. Socialist reformers and avant-gardists believed that the new methods of working together could transform society in general. The simultaneous movement of the workers was understood as a transgressive and transformative poetic form through which the development of the new society could materialize. Such was the conviction of A.K. Gastev, for example, one of the chief engineers and directors of the Central Institute of Labor in Moscow (he became its director in 1920). Gastev not only introduced Taylorist methods to the UdSSR and developed them further, but was also a famous poet, celebrating the new power of industrialized labor and the merging of the human being with the machine. In his poems, he developed rhythmical language to describe the new production process, where the workers would move and transform the entire historical era through their joint work.

"When the morning whistles resound over the workers' quarters, it is not at all a summons to slavery. It is the song of the future.
There was a time when we worked in poor houses and started our work at different hours of the morning.
And now, at eight in the morning, the whistles sound for a million men.
A million workers seize the hammers in the same moment.
Our first blows thunder in accord.
What is it that the whistles sing?
It is the morning hymn to unity." (Gastev/Bogdanov 1932: 357)

It is well known that the movement reforms of the Russian avant-garde (Meyerhold, Foregger, and partially – in the European context – also those of Laban) were heavily influenced by the new production processes, by their abstraction and rationalization. The movement reformers sought to abstract the body away from its interiority and develop an effective gestural language. In other words, they wanted to develop new kinaesthetic dynamics through the efficient use of gesture and a sharp instrumentalization of the body. Meyerhold, for example, began to rationalize the apparatus of movement; the actor's body also became a model for a general optimization of movement. Even though his work was closely connected to Gastev's and Taylor's utilitarian models of production, the methods he used, writes Gerald Raunig, went in another direction: he also wanted to denaturalize theatre (cf. Raunig 2010). Contrary to the psychology of a plot and the presence of an empathetic audience, and also contrary to the singular kinaesthetic experience of the dancing body, which was developing as an autonomous aesthetic language in the West (especially in North America), movement in the concepts of the Russian avant-garde (or the important components of biomechanics) consisted of the rhythm of language and the rhythm of physical movement, of postures and gestures arising from the collective rhythms, which coordinated the movements of the body and that of bodies with one another.

What we observe here are thus two different relationships between the conceptualization of movement and the organization of production (labor itself) in the 20th century. In so-called Western societies, which could be more accurately described as 'capitalist' societies, we see processes of naturalizing movement, which opposed the instrumental use of the laboring body and the rational organization of society. Such naturalization of movement corresponds with the discovery of the singular subject, an individual with desires and transversal and transgressive dynamic movement outside the modes of production (metaphorically speaking outside the factory gates). Most of the time, this individual is conceived as constantly in motion, in the throes of continuous creativity and possessing an autonomous aesthetic language: an individual, who cannot *not* dance.[3] On the other side, there is the proposition of coming through the factory gates – the idea that the modes of production can be intertwined with the transformation of society in general.

The movement reforms of the historical avant-gardes erased the door between work and private life, and revealed themselves as kinaesthetic constructions of larger future worlds. In the movement reforms of the Russian and European avant-gardes (especially the Futurists), a fascination with industrialized means of production led to experiments in denaturalizing movement. The body became a field of experimentation for future social transformation and for understanding a new commonality. Here dance and the production process paved the way to exploring a new generality of people: a generality that comes before any individualization, a sense of the political generality of the future, which has yet to come. Unfortunately, the discovery of the movement of this generality was an enormous failure. It quickly lost its emancipatory, political potential and became a totalitarian unity in the communist regime. Where a clumsy, still, expressive,

---

3 The aspects of kinetic ideologies of modernity are analysed in André Lepecki: *Exhausting Dance: Performance and the Politics of Movement* (2006).

lazy, dreamy, everyday, marginal movement is possibly perceived in capitalist societies as the intervention of a liberated singularity, in the communist regimes, this kind of movement sabotaged the whole social machine. In their utopian pursuit of the future, these societies erased everything that radically existed in the present, because of the cynical belief that the future had already arrived. It therefore comes as no surprise that the communist regimes actually celebrated the most conservative and disciplinary forms of dancing, such as mass gatherings or the authoritarian institution of ballet.

This comparison between two concepts of movement – one that situates the political potential of dance in the movement of a singularity and the other in the discovery of a new (political) generality of the people (especially if we stay with avant-garde concepts) – leads, from today's perspective, to a very interesting observation. We are living in an age that is erasing the doors between factory and leisure time, in a time where individual potential and singular creativity is central to production. The movement of this working rhythm is very different from the description in Gastev's poem, which celebrates exactly the same disappearance of the factory doors. Instead of a synchronized totality of work as a new transformation of society, represented through the image of 'everybody starting at the same time' as described in his poem, today the new transformation of society is taking place with disharmonious working rhythms and flexible working hours, with individualized and displaced work. The factory whistle is replaced by self-imposed and silent deadlines, which drive people to multiple simultaneous and interconnected work and living activities. The movement of the individual, which throughout the 20th century was celebrated as the discovery of the potential of freedom stands at the centre of appropriation, of the exploitation of its affective, linguistic and desirable aspects. Today we are forced to dance in virtuous and conceptual diachronicity when producing; to change places, time, and identities quickly and with only short (but hardly ever destructive) outbursts of crisis. This is the new universality of the post-industrial world and its mode of production.

THE DISAPPEARANCE OF THE GATES AND ITS CONSEQUENCES

This argument leads me to a cartoon from 1980 by the well-known American cartoonist and satirist Dr. Seuss (Theodor Seuss Geisel) – *Pontoffel Pock Where Are You?* In this cartoon we again find a satirical image of workers dancing together; the working process in a pickle factory is actually depicted as a harmonious musical. However, one of the new workers, Pontoffel Pock, is quite a looser. He is clumsy and always disrupting the process, poor and unhappy. Clumsy by nature and dreamy by heart, he tries to push and pull the machine as the other workers do, but in his eagerness to do it well, he destroys the whole factory and is dismissed from the factory in disgrace. Wallowing in self-pity, he is approached by an angel, who presents himself as a representative of a global corporation with branches all over the world. Because, as the corporative angel tells him, his lifestyle is pitiable, he is offered a wondrous piano. All that Pontoffel Pock needs to do is to play a few notes, push the bottom of the piano and he can fly to any exotic destination in the world to experience beautiful and exciting adventures. All that is required is a little tune; with just a little bit of virtuosity, he can fly away into an unknown and exciting future. But again Pontoffel Pock is unable to behave right. He has trouble with unpredictable gestures and movements, with his body, which desires too much and is 'always in the wrong place'. He cannot simply enjoy and be spontaneous. Instead he destroys all social relations with his ill-timed actions. This continues until he finds the love of his life (an Arab princess) and gets one more try at a pickle factory.

The cartoon offers a very good description of the shift that occurred at the beginning of the 1970s, a shift, which can be today be described with the terms post-industrialism or post-Fordism, especially when speaking about modes of working. The main characteristics of this shift have been deep changes in the organization of production and the role of labor, which influences social relations in general. Creative, linguistic and affective labor has become central to production. Labor is no longer organized in an instrumental and rationalized way, behind factory doors, but has become part of the production of social life and relationships among people. What was previously excluded from the de-naturalized movement of the Fordist machine is today at the centre of production: creative, spontaneous, expressive and inventive movement. Contemporary production structures demand creative and capable individuals. Their constant movement and dynamism have become the promise of economic value.

The image of production as dancing together is today an anachronistic one, due also to the ineffectiveness of its social critique. Today Fordist machinery has moved out of our range of vision to countries with a cheap labor force, where there is no escape into leisure time, but only the brutal exploitation of life in all its aspects. The contemporary post-Fordist worker is no longer included in the rationalized machine, but is instead part of affective and flexible networks, with his or her own potential for sale. Italian philosopher Paolo Virno, describes the qualities required of a post-Fordist worker, by saying that such qualities are never qualities

"[...] regarding professional expertise or technical requirements. On the contrary, what is required is the ability to anticipate unexpected opportunities and coincidences, to seize chances that present themselves, to move with the world. These are not skills people learn at the workplace. Nowadays, workers learn such required abilities by living in a big city, by gaining aesthetic experiences, having social relationships, creating networks: all things workers learn specifically outside the workplace, in real life in a contemporary big city." (Virno 2009: n.p.)

In other words, production today is experienced as something spontaneous and flexible. The process of work is always "subject to our own initiative" (id.). In the process of work, "I need to be granted a certain degree of autonomy in order to be exploited" (id.). It is from this perspective that we can also understand another image of dancing together, which has begun appearing over the past years in countries belonging to the post-industrial world: huge flash mobs organized by corporations and television companies. On the surface, it seems that these dances celebrate spontaneity and the emotional strength of human relations. However what really constitutes them are celebrations of commercialized joy and spectacular togetherness.

DANCE AND THE ABSTRACTION OF WORK

If we agree with Virno's observation, then it is necessary to rethink the consequences of such changes in the modes of working for the conceptualization of contemporary dance, especially where I have claimed that dance discovers its political and aesthetic potentiality in relationship to the production process. What are the consequences for contemporary dance with these changes in mind? What could the disappearance of the differentiation between work and non-work mean for the relationship between dance and freedom, which was always somehow the basis of thinking about dance reform in the 20th century?

First, it should not be overlooked, that the relationship between dance and freedom no longer has anything to do with resistance to rigid and disciplinary modes of production. Unexpected, non-hierarchical structures, affectivity and linguistic/physical expression have entered post-industrial production and represent the core of post-Fordism as the new organization of the production processes we are living in. The autonomy of creativity and aesthetic experience, which was so important when resistance to the rationalization of labor first emerged, now represents an important source of producing value. What we thus observe are relationships between contemporary dance and new modes of production, in which movement and constant flexibility play a central role, together with individual expression and spontaneous creativity. Today subjugation is composed of continuous movement, a flexibility of relationships, signs, connections, gestures, bodies – continuous dispersion outside the factory gates with the intent to produce (and spend) even more. Production today encourages constant transformation and the crisis of the singular subject, with the intention of capturing outbursts of creativity and translating them into value. Production encourages ceaseless collaboration, which must be temporary, but not too affective, otherwise it can become ill-timed and destructive.

If this is truly the case, then we must ask ourselves what it exactly is that we do, when we work, or more precisely, when we work with dance. The political potential of dance is not related to the space outside of work, where the body is free to move and disclose its potential of being in time and space, but it must be put into dialogue with the flexible production modes and immateriality of contemporary work. It is common knowledge that the production of contemporary dance is today becoming more flexible through continuous travel. Where the exchange of forever-young and forever-experimental performances (a kind of cheap labor force for more and more globalized performance markets) goes hand in hand with spectacular shows. How collaboration is encouraged for collaboration's sake. How the continuous traveling movement of the labor force is unavoidable. However it is often forgotten that dance and movement have their own materiality, not only that of the body, but also of time and space, which is not abstract, rushed into the spectral kinetic flow, but can also be grasped, located, stuck, rough and ill-timed. This materiality resists the contemporaneity of time and in some ways sabotages the spectral appearance of the 'now' and gives another rhythm to the flow of time. This materiality can be also be brought into relationship with the materiality of work in general and in this sense, dance is again very close to questions of labor.

Thus dance is not close to questions of work, because of its ability to function as a representation of work, an image of the working process, but because it is work in terms of its material rhythms, efforts, in how movement inhabits space and time. It is work in the sense of how bodies distribute themselves in space and time, how they relate to each other and how they spend and expand their energies. The political potential of dance therefore does not have to be sought in an abstract or democratic idea of freedom and the infinite potential of movement, but in the ways how dance is deeply intertwined with the power and exhaustion of work, with its virtuosity and failure, dependence and autonomy. In this sense, dance practice over the last decades has stressed its own ontological propositions (such as dance equals movement, production and collaboration in dance, the relationship between dance and theory) (cf. Lepecki 2006; Kunst 2009; Franko 1995). These are propositions, which all open up dance practice to being aware of the relationship between dance and work. If dance is work (and not something opposite to it, dance freed from the materiality of it), then the political potential of dance can also be understood as an interesting repetition or replacement of the avant-garde gesture: what would that proposition – dance as work – mean for a future society? Is it possible to discover an alternative to continuous movement and speed, to the flexibility of bodies and spaces, to the dispersion of energy and the power of the bodies collected together only for advertisement purposes and massive spectacles? One such answer could be that dance can reveal how kinetic sensibilities not only flow, but open up caesuras, antagonisms and unbridgeable differences. In this sense, many dance performances of the last decade have re-questioned the relationship between movement and dance and broadened the notion of choreography. Another answer could be that dance with its materiality can resist the abstract notion of labor and reveal the problematic relationship between the abstract new modes of labor and the bodies themselves. New modes of labor have tremendous power over the body, especially because they are increasingly erasing every representable and imaginable generality of the body. The dancing body is no longer resisting the dull conditions of work in search of a new society outside of work, but it does have the power to disclose how the materiality of bodies distributed in the time and space can change the way we live and work together. It can use this politically and aesthetically transgressive line between work and non-work to open up chances for a future society.

REFERENCES

Cvejić, Bojana (2004): "How open are you open? Pre-sentiments, pre-conceptions, pro-jections", http://www.sarma.be/text.asp?id=1113 (June 21, 2010).

Farocki, Harun (2008): "Workers Leaving the Factory", in: 1 poor and one 0 (= programme of the performance), Zagreb: BADco.

Franko, Mark (1995): Dancing Modernism, Performing Politics, Bloomington: Indiana University Press.

Gastev, A.K. (1932): "The Song of the Workers Blow", in: Aleksandr Bogdanov, Proletarian Poetry, The Labour Monthly, June 1932, pp. 357-362.

Kunst, Bojana (2009): Prognosis on Collaboration, in: Gabriele Brandstetter et al. (eds.), Prognosen über Bewegungen, Berlin: B-Books, pp. 336-347.

Lepecki, André (2006): Exhausting Dance: Performance and the Politics of Movement, Routledge: Champan and Hall.

Martin, John (1990): The Modern Dance, Hightstown, NY: Dance Horizons.

Raunig, Gerald (2010): A Thousand Machines: A Concise Philosophy of the Machine as a Social Movement, trans. by Aileen Derieg (= Semiotext[e]) Cambridge, MA: MIT Press.

Virno, Paolo (2009): "The Dismesure of Art", in: Open 17, A Precarious Existence, Vulnerability in the Public Domain, http://www.skor.nl/article-4178-en.html (June 21, 2010).

FILMS

Arbeiter verlassen die Fabrik (1995) (DE, D: Harun Farocki)

Modern Times (1936) (USA, D: Charles Chaplin)

Pontoffel Pock, Where Are You (1980) (USA, D: Gerard Baldwin)

The Collective That Isn't One

LIGNA in conversation with SANDRA NOETH

SANDRA NOETH: In your performative audio play *Der neue Mensch. Vier Übungen in utopischen Bewegungen* (*The New Human. Four Exercises in Utopian Movements*)[1], which was also presented during the Dance Congress 2009, you strongly focused on concepts of collectivity and the choral. The piece is a collective choreography designed with the help of various traces of instructions and absent references, which the members of the audience experience and execute individually via headphones. How is this relationship between the individual versions of the movement instructions and the formation of the groups organized?[2]

OLE FRAHM: Our question is aimed at the audience as a collective. One starting point was the idea that in theater the audience situation is rarely brought into play. In other words: you always have the presence of a crowd of people, who have more or less randomly met in the auditorium, without really having gone there together. There is a certain recognizable middle-class audience, who are there on a regular basis, but ultimately it is dominated by a necessary anonymity,

---

1   *Der neue Mensch. Vier Übungen in utopischen Bewegungen*, premiere October 2008, Kampnagel Hamburg.

2   The conversation between LIGNA and Sandra Noeth took place on February 7, 2010 in Vienna. LIGNA is Ole Frahm, Michael Hüners and Torsten Michaelsen and exists since 1997. The group develops situations between theater, dance, installation and performance, which establish new spaces of action, enable unlikely, collective movements and reinvent the role of the audience. With their models of performative radio use, such as the radio ballet, they intervene in the public sphere and question its norms and controls.

so that the individual can focus on what is happening on stage. So there's this collective, which doesn't act, but only observes and which is physically attacked by the stagnant air in the very narrow corridors. We wanted to cast the spotlight on precisely this group – and for this, we of course looked to Bertolt Brecht and his *Lehrstücke* (teaching plays). What interested us most was how the audience can be moved to become aware of itself. Namely by putting them into contact with one another ...

TORSTEN MICHAELSEN: ... and allowing them to become an audience for the others. The audience is thus split up into four groups, who perform different things parallel. In doing so, they follow four different movement concepts – by Rudolf von Laban, Vsevolod Meyerhold, Bertolt Brecht and Charlie Chaplin – and because these groups are set in a certain relationship to each other and watch each other during the performance, every participant is both actor and spectator. You see things that you have already performed yourself or which you will be performing and after a while you understand the structure of the piece. We create a situation in which you can, so to say, play with the others, but in which something always evades capture, something that can only be accessed bit by bit through the process. However, it's not necessary the case that you can grasp the totality of the piece after seeing the four parts. I believe there is always something left over that you don't have, which maybe didn't quite work out, which is random for all in each and every performance.

OLE FRAHM: The decisive aspect is that the singular experience of the spectator cannot be replaced. It is always singular. You may be part of a collective, but will always remain within your own realm of how you perceive the space and your own body in relation to everyone else. This subjectivity is something that is created by the headphones. It would be a completely different situation, if we would use a single loud radio. But it is precisely the internalization of the external radio voice, which creates the personal space of perception, which in turn produces one's own irreplaceable relationship with the world.

If I am part of the Laban group for instance and I see how the others raise their hands, I know that we're hearing the same thing and yet nevertheless I don't know for sure how the others interpret what they are hearing. Especially in the case of the Laban swings as presented in the piece, it's not quite clear to amateurs how to execute them. At the Dance Congress it was of course very nice to see how the many dancers present in the audience performed these swings.

On the one hand, there's this singularity of perception, on the other, there is a collective moment of awareness, which is somewhat scary. In the performance, we repeat the choreography of the first *Radioballett*[3] four times. In the video documentation, we can see how in the first round, in which people are supposed to point upwards, some point up with a straight finger, other with an outstretched hand.[4] Over the course of three-quarters of an hour, the mass forms itself and unconsciously agrees on how each individual should point. This harmonization definitely has something to do with the principle of mimesis. It is the mimetic ability of humans, which evidently articulates itself as a desire to be formed – almost as if there were such a thing as a correct execution of the movements. This mimetic force is also in *Der neue Mensch* – for example in the previously mentioned swings.

SANDRA NOETH: My impression is that failure plays a major role. Thoughts such as: "I'm too slow", "I can't follow", "I missed something in between". In the beginning, the audience is very occupied with trying to understand the structure of the piece and then gradually slips into its role, learns to handle the theatrical space, has maybe already repeated some movements. What surprised me is that apparently the audience usually very quickly accepts what you're suggesting. Even if everyone is free to act as they wish, the authority of the voice in the headphones takes effect. Regarding the dance context and the dance and art historical dimensions that you are addressing as a group, this observation reminds me of choreographic processes of creating unisono and group figures in connection with concepts of subjectivity and individuality as are currently being intensely discussed.

OLE FRAHM: Yes, the work of Rudolf von Laban was one starting point, which had a couple of aspects that we found difficult. But then there are also moments in his work, which really impressed me. When Laban joined those veggie communes near the Lago Maggiore, he developed a radicality in his art, which is truly uncompromising. But which still – and that is the decisive difference to the other three positions – really searched for attaining unity with the cosmos through dance. Laban's modernist 'We-must-return-to-the-fundamental-structures-of-movement' and his conviction that dance needs no music, were very controversial positions in his time. He had a modernity, which far surpassed his

---

3 *Radioballett. Übung in nichtbestimmungsgemäßen Verweilen* (*Radio Ballet. Exercise in Lingering Outside of Regulations*), Hamburg 2002.

4 See also: *Übung in unnötigem Aufenthalt* (*Exercise in Unnecessary Residency*), Installation, Group exhibition *Art on Air. Radiokunst im Wandel* (*Radio Art in Flux*), Neues Museum Weserburg Bremen 2008/2009.

aesthetic horizon. That, which he really performed, is, in descriptions, often quite banal and above all reactionary, such as reproducing the stereotypical images of the city as juggernaut verses the harmony of nature. Interestingly enough, the performance situation of the movement choirs attest to a kind of grotesque aesthetic that allows associations to Chaplin, Brecht and Meyerhold.

TORSTEN MICHAELSEN: These four positions handle the subject, this civil subject, the First World War and the social changes taking place in this period, as well as the challenges of an audience, which is largely no longer a middle-class one, very differently. These are not somehow positions that we want to measure with the same yardstick just so as to extract a LIGNA message out of them. Instead it is interesting for us to create a constellation in which their disparities become clear and which also relates to them on a formal level. What we're doing is concerning ourselves with question of subjectivity. How can we conceive a non-authentic, playful subjectivity, which creates itself through the execution of movements? In this respect, the formal structure of the piece always refers back to the positions we have chosen.

SANDRA NOETH: An important aspect is the how you address the body – between the present bodies of today's audience and those of the 1920s. One the one hand, it contains the formulation of various concepts of subjectivity and community, but it also plays with representations, symbolisms and fiction. Moreover, a certain additional moment of translation seems to play a role – through the language, i.e. the original quotes, but also your contemporary narrative relating to the movement concepts. How do these various discourses and levels come together in the piece?

OLE FRAHM: What interests us is how the audience forms this shared body within a discourse, which may not be very accessible for most of them in the beginning. And which is composed of entirely banal things such as shaking hands with the right hand, walking forward, etc. To state it more precisely, we superimpose two discourses. There is the everyday discourse, which creates the bodies, the subjects and which brings into play a specific, never quite conscious form of subjectivity. On the other hand, we try to find out whether and how this can be contrasted with, disrupted by the discourses on the body from the 1920s. To find out what kind of body should shape the new human. The really interesting thing is to what degree artists in the 1920s were completely confident in their own aesthetic and its social power of effect – from the Futurists right down to the writings of the avant-garde until 1933. You didn't just make a good piece; you were immediately connected to the entire universe. The Futurist painters truly believed that they could paint the laws of the cosmos. And by doing so burn them into the consciousness of the spectator. This discussion is very exciting when we realize that certain questions have been forgotten, namely whether certain collective processes can also be changed collectively and not only be changed top down, as for example through physical education in schools. To bring about change truly as a collective, so that moments can occur with which the institutions and discourses that form the body themselves become negotiable. That means the individual in his or her own body is however only relevant if the social situation is also taken into consideration. Theater rarely takes into consideration the physical situation of the spectator, ignores or forgets its physical situation in the space and reduces him or her to his or her audio-visual apparatus or perception.

For me these aesthetic models are so interesting because they began as early as the 1920s to rethink this relationship differently and didn't limit themselves to the statement that reception is active, because things are assembled in perception. Instead they insisted that we ourselves have to be in the situation, must act for ourselves in the situation. And in *Der neue Mensch* we mainly began thinking about how our own subjectivity is constituted by the body. I find the Brecht sentence – we think differently when the feet are higher than the head – quite revealing. It does work in a certain way; when the spatial situation changes, we are physically different.

MICHAEL HÜNERS: Of course that is nevertheless also just simply a statement. But trying it out, that's what's so exciting. To see whether something happens, to test it. And then it's also quite important that it is still the body acting as the site of resistance. In other words, we could use this body as a starting point to arrive at a political body. What we're looking at in the piece is a social issue. The question of a utopia, of renegotiating society anew or simply projecting it differently. And in this, the body is of course very crucial.

OLE FRAHM: We also discussed whether the piece might be problematic in this day and age. You can't even go to the theater without being accosted. Like those websites, where you have to write your opinion. And that is exactly where the distinction lies. Namely that there is a difference between what we do and this activation of the spectator by the media, which is based in principle upon collecting statistics on the viewer as consumer, in a manner of speaking. In our case there's no surplus value in this respect. On the contrary: you can simply begin to think about what kind of society you want to live in generally.

MICHAEL HÜNERS: These four positions are also outlines. We don't want to lay claim to the fact that if you assemble these four positions something completely new could emerge. And we could question the selection. Why did it have to be exactly these four positions, it could also have been done in a different way.

OLE FRAHM: These four really very different positions surprisingly share an aesthetic, which was not yet authoritarian in the 1920s, and converges on the grotesque, as Chaplin articulated it in his early films, in the display of gesture. The notion of the new human is often prematurely associated with totalitarian regimes. The aesthetic of the grotesque with its discovery of stasis, of interruption doesn't toe that line, however. Laban accordingly dispensed with grotesque elements in his choreographic work under the Nazis. In the course of our research, we discovered that our own aesthetic has also always contained a certain moment of the grotesque.

TORSTEN MICHAELSEN: Ultimately we have always worked in the style of the grotesque. Even in our first performative pieces, we used the radio in such a way that it didn't demand from the people that they really act out theater. It was always about performing gestures. As for example at the Main Train Station in Hamburg, where we presented the *Radioballett* and wanted to let the people perform gestures that subverted or transcended the regulations of the space.

For us, it has always been about discovering that movement always has a real effect on the space even when it is performed mechanically. You don't have to be the person sitting down, so to say; you don't have to perform what you're doing. You simply do it and that in itself has effect. Basically, it is always an invitation to non-emphatic acting, which seeks to challenge you to observe yourself doing something instead. And to see what happens when you do. It's a very Meyerhold-like thought. The movement is what matters and the truly conscious execution of this movement and then the reflection of the effect of the entire thing. And that is – I would say – already an aesthetic, which is entirely more grotesque than any kind of emphatic aesthetic. This is also always our answer to the questions: "You create robots or soldiers, don't you ..." and "Isn't that dangerous?" – We would answer with Brecht from the *Messingkauf* (cf. Brecht 2003) that investing emotional energy in the actor or in the Fuehrer, to whom Brecht comes in the end, is ultimately what makes one passive and what is so dangerous. And he responds to that with an aesthetic, which refuses to do exactly that. Which instead discovers the possible distance more in one's own acting. What we're also trying to do is open up the space by playing with subjectivity.

SANDRA NOETH: This detachment in the historical text sections, the voices of the narrators, but also the formal detachment in the piece's performance concept seem to me to be very important and the idea that an encounter can only become possible through this detachment, that only through distance is infection possible. What is interesting in this respect is also that radio as a medium produces diversion. If we read the choreographic as a focused inscription, then we are confronted in your practice with that fact that many things – spaces, structures of receptivity and time – are being dissolved and sent back to their original location and that the location of the choreography is constantly changing and shifting.

TORSTEN MICHAELSEN: We began working with the term choreography, when he started calling them 'choreographies of forbidden and excluded gestures'. We don't choreograph in the sense that we arrange the participants in the space and purposefully create movement in most sections of the piece. It can happen that a very direct movement materializes, there is the alignment along the outside edges of the space, an orientation towards the middle, and this is in principle choreographed without us really specifying and determining positions. This kind of thing has to create itself in some other way. By all means, there is a certain composition of the space, whereby the main impression of the piece is that actually very diverse things are happening at the same time and all mixed up with each other and that the positions also occasionally get confused and don't comply with an overall view, but instead are carried out parallel in a disorderly fashion.

MICHAEL HÜNERS: That is why the term choreography is somewhat difficult, because it can't be thought of as a central perspective directed at a single viewer. It is more about the possibilities of the space or rather the possibility of creating certain situations within the space between and together with these four separate groups. And that is why we don't really have the intention of creating a choreographic scheme for a single spectator.

OLE FRAHM: The four positions each follow a different sequence. It is therefore as if we were talking about four pieces. The first position shapes the perception of the piece. Accordingly the overall dramaturgy presents itself different depending on which position that it. At the same time there is a precise rhythm in each of the four repeating parts. At the premiere, we were surprised at how long the Laban people did their swings in that part. It was great for the spatial situation, because it established a funny consistent structure. At the same time, we fixed certain clear points – especially in the stage performance at the end of each respective part. We chose a very simple situation, namely two rows of chairs, which structure the space, emphasized by a spotlight, which illuminates the middle of the space. Moreover it is striking how people never go into the corners of the space, even when the space is completely illuminated. They orient themselves towards the center. In contrast, it's different in the walking part; everyone walks along the edge on purpose, so as not to bother the others in the middle. But there are also a few things that even today aren't quite clear. Chaplin claps his hands on the stage and Meyerhold should – as practiced beforehand – jump. But that only happens in rare cases.

TORSTEN MICHAELSEN: I really like it when the last jump by the Meyerhold people is accompanied by the humming of the Brecht people. This creates a rhythmisation. And really there are a great number of overlapping moments, which converge by accident. Ultimately we just brought those things together, which clearly refer to one another – the one side, which does something and the other, which produces the effect. The rest is simply not so precisely choreographed.

MICHAEL HÜNERS: The question is simply, whether a piece shouldn't always have unintended openings, intervals, accidents, interruptions. – A precisely timed, fully choreographed piece aspires towards being something completely self-contained.

OLE FRAHM: It really is difficult. We developed various notations, while writing the piece. In the end it was the sound program, which emerged as the most precise form of notation, this strict synchrony of the track. For us the technical element plays a large role. What situations does the radio create, which no other apparatus can create? Our choreography was based on the question of how the apparatus can be used to produce a particular situation that exceeds one's own power of imagination.

SANDRA NOETH: In this light maybe the choreographic as a space-time structure applies more to radio than to a concrete movement score. At the same time 'reading' notation via hearing demands a more specific form of translation than for example deriving movements from one body to another. What is it that is being transmitted? Words, text, references and ideas, but also simultaneously rhythm and pitch of the voice …

TORSTEN MICHAELSEN: It is interesting that a movement also has to be described very differently when it is intended for a situation such as this one, in which it simply runs linearly past the ears and the listener then has to execute it. That is also something we firs had to experience for ourselves. You can brilliantly write the movement down on paper, so that it sounds good when you read it. But when you hear it, it doesn't work. First of all, the capacity to absorb information is very limited. In the Laban part for instance, three orientations in the space are explained and that already is quite a lot of information. Then there's the problem of missing parts. Is it then at all possible to retain one's orientation, can you then still continue?

OLE FRAHM: According to Brecht, a great deal of the pleasure comes from precise interaction with the apparatus. Of course we try to build up tension between the things that must be executed very precisely, where you really know that you're doing them correctly and those things, which are simply somewhat less clear. If we had open, poetic instructions the whole time, then people would think, "What do they want from me?". And on the contrary, a constant imperative would be just as boring. The format of the *Radioballett* has been presented by other people on various occasions and it has been interesting to see that, from our perspective, if something didn't really work aesthetically, it was either because it had transformed into a kind of street theater or into a pure simple imperative. It is a fine line that we work on. I truly believe that our subjectivity is constructed in such a way that there is pleasure in the correct execution of something, but that it also needs this detachment.

SANDRA NOETH: ... in order to still identify it as a game, as acting?

OLE FRAHM: Brecht said, "It is possible to also live in third-person". There have to be these audience spaces that are indeterminate. For me, one of the most interesting moments is when Brecht rebuilds the set out of chairs. In this moment, it is all about the audience reaching consensus among each other and how the space is truly restructured into something new. These are the moments in which we ask ourselves, what really is our responsibility in continuing to allow this piece to be enjoyable. And that also brings up the question whether there are people who don't participate at all. And if there are such people, are they spoilsports, almost in a Chaplin-esque sort of way, precisely because they don't take on any form of responsibility? On such a note, we can also reflect the institutions that create our subjectivity. Some truly believe in their subjectivity as citizens – I am utterly original, I am not replaceable. Of course, this runs contrary to our approach. And it is quite surprising to a degree, because it is a theory of subjectivity, which is fundamentally embedded in the 19th century and is apparently still being cultivated, instead of making use of the freedoms provided by the 21st century.

SANDRA NOETH: There is after all also the question why the piece is made for a theater institution and not for a different space.

TORSTEN MICHAELSEN: We made the piece for the stage or rather for a theatrical space precisely because the piece deals with that same space of theatrical reception.

OLE FRAHM: We resisted the stage for a long time. In the first piece that we created for Kampnagel, the stage there seemed too small for the wild strike that we wanted to retell. We thought that we had to leave the theater, go out into the public sphere – in other words, interrupt the representation, bring the actual materiality of the body into play. Which also happens now, but on the interior, as we have discussed. Brecht was very helpful in this regard by pointing out this function of theater: you have a spatial situation, which is completely artificial in its artificiality, but which – if its artificiality is taken seriously – suddenly establishes entire discourses. Of course, we could perform *Der neue Mensch* in schools, for example, but that would be a completely differently affair.

TORSTEN MICHAELSEN: Then we would really have to make a piece about school. *Der Neue Mensch* is a piece about the audience and therefore it makes sense to perform it on a stage and to see what form of audience could actually come after an audience – so the proposition of the positions from the 1920s – which has simply outlasted itself, wasn't able to follow through with its transformation in mass society. Thus the audience is called upon to put into practice a new approach. This is exactly what Meyerhold and Brecht were looking into. And Laban ultimately did so as well, by letting the audience disappear altogether. And Chaplin too – by presuming that an audience simply needed a really good joke every 30 seconds in order to be emotionally involved.

REFERENCE

Brecht, Bertolt (2003): The Messingkauf Dialogues, trans. by John Willett, 2nd edition, London: A&C Black.

HYBRID SPHERES

Jérôme Bel and Myself:
Gender and Intercultural Collaboration

Susan Leigh Foster

In what follows, I stage a three-way conversation between French choreograph-
er Jérôme Bel, myself as a feminist scholar writing about a piece he created in
collaboration with Thai dancer Pichet Klunchun entitled Pichet Klunchun and
Myself *(2004), and myself watching the performance of the lecture along with*
Bel.

When I performed this imaginary conversation with Bel at the Dance Con-
gress in Hamburg 2009, the two versions of myself shared one microphone at a
podium and I impersonated 'Bel' speaking from a different microphone at the
same podium, with each 'person' articulating a different style and tone. At that
presentation, Bel was in the audience, and we began a dialogue afterwards that
is ongoing, and for that reason, I chose to retain the conversation format used in
the conference for this published version of the text. Since the conference presen-
tation, I have viewed a subsequent collaboration that Bel undertook with Klun-
chun, About Khon *(2009), in which he takes on a role very different from the one*
in Pichet Klunchun and Myself. *The conversation that follows gestures towards*
the ongoingness of both his artistic research and my scholarly inquiry and to the
ways in which artists and scholars might enter into dialogues of great mutual
benefit.

Like Bel, I believe that both choreographers and dance scholars engage in
research. They propose hypotheses about the nature of corporeality and the con-
struction of identities, both individual and social, and they investigate the rami-
fications and consequences of their various propositions. Whether this research
issues on the concert stage or the printed page, it offers different and equally va-
lid ways of knowing. Therefore, I have attempted to adapt the format of Pichet
Klunchun and Myself *in this essay, 'choreographing' the writing so as to affirm*

the importance of performance as a form of knowledge production and, at the same time, de-stabilizing scholarship so that it is not construed as 'having the last word'.

About a half hour into his conversation with Pichet Klunchun about his career as a dancer, Jérôme Bel asks Klunchun to teach him some dance. Declining to learn the role of the demon, because he is not in good shape, Bel requests, instead, to be instructed in a phrase from the female repertoire, one of the three other principle character types in Khon, classical Thai dance. Klunchun then takes him through a phrase, explaining in detail the positions and actions of legs, torso, arms, hands, fingers, and head. Although designed to illustrate the complexities of the form, this pedagogical moment also demonstrates Bel's ability to pick up the movement and execute, at least superficially, a relatively accurate, for the untrained body, version of the phrase. It also secures the notion of gender as performance as these two renowned male artists pursue a seemingly spontaneous cross-cultural conversation about their work.

JÉRÔME: You read that one sentence quite well – it had a lot of commas and halts and awkward turns, but you managed it. Were you trying to choreograph the sentence so as to suggest the way that a dancer learns movement?
MYSELF: Yes, it's very nice that you noticed.

Touring for the past five years internationally and to adulatory reviews and standing ovations across Europe and North America and to more mixed reviews in Korea, Singapore, and Indonesia, *Pichet Klunchun and Myself* stages a dialogue between two artists, who ask each other questions and demonstrate their work to one another as a way of finding out about each other's worlds of dance.[1]

JÉRÔME: This seems like a congenial gathering of people. Does it make you nervous, standing up in front of them and delivering a lecture?
MYSELF: Always.

In what follows, I want to examine *Pichet Klunchun and Myself* in relation to its representation of gender and, even more, the gendered division of labor that it embodies in order to discern what I see as serious obstacles to intercultural col-

---

1 *Pichet Klunchun and Myself* had its premiere at the Patravadi Theatre's Studio 1 as part of the Bangkok Fringe Festival. Singaporean producer Tang Fu Kuen initiated by collaboration pairing the two artists who were unfamiliar with each other's work.

laboration. I use gender as an analytic framework for categorizing action throughout the performance in order to reveal the underpinnings of the euphoria produced by this display of cross-cultural conversation and understanding. *Pichet Klunchun and Myself* performs the felicitous heterosexual marriage of two cultures whose histories of privilege, wealth, and access to global circulation of products and ideas have been markedly different. It also reaffirms and reinvigorates hierarchies of civilization implemented in Europe's colonization of the world. Although the association between the feminine and the Other and the ways in which the two are used to mutually marginalize one another have been demonstrated innumerable times, I still find it illuminating to move across this territory, yet again, especially in the context of the recent explosion of intercultural collaborations in the arts.

JÉRÔME: And you have to stand very still and look very serious while you read?

The feminine is referenced in this performance seven times: 1) as Klunchun's description of his mother who wanted a son, the more desirable gender, especially after having had three daughters; 2) as one of four types in the classical Thai repertoire of characters; 3) as a character demonstrated by Klunchun who has just been told about the death of her husband; 4) as a form that it would be easier for Bel to learn than the demon form; 5) as the child bearing, non-married partner of Bel and as the vehicle for a family desired by Klunchun, but who does not want to marry, a prerequisite for having children in Thai culture; 6) as the transgendered character of Bel lip-synching Roberta Flack's performance of the song *Killing Me Softly with His Song* in order to demonstrate death onstage;[2] and 7) as the nearly naked dancers performing in a sex bar in Bangkok.

In addition to these appearances of the feminine on stage and in the dialogue, I am also interested in the performance of the feminine that occurs throughout the piece in the form of a set of dichotomies that align systematically with the masculine-feminine dyad. In this dyad the feminine is fleshed out through its association with tradition, unquestioning allegiance to larger social order, the non-technological, the desire to explain and be understood; the contorted and unnatural cultivation of the body; and as the object caught within representation. In contrast, the masculine is embodied as experimental and contemporary; as al-

---

2   *Killing Me Softly with His Song* was composed by Charles Fox and Norman Gimbel in 1971. Roberta Flack recorded it in 1973, and her version won Grammy Awards for Song of the Year, Record of the Year, and Best Pop Vocal Performance by a Female Performer.

ways questioning, conducting research, presenting the latest reality; as hi-tech; as privileged to initiate questioning and to evaluate answers; as eschewing all refinement, exaggeration, or premeditated self-presentation; and as dwelling outside of representation.

JÉRÔME: That's a very impressive set of claims. I can see why you want to be very quiet in your body.

The performance begins with Klunchun and Bel entering the stage and seating themselves on two chairs facing one another. Barefoot, and dressed in loose, cropped pants and T-shirt, Klunchun carries a bottle of water. Bel, in jeans, boots, and shirt, glances briefly down at the laptop on the floor beside his chair, before beginning a set of questions to Klunchun. The 90-100 minute performance consists entirely in a mutual interview, conducted informally, first by Bel and then, in the second half, by Klunchun. The conversation proceeds methodically from personal background to training, to opportunities to perform and make a living as an artist, and the parameters for how various subjects might be represented in dance. Each artist, familiar with the answers he will deliver, nonetheless proceeds in a seemingly spontaneous manner, creating a dialogue that is more organized than a typical conversation, yet unpretentiously straightforward and dedicated to the task of finding out about the other.

JÉRÔME: But I have to say that it strikes me as very odd, this custom of standing up in front of people and reading a piece of paper. Do people ever extemporize their lectures?
MYSELF: Yes, some professors are very accomplished at that, especially here in Europe. I find it most impressive, the way they form such perfect sentences spontaneously. But I'm no good at it, and I only have twenty more minutes.
JÉRÔME: Well then, I suppose you should continue, if you want to make all those points.

We learn that Klunchun became a dancer to give thanks to a deity associated with dance after his mother had prayed to it to become pregnant with a boy. Expert in the demon repertoire, Klunchun explains that nowadays he typically performs excerpts of the classical court danced narratives for tourists who book dinner and Thai dance for a given evening. A recent Prime Minister dedicated to modernizing the country, abandoned the classical arts in favor of cha-cha and tango. Klunchun, however, remains dedicated to the project of revitalizing this classical repertoire and demonstrating its value to Thai culture.

At Bel's request, Klunchun demonstrates various aspects of Khon – basic training exercises, character types, and ways of representing death onstage. Differing positions of arm or hands designating different characters are seen by Bel as almost imperceptible, however, Klunchun assures him they are enormously distinct. Scenes of violence and destruction remain opaque to Bel until Klunchun describes the action while dancing it. Once he is initiated into the symbolic system, Bel is better able to follow along, sometimes correctly guessing the meaning of Klunchun's actions. Still, Klunchun must explain to a disbelieving Bel the refusal of the form to represent death onstage. Bel also queries the strenuous, even grotesque, demands placed on the hand when he attempts to reproduce Klunchun's intense curvature of wrist and fingers. Klunchun responds matter-of-factly that the dancer's training constructs analogies between the body and temple architecture. The curves of the hand serve to re-channel the energy back towards the center of the body, so that the dancing establishes a continuous recycling of effort. Klunchun contrasts this aesthetic with the Western propensity to throw energy away in various leaps and extensions of body parts.

Here, for the first time in his interrogation, Bel expresses admiration: "I'm very impressed; this is something I had never thought of before." Up until that moment, Bel alternates most often between silence and skepticism, confusion, dis-belief, and perplexity in response to Klunchun's answers and demonstrations. Requesting to be shown a violent scene, for example, Bel initially rejects Klunchun's performance as insufficiently violent until Klunchun decodes it for him. Responding to the idea that death could be signified by a long and exceptionally slow walk across the entire stage, Bel is at a loss to imagine how meaning can be conveyed within the form. Even the "Good luck" that Bel offers in response to Klunchun's expressed desire to vivify Khon for a younger generation belies his uncomprehending incredulity.

JÉRÔME: Do you think you change people's minds when you give a lecture?
MYSELF: Do you when you present a dance performance?
JÉRÔME: Maybe I just give them something to think about.
MYSELF: And some parameters for thinking about it?
JÉRÔME: I suppose so.

Bel then invites Klunchun to question him, and we learn that Bel, although unmarried, has a child. Expressing a desire for children, Klunchun rejects Bel's proposal to bear one out of wedlock. Bel's raised eyebrow and shrug of the shoulders renders Klunchun's response prudish and old fashioned. Asked to demonstrate some dancing, Bel replies with beguiling modesty that he is not a 'real' choreographer, nor does he perform. After Klunchun objects that he has shown Bel a great deal, Bel offers one of his favorite scenes: he stands unassumingly gazing out at the audience with interest but no affect. Deploring the society of spectacle in which we are living, Bel explains that such an action is "not a representation". In a second demonstration, Bel uses his computer to play a soundtrack from David Bowie's *Let's Dance* to which he moves with a marked absence of energy, commitment, or fervency, thereby exposing the traditional association of rock music with abandoned physical display.[3]

MYSELF: How are you finding the lecture thus far?
JÉRÔME: You're making some interesting points, but there's someone who's almost asleep over there, and I can see why – listening to this complicated prose has a kind of numbing effect. And there are no pictures or video excerpts ... seems a little dull.

When Klunchun expresses disappointment at Bel's performance, Bel retorts that he is not surprised. Advocating for his anti-virtuosity approach, Bel aspires to create more egalitarian relationships using pop music, a form that belongs to everybody. Bel continues by explaining that whereas Klunchun dances about and for a King, Bel's country beheaded theirs two hundred years earlier so as to live in a more egalitarian society. Sponsored by that government, Bel conducts research within the 'contemporary arts', producing new works, whose form and content are unforeseen, and whose reception is frequently mixed at best. Nonetheless Bel aspires to make space for viewers to have their own response to life's enduring challenges. He illustrates this invitation by performing a very slow slump to the floor while singing along with *Killing Me Softly with His Song*, and then remaining inert for the last verse. Klunchun admits to having been moved by this action since it reminded him of his paralyzed mother's death, and Bel is pleased that his aversion to virtuosity and the quiet and matter-of-fact display of the body lying onstage as the symbol of death has been successful. Having agreed that they are very good viewers, even ideal, of one another's work, Bel reminds Klunchun that he cannot tell him anything. It must be discovered.

In one final example of his choreography, Bel begins to demonstrate a dance based on the manipulation of pieces of his own flesh. But when he moves from his ample stomach to take down his pants, Klunchun refuses to view anything further, claiming his culture's standards of aesthetic decency. Bel responds that

---

3   *Let's Dance* was the title track on David Bowie's hit album *Let's Dance* which issued in 1983.

he has seen considerable nakedness in Bangkok in the bars, but Klunchun explains that these dancers are working for tourist dollars. At this point, Klunchun and Bel agree to end their conversation.

JÉRÔME: It also seems to me that the whole set-up with the podium and the microphone is rather, if you don't mind the expression, phallic.
MYSELF: What would you do instead?
JÉRÔME: Well, I'm not sure, this is your gig, and I don't usually perform in this kind of situation. Maybe you should have a microphone that no one ever speaks from. Or you could circulate through the space rather than standing in one place … Or so something with the paper you're reading from … I'd have to think about it.
MYSELF: Well, do. I'd like to know how we might make it different.

All of the appearances of women in the piece cast them in highly traditional roles – as mothers, as members of the social whose roles are well established and who take responsibility for grieving for the loss of others, as sex workers, and as roles inhabitable by men when the need arises. And each role locates women in an inferior relationship to men. As mothers their labor is erased, for it is Bel who 'has' a child, and Klunchun who became the dancer. As sex workers, they are betraying their country's standards of decency. As theatrical roles, they demand less physically than other character types, or else they serve as vessels easily occupied by the male artists to demonstrate their form's aesthetic proclivities. The fact that these two male artists find so much in common in these archetypal feminine images permits them to establish a tacit familiarity and a tenuous equality to one another. The ease with which they reference the feminine and move in and out of her roles confirms their privilege and superiority.

At the same time, the masculine-feminine binaries operating in the guise of oppositions such as tradition/experimentation and representation/beyond representation work to place Klunchun in a distinctly inferior position. Klunchun's unquestioning acceptance and pursuit of dancing as a life calling, his devotion to resuscitating an outmoded form, the rigidity of the form itself with its detailed specifications for roles, stories, and modes of representation – all seem quaint and naïve at best when compared with Bel's iconoclastic vision. Klunchun's pliability, both in terms of how he has worked to cultivate the body, and also his amenability to explaining and demonstrating his form, signal a willingness to connect to Bel and to the world that Bel's aesthetics, in their guise as pioneering research, disdain. Where Klunchun has dedicated much of his life to the acquisition of technical facility at dancing, Bel has devoted a comparable amount of

time to learning and then unlearning how to dance. Where Klunchun can effi-
ciently decode the meanings behind each gesture and phrase in his danced dramas, Bel aspires to create space for the ordinary and the everyday as actions that
cannot be decoded because they simply are what they are. Staring straightfor-
wardly at the audience, lying quietly on the stage, Bel claims to eclipse representation by presenting things that cannot mean anything else. Yet even these claims
are vivified and fortified by the prior revelations of Klunchun regarding how
dance signifies.

JÉRÔME: Then why didn't you let me begin this presentation?
MYSELF: Because I believe that even if you gave an anti-lecture first or even
without my lecture, you'd still be operating within representation and, here,
within the frame of an academic lecture.

Bel stakes his claim to choreographic originality by implementing a distinction
between that which is caught within representation and that which resides outside of it. Claiming a naturalness equivalent to that of the early modern dancers a
century ago, Bel obfuscates his heroic aesthetic quest through beguiling inept-
ness and a willing confession of his lack of competence at dancing and his marginal status as a choreographer. In so doing, he secures a prestigious position for
himself on the vanguard of the avant-garde. From this position Bel serves, not a
monarchy, but rather the 'people'.

JÉRÔME: They don't have to come to my performances anymore than they have
to listen to this lecture.

Bel's location beyond representation, however, depends upon the prior establishment of the mutual interview as the format in which intercultural collaboration will be displayed. The dialogue-as-performance recapitulates Bel's dedica-
tion to arranging the 'spontaneous' onstage. The two artists have not met, ex-
changed ideas, and then developed something for presentation. Instead, they represent onstage their initial encounters and explorations with the same quality of
unpretentious straightforwardness that Bel invokes when staring at the audience
or lying on the floor as if 'dead'. Bel has thereby established the representational
grounds on which their exchange will take place and then located himself outside that framework as an artist who eschews representation. In so doing, Bel
uses the comparison of his own approach with that of Klunchun in order to ex-
pose, most humorously, the intentions of his artistic practice in relation to the
general workings of contemporary concert dance. However, he also creates for

himself a special place of privilege beyond the roles of masculine and feminine from which to display the brilliance of his artistic vision.

JÉRÔME: Well, isn't that what you're doing to me?
MYSELF: It's true, I invited you to this lecture. But I'm trying to find a space where we can have a discussion that does not advantage one of us at the expense of the other.

Throughout the performance, even as he is positioned within this representational system, Klunchun preserves his dignity, integrity, and worldview. He quietly rebuts Bel's dismissal of the different positions of the arm for different characters by asserting their dramatic effectiveness. He likewise rejects Western dance as a practice that throws energy away. And he steadfastly maintains his modesty in the face of invitations to produce a child out of wedlock and to view Bel's naked body. Although located within the apparatus of representation, he nonetheless perseveres in the commitment to his art and his willingness to share it with anyone who expresses interest. He even challenges Bel's theory of representation by continuing to decode, in the same way as he has his own work, Bel's performance of death.

According to Klunchun's aesthetics, the dialogue with Bel places him at no disadvantage nor does it demean his art form or way of life. He never attempts to ingratiate himself or his dance with either Bel or the audience. He presents the facts of his life and dance form with care and confidence. Similarly, for Bel's aesthetics, given the limited amount of time allotted for the two artists to get to know one another, the most honest plan, one preserving the integrity of each practice, would be to present a simulated version of their initial encounter onstage. Yet the collision of these two worldviews and their assimilation into Bel's conception of representation reinvigorate the first-world's heritage of privilege based in colonial histories and the stereotypes that enabled colonization.

JÉRÔME: But if we're always operating within the realm of representation, there isn't any place for hope, any imaginary where we could get away to a different world.
MYSELF: There's always irony.
JÉRÔME: You mean, reflecting and commenting on things while you're doing them?

Transnationalism and Contemporary African Dance: Faustin Linyekula

SABINE SÖRGEL

TRANSNATIONALISM AND CONTEMPORARY AFRICAN DANCE

"Transnationalism involves a loosening of boundaries, a deterritorialization of the nation-state, and higher degrees of interconnectedness among cultures and peoples across the globe. As people make transnational voyages and live lives of flexible citizenship in two or more cultures, they adhere to a new type of nationalism that creates an exclusionist discourse and builds 'the Other' as conservative defenders of cruder territorial loyalties. This rhetoric disturbs the social fabric as traditionalists and transnationalists create 'imagined communities' defined in particular ways." (Duncan/Juncker 2004: 8)

In the age of globalization contemporary identities emerge from diverse corporeal sensations and cross-cultural inscriptions, which increasingly build 'imagined communities' beyond national confines. Discourse on contemporary African dance may serve as a lens through which dancers and choreographers from the African continent explore a transnational politics of belonging that transcends earlier discourses of post-independence African nationalisms of the 1950s and 60s. The question of contemporary African dance is a much debated one among dancers and choreographers on the African continent since the mid-1990s (cf. Sanou 2008; Douglas 2006; Tiérou 2001), which presents a choreographic quest that creates new epistemologies of creativity and freedom between tradition and (post)modernity.

Alphonse Tiérou's *Si sa danse bouge, l'Afrique bougera* (2001) gives an example to illustrate this argument, as he outlines a new transnational politics of dance that considers contemporary dance as an 'imagined community' outside (neo)colonial discourse and racist representation. "Lorsque la danse paraît le masque tombe, dit un proverbe africain" (Tiérou 2001: 161), he states in the concluding chapter to his book which outlines the challenging politics of an emerging African contemporary dance form. As it turns out, Tiérou's query into the meaning of African contemporary dance propagates nothing less than the up-coming therapeutic against the persistent inferiority complex of the colonized.

As was first outlined by Frantz Fanon in his *Black Skin, White Masks* (1967) and is meanwhile well known, colonialism suppressed the many facets of Afri-can cultural expression. Languages, religions, philosophical views, and dance were misrepresented by colonial discourse and its pejorative misconceptions de-nied African identity on equal terms. Yet, Tiérou's analysis goes beyond the la-mentation over an irrevocable loss as he demonstrates how to overcome this de-pressing state of affairs in a self-confident appropriation of Western choreo-graphic models. While the colonialist negation of African humanity and culture persists in the current debates on dance – which more often than not reiterate ste-reotypical views on African dance as being tribal, primitive, sensual, and exotic (Tiérou 2001: 14) – he suggests that a knowledge of choreographic practice will provide a base for further theoretical investigation as well as documentation of African dance forms in a global setting (id. 2001: 46).

Western misnomers for African dance forms have long since falsified its complex philosophical conceptualization, he argues, which is neither animalis-tic-mimetic nor exclusively ritualistic, but rather outlines a highly sophisticated mode of being-in-the-world (Tiérou 2001: 33-34). One of his examples of this complexity is taken from Wèon (Ivory-Coast) culture and refers to its many name-giving dances which demonstrate how deeply embedded they are in the complex philosophies of griot (story-telling) culture. In that sense, dance origi-nates identity and embodies so much more than language could ever express. As Tiérou comments:

"La danse africaine est un moyen d'expression, mais un moyen d'expression plus fort que le geste, plus éloquent que le langage, plus riche que l'écriture. Elle va au-delà du mime. D'ailleurs il existe une différence irréductible entre le mime et la danse. Le geste du dan-seur est projectif, il induit une expérience non réductible à la parole. Celui du mime est descriptif. Le mime est comme le mot ou le concept. Il se compose d'une réalité déjà exis-tante ou résume un fait. La danse dépasse ce qui est pour suggérer un possible, un imagi-naire […]." (Id. 2001: 33-34)

African contemporary dance thus appears to zoom in on the pre-representational qualities of dance as to emphasize the dancer's agency over his or her objectification by the colonialist gaze. Hence, Tiérou encourages a fresh perspective which derives from an embodied understanding of African traditional dance forms and their oral histories, yet combines these with contemporary European dance training and technique in a strategic appropriation as to defend African culture in a competing struggle over global legitimacy and copyright.[1]

After all, there is no turning back to innocent origins anymore, neither for the contemporary African choreographer, nor his or her Western audience. While there is no outside to the traditional dancing circle, colonialism's alienating gaze enforces a separation that irrevocably divides the dancer from the dance. Likewise, dances presented within the Western proscenium arch frame their performers as visual objects and/or artifacts, once that these traditional dance forms are presented on the world stage.

African contemporary dance thus seeks to remedy earlier post independence efforts of the 1950s and 60s which established national ballet companies in veneration of traditional dance forms, but were often stifled by a static notion of cultural heritage. Although process and exploration are considered key elements of traditional African dance in its community context, such development was denied in the name of national treasure building. Ironically, many national ballets on the African continent thus featured dance as a form of auto-chauvinism by adhering to Western models of art objectification and the cultural museum (Tiérou 2001: 44-45). This raises the pressing issue then of how to define contemporary African dance without adhering to Western hegemonic models of representation. Is it possible?

Postcolonial theory seeks to redress this double-bind by arguing that colonial hegemony may be undermined from within its own framing. Homi K. Bhabha's critical concept of colonial mimicry thus introduces an emancipating trajectory by which an appropriation of Western contemporary dance forms by African dancers and choreographers should not be regarded as a form of neocolonialism, but rather decolonization. In fact, as the following example of Faustin Linyekula's *Dinozord: The Dialogue series III* suggests, the dancing body emerges as an ennunciative presence from which a transnational dance politics may be developed.

---

1   Such strategic efforts appear increasingly important as to acknowledge, preserve and further develop dance forms that are constituted by improvisation and repetition rather than writing/notation (cf. Foster 2009).

FAUSTIN LINYEKULA:
DINOZORD: THE DIALOGUE SERIES III (2006)

"Il y a longtemps que je voulais trouver une façon de raconter le Congo …"
(Linyekula 2007: 2)

Faustin Linyekula's *Dinozord: The dialogue series III* interrogates the possibility of accounting for the traumatized history of the Congo after colonization, dictatorship and the ongoing civil war, when there is hardly a sense of nation anymore, but instead the haunting notion of a state of ruins. The performance begins with a pre-performance installation of photographs and documentary film-clips, as well as interviews, taken from Faustin's home village Kisangani.[2] While audience members slowly assemble in front of the stage doors, one may not yet be aware of it, but already one has entered a transnational performance-space which aligns Kisangani and the local venue (which in my case was part of the Utrecht Springdance festival 2006). Faustin is dancing among our midst, wearing whiteface make-up, black jeans and a white shirt. His ongoing movements between the Kisangani photographs and the audience members mediate between the documentary footage from Kisangani and the international festival world. On the floor then, one discovers pictures from an African village as bits and pieces from the monitored interviews on the screens are audible. A little undecided whether deciphering Dutch subtitles will be easier than discerning the French accents I hear, I move closer to the monitors and actually now see some of the Kisangani villagers narrating their stories as I pass along. When I finally move on into the actual theatre space, I have already become a momentary inhabitant or visitor to the world of Kisangani, as I listened to the villagers' stories and encountered traces of their private lives.

This pre-performance set-up suggests a spatial concept that has recently been described under the rubric of contemporary cosmopolitan performance. According to Paul Rae (2006), audiences in such a globalized theatrical setting must find ways to communicate across cultural affiliation and national divides as to allow for an "experience of theatrical spatiality that expresses the intertwined experiences of place and identity in an age of complex connectivity" (Rae 2006: 10-11). With regard to Linyekula's multi-media installation as an example of this, we may thus assert Rae's observation that cosmopolitan performance aes-

---

2   For the following performance analysis also compare DVD *The Dialogue Series III: Dinozord* (Linyekula 2007).

thetics introduce a shift of theatrical spatiality bordering on the transnational in the sense that they

"[…] provide the context within which the individual can find an experience of spatiality that reconciles the fact of interconnectedness to the inconceivable extensivity of those connections, and an experience of sociality that recognizes the stranger without compromising the disinterest upon which their identity as stranger must, at some level, be maintained. An experience, that is, approaching the cosmopolitan." (Rae 2006: 20)

As Faustin dances between us, he thus allows for a shared moment of recognition, where although we may have never been to Kisangani we feel invited to join in conversation with his community that he mediates for us rather than the other way round. In a way then, this set-up includes us almost as a dancing member as we move in-between their chosen stories and images. Even though we are geographically separated by ever so many miles, the installation makes us aware of their presence and agency as performers in their own right.

Yet, once inside the theatre my assigned seat places me again within the imperial gaze of the Western proscenium frame. When Faustin enters from the wings, he thus introduces himself more formally, as he demonstrates a keen awareness of the convention by finding his stage-managing position behind yet another wooden frame on stage. He refers to himself subtly as "a multi-dimensional songster", who "sings everything, religious songs, traditional songs, Congolese" (Linyekula 2007) as to tease his audience into the world of disbelief. The stage set-up is quite simple: a multi-media desk, operated by Faustin from behind a wooden picture frame, a laptop and digital-beamer for projections onto a white canvas at the back wall of the stage, a chest, a microphone and a typewriter – minimal props for the five performers (Serge Kakudji, Dinozord, Papy Ebotani, Djodjo Kazadi, Papi Mbwiti) who have now also appeared on the left side of the stage to engage with. As was already mentioned, there are frames within frames in this set up and one already senses that there will be no full picture presented as to grasp the meaning of this playful deconstruction of the proscenium's imperial gaze.

As sound-operator Faustin continues to set the mood and atmosphere of the choreography; he introduces the members of his company by name and profession – a counter-tenor, an actor and two dancers – who will from now on join him on his return to the village of Kisangani. Finally, so Faustin tells us, he wants to give a funeral for Kabako, his long-lost friend, who died from plague twelve years ago. Originally commissioned for the 2006 Salzburg Mozart festival, the choreography evolved from the solemn sounds of the Catholic high mass requiem which we now hear being introduced from off-stage. Simultaneously, I hear frantic typing which performs an underlying score to Mozart's organ, ominously connected to the presence of the type-writer on stage. Linyekula's performance uses motifs from the Mozart requiem, such as the *Day of Wrath* and *Final Judgement*, as yet another unsettling frame through which we, the international audience, become attendants to this curious mass service. Although we are most probably a rather unholy congregation, we are nonetheless cleverly summoned in our role as international witnesses, and after all in the vicinity of the International Court of Justice in Den Hague.

The Mozart requiem is divided into fourteen movements, which the choreography basically takes as its point of departure for the performance which becomes more and more of a contemporary passion play. Dramaturgically this structure presents different stations of suffering, abstract images from Congolese history, commemorated in front of an international public. The performance further evolves as a complex mix of diverse cultural signifiers, which Faustin guides us through by controlling the sound board and digital projections from behind his picture frame. There is much information to absorb over the next hour: abstract contemporary dance vocabulary, electronic sounds, images from a prison in Kinshasa, excerpts of Mobutu in French which taken together present the hybrid nature of contemporary African culture between tradition and modernity.

The performers' face-masks and body paint thus appear as abstractions from African traditional rituals though likely misleading as we name them according to Western misconceptions, and as in fact we may learn from the interview Faustin gave to Irene Filiberti in 2007. Here, he explains that the numbers on the performers' backs simply emerged from adolescent memories of happy soccer games and have nothing to do with Western desire for exoticism. In this respect, the prevalent colors of black, white and red are as open to interpretation as they would be in any other abstract contemporary performance, especially if we take up Tiérou's comment that African dance is in fact no more mimetic than European contemporary forms. The color symbolism can hence represent death, innocence, and blood, but it may also be perceived as an affect that adds to the overwhelming sense of trauma that the performance presents.

It seems no accident then that the conscious choice of loin-cloths plays to the same stereotypical audience expectation. And yet, no performance could be further removed from the Western misconception of 'tribal' dance. There is no mistaking this for a traditional burial rite, even though some of the movement vocabulary is derived from there as the performers rotate their pelvis ever so subtly moving around the chest of hidden documents. The traditional dancing-circle as a continuum between the living, the dead and the yet to be born is irrevocably broken in today's Congolese society and therefore demands new vocabularies and names as Faustin's comment suggests:

"My dance will be an attempt to remember my name. I must have lost it somewhere along the dark alleys of Memory. I've been wandering ever since […] Thus I was born in a land called Zaire, the most caring hand I could ever find under the sunlight. I grew up believing this, until … 1997, lines from a conversation with History Zaire was but a lie invented by Mobutu, a dead exiled land. Perhaps my name is Kabila; perhaps I'm a bastard son of King Leopold II and the Independent State of Congo. I'm a kid soldier scavenging through a heap of lies, raped virgins and cholera. Democratic Republic of Congo was my real name, rectified my fathers […] My glorious legacy […] Where is the truth? Is there a stone or owl or river or sorcerer out there to teach […]? One possible answer: land of exile or native land, perhaps everywhere is but exile; perhaps my only true country is my body. I'll thus survive like a song that's never been written." (Linyekula 2008: n.p.)

Celebrating the pelvis traditionally signifies the continuation of life, however, here this familiar movement enters into a strange dialogic combination with the solemn choir music. Instead of invoking a false nostalgia for an Zaire as an imaginary homeland, Faustin's personal memories evoke the political presence of Kisangani in a transnational setting. Hence, the performance is not only a funeral to Kabako, but becomes an accusation against the auto-chauvinism of African nationalist discourse and its horrors of dictatorship and civil war crimes in the face of human dignity.

Throughout the performance there is a chest on stage, full of documents, which becomes a pivotal object in this respect. At first, when the performers circle their hips very slowly around it, the wooden chest is used as a coffin, but later it resembles an archive of civil war atrocities, when the performers tear away at those letters like howling dogs. These papers are haunting though we never quite know what is written on them, for the dismay alone is enough for us to imagine the atrocities and unaccounted crimes against international law and human rights. In that sense, we are confronted with precisely that "non-signifying presence" Paul Rae defines as the surplus of insoluble difference within cosmopolitan performance.

As spectators we are actively summoned to listen to the testimony at hand, and as soon as Faustin consciously switches into English for some of the passages of the performance, one realizes the urgency of this performance to find the ears of international audiences worldwide. The mechanical sound of the typewriter over Mozart's requiem makes sense then, as we can read it as the somewhat desolate attempt to keep track and document the pain that we feel expressed through the music and in the dancing bodies. So if I am indeed cast as a member of some kind of a transnational jury here, then this Mozart requiem is not only held for Kabako, Faustin's friend, but also a commemorative service to the unburied dead of the Congo.

Faustin Linyekula's pre-representational return to the body as an individual's protective shield of intimate knowledge and experience reverberates with Tiérou's dream that African contemporary dance will allow for an expression of freedom beyond national confines and racial stereotypes (Tiérou 2001: 162). African contemporary dance thus becomes the imaginary home for Faustin and his dancers at a point in Congolese history, when all other systems of representation and communal affiliation have failed. It seems ever more important therefore to realize that this emphasis on the experiential rather than representational mode of dance cuts right through Western politics of objectification as it articulates the artist's only strategy for survival. As Faustin's persisting questioning of all representational frames contests, dance is the only mode of potentially being free as each new movement allows for an agency on one's own terms:

"Is this Art? Is this Dance? Is this Contemporary African Dance? How will I know if this is art? Do you call Art one's attempt to resist the cycle of destruction by planting seeds of beauty/seeds of dreams in a hopeless context? What then when this resistance is written in one's body? The body as the last shield for freedom." (Linyekula 2008: n.p.)

DANCE: THE EMBODIED POLITICS OF TRANSNATIONALISM

Faustin Linyekula's example presents the transnational politics of dance from an experiential perspective that situates the dancing body at the originating moment of representational meaning and identity. In line with Tiérou's theoretical framing of an emerging African contemporary dance aesthetic in the beginning of this article, my analysis of *Dinozord: The Dialogue series III* attempts to show how this ethical shift towards the performer's agency is closely aligned with the complex conceptualization of traditional African dance forms, where there is no outside to the dance, but everyone participates. African contemporary dance thus appropriates Western theatrical forms as creative mimicry (cf. Bhabha 1994), whereby choreographers like Faustin Linyekula or Salia Sanou present a contemporary ritual of counter-memory (cf. Roach 1996) and hope. While this aesthetic choice confirms Western hegemony to some extent, it undermines prevalent discourse of inferiority/superiority as these choreographers combine African traditional dance forms with European contemporary idioms. In that sense they perform nothing less than the alternative to a postmodern cynicism of resignation to the status quo. African contemporary dance is hence characterized by a mixture of Mozart and Ndombolo which makes dance from the African continent visible on the world stage from Kinshasa, to Berlin and San Francisco. Less concerned with the rhetoric of post-independence nationalisms, African contemporary dance introduces a politics of transnational affiliation between dancers and their audiences worldwide. To summarize then, Faustin Linyekula's choreography establishes a sense of communal belonging beyond national confines and thereby creates the possibility for a deterritorialized transnational politics to emerge.

REFERENCES

Bhabha, Homi K. (1994): The Location of Cultures, London/New York: Routledge.

Douglas, Gilbert et al. (2006): "Under Fire: Defining a Contemporary African Dance Aesthetic – Can It Be Done?", in: Critical Arts Volume 20, Number 2, pp. 102-115.

Duncan, Russel/Juncker, Clara (eds.) (2004): Transnational America. Contours of Modern US Culture, Copenhagen: Museum Tusculanum Press.

Fanon, Frantz (1967): Black Skin, White Masks, New York: Grove Press.

Filiberti, Irène (2007): "Entretien avec Faustin Linyekula", http://www.kabako. org/txt-entretiens/entretien.html (August 12, 2009).

Foster, Susan Leigh (ed.) (2009): Worlding Dance, Basingstoke: Palgrave Macmillan.

Linyekula, Faustin (2007): DVD "The Dialogue Series III: Dinozord", Utrecht April 2007, Kinshasa: Studios Kabako.

_____ (2008): "Corks and Memories", http://www.kabako.org/txt-entretiens/Corks.html (May 13, 2008).

Rae, Paul (2006): "Where is the Cosmopolitan Stage?", in: Contemporary Theatre Review Volume 16, Number 1, pp. 8-22.

Roach, Joseph (1996): Cities of the Dead. Circum-Atlantic Performance, New York: Columbia UP.

Sanou, Salia (2008): Afrique Danse Contemporaine, Paris: Éditions Cercle d'Art.

Tiérou, Alphonse (2001): Si sa danse bouge l'Afrique bougera, Paris: Maison-neuve & Larose.

Flee(t)ing Dances!
Initiatives for the Preservation and
Communication of Intangible World Heritage
in Museums

ANETTE REIN

Holistic, or so-called traditional worldviews are characterized in particular by how the material, everyday realm and the immaterial, spiritual realm are experienced as inseparably intertwined, as two dimensions of one reality. In this sense, a dance performance – since it has its roots in both worlds – embodies a special type of medium, which allows these two dimensions to communicate (cf. Rein 2010).[1]

The task of collecting, exhibiting and communicating tangible and intangible world heritage – in this case, dance events – presents museums with a special challenge – one that I will further elucidate below.

A museum collection mainly consists of tangible things. If we look at the history of ethnographical museums, we must ask ourselves: to what extent have traditional dances, as largely intangible forms of cultural knowledge, been collected despite their ephemerality and been given equal status to tangible objects? To what extent are and have they been archived and used in museums to represent cultures?

1   I would like to thank Gabriele Klein and Sandra Noeth. Their critical questions caused me to develop further perspectives on the subject. I thank Heide Lazarus, Annette Hornbacher, Leontine Meijer-van Mensch and Reiner Zapf for their constant willingness to discuss the issues further with me.

All dances contain tangible (e.g.: dancers, costumes, stage, audience, etc.) as well as intangible aspects (timing, religious practice as an expression of an ontology, sequences of movement, music, etc.). Only when all components interact seamlessly is a traditional dance event judged successful by its participants.[2]

At the beginning of the 20th century, museums began commissioning collectors to document data on the material, origin and function of things. At this point in time, the museums realized that objects without accompanying data were without value for the institution – empty material shells, so to say (cf. Laukötter 2008: 4). With the advent of increasingly improving technical recording equipment, collections of intangible world heritage, e.g. large music archives, were for this reason established to supplement the collections of tangible artifacts.

"The inclusion of other legacies has been common practice, at least in leading institutions, for many years. They are no longer – or at least, no longer only – to be considered storage spaces of tangible traditions. Instead, they have defined themselves as the agents of cultural values and perspectives in a more comprehensive sense." (Beier-de Haan 2007: 56)

In contrast, the documentation of dance only became more widespread with the advent of more sophisticated film equipment, which also allowed their meanings within the respective indigenous contexts to be grasped and recorded in more diverse ways (cf. Rein 1994). It is the fleeting nature of a dance event that contains special potential within the diversity of cultural production and thus also requires a special approach.

In this sense, let us take an exemplary look at a film sequence of the Balinese temple dance *Rejang*[3] and its context as stored in a museum archive. Then we will examine the three steps in the musealization process, to finally explore what – in my opinion – other dimensions of action can be included in the museum's

---

2   After returning from field research, ethnologists have at their disposal the material brought back by them or their colleagues to analyze cultural events. In the case of dance, these are collected material accessories, notes, photos, music recordings and ideally film and video documents archived in an ethnographical museum. Here the documents are further analyzed and prepared for presentation in accordance with the museum's mandate to educate the public on traditional cultural production.

3   The results of my field research in 30 Balinese villages from 1985-1987 forms the ethnographic basis for this text. All of the cursive words in the text are terminology from ethnology or museology that are not explained further. The above film sequence was recorded by Reiner Zapf on October 19, 1985 in Subagan, an Eastern Balinese village.

educational mandate if we wish them to fulfill the expectation of translating and communicating non-Western world views and life practices.

BACK – FORWARDS – A LITTLE FURTHER BACK – PLAY!

Illustration: Rejang in Subagan (Bali), October 19, 1985

Photo: Anette Rein

The following film scene unfolds before my eyes:

Young girls stride in a circle around a shrine, while alternately raising their right or left arm. When their hands are down, they grasp the shawls hanging from their hips, lift them briefly and let them go when their arm is lifted to its highest point, so that the colorful floating fabric highlights the girls' movements. The sound of an orchestra can be heard; the shadows on the ground indicate that it must be around midday.

The film sequence ends and I press repeat. I watch the film again and again. I study the textiles that the dancers are wearing, individual details of the stairs that lead to the shrine that they are circling, and the temple wall in the background. The same events seem to happen over and over again, and they appear to be endlessly repeatable. The cameraman's perspective decides what I can see.

There is no camera pan to show me the wider surroundings of what I had observed at the time: the way the mothers stood around the circle and how they were bursting with pride watching their daughters dancing. No one tells us that some of the girls took part because they had been healed from a severe illness and that their participation was part of their parents' vow to attain the help of the Gods.

It remains unclear why the girls in Subagan were still little children, while in the next village Timbrah, it was only young women, who danced at the *Rejang* until they married. Who is there in this film to tell me that each village had its own rules stating that in Subagan, the dancers stopped dancing the *Rejang* upon the onset of menstruation, while in Timbrah, they only began participating in the temple dance after menstruation had set in?[4]

The smell of the blossoms in the dancers' headdresses and the siblings' laughter in the temple's neighboring courtyard, unexpectedly chasing a chick that was to be sacrificed after the dance – none of this reveals itself to me while watching the film. The camera team determines what you see and hear; it reduces the complex *Rejang* dance to the girls' flow of movement. The musical accompaniment doesn't provide any further insights.

Still, this film sequence could be a part of an exhibition about Balinese dances. However, before this dance can be made public as an exhibit in a glass case or shown on a screen, it has to go through the process of musealization. This process removes the tangible and intangible cultural expressions from their original context in order to integrate them into the academic environment of the museum institution.

PROCESSES OF MUSEALIZATION

According to Anja Laukötter, the act of musealization takes place in three steps (cf. Laukötter 2010: 120ff). Figuratively they correspond with the classic model of liminality in rituals that, according to Arnold van Gennep[5], can be summarized colloquially as: *remove – recreate – reintegrate*.[6]

---

4   The use of past tense is here a conscious decision. An *ethnographic present tense* would suggest that the dance that was recorded many years ago still takes place in this form today. In fact, even these dance traditions have always changed over time.

5   In 1909, van Gennep described the structure of rites of passage for the first time. In the exhibition *Reisen und Entdecken. Vom Sepik an den Main* in the Museum der Weltkulturen Frankfurt am Main (October 27, 2007 – August 30, 2009) the various steps of musealization were staged and explained in a companion book to the exhibition (cf. Raabe 2008).

6   I wish to thank Dr. Matthias Jenny, director of the Palmengarten in Frankfurt am Main

First: 'removed' from their original context, the things are robbed of their function – they are taken out of time and space – in order to be exported in this still 'unclean' condition for further processing.

Second: the semantic change of the objects takes place along a prescribed path through the various departments of the museum: in a process of gassing, inventory, conservation, restoration and declaration. They are integrated into the museum's system of rules and regulations in the workrooms far from the public eye. Dislodged from their true symbolic context, the objects are sorted according to principles of materiality, authenticity, analogy, causality or functionality and then assigned to a culture – *ergo*, 'recreated'.

In this second step, the prerogative of interpretation is defined after physical appropriation has taken place. The objects become scientifically legitimized and are often declared exceptional. Especially chosen pieces are given this mark of quality by labeling them as *top exhibit* or *masterpiece* for the general public.[7] An object that has been sanctified in this way comes to represent an entire culture, since ethnographical museums never show the people themselves, but only their forms of cultural expression (cf. Köstering 2003: 17).

Third: the last step of musealization is its exhibition. The visitors' individual perspectives give the things their exclusive aura and thus turns them into museum objects (cf. Laukötter 2010: 121). Their new status is now also perceived by the public and thus they are 'reintegrated'.

"For the museum context, a single object was not sufficient. Instead, it needed […] an exhibited collection in order to fulfill the expectations that had been created." (Id.) Only with the help of the presented objects, a sheer vast mass of things, could e.g. ethnographical museums convincingly demonstrate to the public their expertise in the mastery of knowledge and the interpretation of the world in the midst of the ostensible chaos of cultural diversity. The final decision of what is shown in an exhibition, and in what way, resides with the curator – the established scientific expert (cf. Laukötter 2010: 122).[8]

---

for the information that these three steps of musealization not only apply to things, but also to plants. The arrangements of plants in public shows are not to be equated with nature, but rather represent our Western idea *of* nature. The composition of arrangements and collections also lies in the responsibility of curators. In German the terms are *raus – rüber – rein*.

7   See *Being Object – Being Art. Meisterwerke aus den Sammlungen des Museums der Weltkulturen Frankfurt am Main*, http://www.mdw-frankfurt.de/Deutsch/ (March 21, 2010).

8   Only thanks to the demands of New Museology since the 1970s has the sole claim to

EXHIBITING AND COMMUNICATING

Even today, the collected objects with their static materiality remain at the center of interest in many areas. Interactive methods such as *hands-on* and *minds-on* seek to directly communicate the scientifically gathered knowledge about the objects, as demonstrated in the following play on words: 'grasping', under-'standing' and re-'living' knowledge.[9] In contrast, although dance is an undeniable cultural phenomenon – it simultaneously cannot be 'grasped' nor 'held tight'. A dance is an ephemeral 'in-between' shrouded in all sorts of manifestations that lend specific points of memory (cf. Kuhnt-Saptodewo 2006) to the ephemeral – and pose a great challenge for the museums' mandate to collect and communicate.

Despite existing knowledge of the many aspects of original dance events, we find isolated objects, such as dance masks, hung in glass cases like art objects even today. A complex dance event is in most cases still reduced to tangible aspects confined to glass cases after having run though the process of musealization and forced into an immobile, frozen form. They die the museum death (cf. Pazzini 1989: 124) in order to be reborn in a second life as a museum object.

The following situation illustrates the complexity of a dance event.

"A visitor standing in front of a glass cabinet illuminated by neon lighting, is peering into it with curiosity. A mask, a skirt-like brown costume, a foot rattle and a photo of dancing Indians are exhibited there. The text on the wall explains that the mask represents a spirit of the nature, who plays an important role in the initiation of Turkana girls. A foreign world opens up before the eyes of the observer; however, its vitality remains inaccessible. She doesn't see the squirming wild demons, doesn't hear the yelling of the crowd, the roar of the music instruments, doesn't feel the vibrating, buffeting bodies around her, doesn't smell the smoke of the fire and doesn't perceive anything of the fascination of the spectacle that possesses the revelers." (van Elsbergen 1998: 537)

---

expert status in dealing with 'the world' been broken by the active participation of those affected (producers, users, etc.) from the countries of origin in the interpretation of the world. This was the beginning of the ongoing process of deconstructing expert knowledge and the role of the curator versus the knowledge of laymen.

9   Both of these terms stem from museum pedagogy and characterize the specific interactivity of programs in which touching things and being addressed by them are central.

Let me summarize specific aspects of ritual dances and their role in the ritual. Using the example of the ritual Balinese dance *Rejang*, I will argue that we have as yet no sufficient methods available to archive this phenomenon in an appropriate way – by which I mean the possibility of reproducing it in its original sense.

Ritual dances are always performed when extraordinary, exceptional areas of experience are meant for display. These dances, which are in the broadest sense improvised when seen from a Western perspective – are a "cultural setting" (Huschka 2009: 8) whose movement sequences are memorized by observation over many years. If we examine ritual dances with this aspect in mind, then it is clear that a specific form of knowledge transmission is taking place here: not by showing and repeating concrete sequences of steps and positions (cf. id. 2009: 19) – as in academic dance – but by imitating role models who, for their part, are also emulating a memory (cf. Rein 2000/1).

As described above, holistic worldviews see the ordinary and extraordinary dimensions of reality as constantly present and inseparably intertwined. In the case of Balinese ritual dances we can say with some certainty that dances take place in a ritual when spiritual entities manifest their presence. Dance steps that appear to be spontaneous represent a non-ordinary, spiritual dimension of reality that follows the spiritual beings presented in dance. It is the staged alternative to the ordinary human order (cf. Hanna 1987; Rein 1994; Kuhnt-Saptodewo 2006). This is expressed in the fact that profane dance movements are seen as owned by humans and are actively taught and trained. In contrast, ritual dance movements, in which the talent of an individual is meaningless, are seen as an expression of a holy choreography in which humans are the medium for the embodiment (cf. Rein 2000/2).

Central aspects of a three-phase temple festival on Bali may illustrate this better: the decoration of the temple; the arrival of the Gods and ancestors who come to rest on the seats that have been prepared for them; and the hospitality towards the spiritual guests and their return to their residence, the holy mountain *Gunung Agung*. According to Annette Hornbacher, during their stay in the temple the spiritual guests accept

"[...] smell and luster, or as the Balinese understand it, the essence (sari) of the aesthetically transforming material offerings and performances [...]. In return, they leave their blessings and revert to their invisible state [in the end] (Hornbacher 2005: 358). The manner of ritual configuration [is not] unconscious performance, but rather an act of insight [...] (id. 2005: 362). The body [of the dancers] becomes the kinaesthetic form of representing metaphysical knowledge." (Id. 2005: 386)[10]

All of the media or 'configurations' used in the ritual – the decoration of the temple, the music groups and the ritual dances – communicate an aesthetic transformation of material reality to impart metaphysical knowledge (cf. id. 2005: 358). The dances don't provide symbolic images; they show the human body as a visible aspect of cosmic energies that can't be concretely represented. These dance movements are cosmic movements (cf. id. 2005: 387). They communicate the unity of *sekala* und *niskala* (cf. id. 2005: 385) of the tangible (ordinary) and spiritual (extraordinary) dimensions of reality (cf. Rein 2010: 9).

Against this backdrop, I would like to return to the museum as an institution with its various functions to offer a perspective of how a museum can comply with its educational mandate in the context of traditional dances.

THE EDUCATIONAL MANDATE OF MUSEUMS

The complex institution museum is composed of various central parameters: cultural heritage (in the form of collections and archives), functions (collecting, conserving, documenting, exhibiting and educating) and society (cf. Meijer-van Mensch 2009: 20). Each specific mandate is the consequence of a certain set of priorities and how the contents of individual parameters are defined. If we go along with the work groups on the homepage of the *Deutsche Museumsbund*, then we can differentiate between scientific museums, historical museums, museums of cultural history and art museums, museums for the history of technology and open-air museums (cf. Museumsbund.de). Irrespective of the subject, which a museum is devoted to, the initial foundation is a collection.

Museums have their origins in the royal art and curiosity cabinets of the Renaissance; to fill them, things were collected world-wide on the basis of personal preferences and research interests, arranged freely according to material and the diversity of form and presented, in constantly new variations, to only a select

---

10 "Duft und Glanz, oder nach balinesischer Auffassung das Wesen (sari) der sich ästhetisch transformierenden materiellen Gaben und Aufführungen entgegen [...]. Im Gegenzug dazu hinterlassen sie ihren Segen und kehren [am Ende] in die Unsichtbarkeit zurück. [...] Der Weg der rituellen Gestaltungen [sind keine] bewusstlose Performanz, sondern ein Akt der Erkenntnis [...]. Der Leib [der Tänzer] wird zur kinästhetischen Repräsentationsform von metaphysischem Wissen." Additions and edits by the author.

group of people. In compliance with an encyclopedic principle of collecting, these things were supposed to showcase the entire world in all of its different manifestations (cf. Bredekamp 2009: 28). The spaces that housed the collections became places of an imaginary appropriation of the world. Exotic objects represented foreign worlds and made them seemingly accessible (cf. Bräunlein 2004/1: 32).

From the 19th century onwards, the objects were made accessible to a broader public according to a system influenced by the natural sciences during set opening hours in newly constructed buildings for presentation (i.e. museums) as national cultural heritage. However, the museums' own focus was still directed inwards and concentrated on the upkeep of the collections and on research.

In the 1979s Hilmar Hoffmann issued the slogan "culture for all" (cf. Hoffmann 1979), which formulated a shift towards a form of socio-pedagogical mandate for museums as "social places of learning" (Bräunlein 2004/2: 56). Museum educational service was professionalized as the social medium for knowledge transfer concerning all objects in the collections (cf. Meijer-van Mensch 2009: 21f). Museums developed into public, social institutions of learning that proclaimed an active role from an emancipatory point of view (cf. Bräunlein 2004/2: 57). According to Leontine Meijer-van Mensch, "the recommendations of the UNESCO for the involvement of all people in the shaping of cultural life [...] (Nairobi 1976) [...] was a further important milestone in that period" (Meijer-van Mensch 2009: 22).

Despite these recommendations, the perspective on the objects of the Others continued to be primarily aesthetic and relationships of power were mostly ignored. Despite this fact, the necessity to 'understand one's Own and the Other' transformed museums from places of learning to spaces of cultural tolerance and understanding over the following years. Ethnographical museums in particular were discovered as protagonists of multi-cultural enlightenment (cf. Bräunlein 2004/2: 59).

Accordingly, the work of ethnographical museums in the early 1980s concentrated on the presentation of collections in the context of current, socially relevant and comparative cultural issues. However, the *native point of view* still remained stuck in its reconstruction from a European point of view and the voices of the Others are even today not yet systematically incorporated in museum presentations. This concentration on data about material culture presents itself as a shortcoming in communication about complex indigenous systems of knowledge in the context of the (historical) artifacts in museum collections (cf. Rein 2009: 18; Rein 2010).

DANCE AS AN INDIGENOUS SYSTEM OF KNOWLEDGE AND OVERSTEPPING OF MUSEUM BOUNDARIES

The UNESCO Convention of 2003 raised worldwide awareness for the impending loss of the diversity of intangible world heritage due to the spread of globalization. Indigenous peoples suddenly had a voice – something no one had reckoned with at first (cf. Alivizatou 2007). Now their knowledge of oral history and cultural practices that had not previously been recorded in writing was much sought after. The call was also to document contexts in order to gain a better understanding of cultural diversity (cf. Seyppel 2007: 77).[11]

Traditional systems of knowledge and their oral transmission are directly tied to age, descent and gender. The small girls who dance *Rejang* in Subagan participate, because their parents want them to – they know little more than that about dance as a religious practice in life. Even the nubile dancers from the neighboring village Timbrah only know excerpts of religious knowledge about dances and temple rituals. They learn the holy songs, but don't understand what they mean. Only the village elders have this knowledge. As is standard in *geronto-cratic* societies, one has to have reached a certain social status (i.e. marriage and children) and biological age in order to be completely able to participate in the respective gender-specific pool of knowledge.

The traditional knowledge tied to dance movements in Bali, is part of the intangible world heritage that was first publicly recognized this last decade for its importance as an autonomous system of knowledge and as a contribution to cultural diversity. Part of the knowledge of the meaning of dance movements is the temporally limited appearance of Gods during the dancers' flow of movements – after the dance, at the end of the ritual, daily life begins anew until the next ritual.

Documented through media and analyzed by academia, 'dances' are available in museums and archives for researchers and are also subject to their interpretations. Their previous ephemeral quality as an expression of a different, holistic worldview doesn't seem to matter anymore. Conserved on tapes and reduced to the material dimensions, dances, as well as objects die the museum death.

Ethnographical museums, who are committed to the transmission of non-Western traditions, are involved in an almost impossible balancing act between the demands of collecting, storing and presenting the diversity of world heritage

---

11 In the UNESCO list, rituals and festivals are in third place – after the performing arts.

on the one hand, and presenting non-Western systems of knowledge to local visitors in an understandable way that respects the original intentions of its producers on the other.

NEW PATHS

In my opinion, the following paths exist when dealing with museum collections (and dance) in order to integrate them as indigenous carriers of knowledge systems in the museum's educational mandate and to conform to the objectives of the UNESCO Convention from October 17, 2003 on the conservation of intangible cultural heritage:[12]

First: The direct involvement of knowledge producers in the archiving of their cultural products is essential. All aspects of documentation and collection should be discussed and realized together with them.

Second: Indigenous representatives should be invited to discuss historic collections and to tell their own stories about them (cf. Rein 2010).

Third: All (dance) performances that take place in the context of museums should be organized together with the performers (producers of culture), so that all participants are given a forum for inter- and trans-cultural dialogue.[13]

Fourth: Unlimited respect should be first granted to indigenous worldviews and systems of knowledge before the academic museum mandate and so-called expertise takes hold. New insights can only be discovered in mutual dialogue.

Even if these paths towards an 'inclusive museum' are strictly followed, the conflict – between collecting and storing, and the ephemeral quality of dance movements that is characteristic for the short-term, imagined presence of spiritual entities in a ritual – remains. The museums' attempt at archiving this concept of ephemerality in some way or another in order to communicate it through objects in its preserved state is doomed to fail – except if the institution museum expands its educational mandate to explain to visitors how to concentrate on the

---

12 Beier-de Haan states a difference between collection strategies and exhibition practice. For some years now, the latter has been attempting to secure a greater involvement of indigenous statements – whereby a generally required practice of participation does not yet exist (Beier-de Haan 2007: 57).

13 From 2000 to 2008 international musicians appeared in the Museum der Weltkulturen Frankfurt am Main in the *Musikalisches Wohnzimmer* and *Jardin du Monde*. The extraordinary thing was the close contact between the artists and the audience with many stimulating and very personal conservations about traditional music and world music.

staging of the ephemeral in the present, to enjoy it, absorb it and remember it themselves. This would mean allowing a dance event to simply occur in the here and now and to only remain stored as a fleeting event in individual or collective memory. A museum mandate that is expanded in such a way (beyond the museums' collections) would, in my opinion, equally contribute to preserving *and* communicating world heritage on the basis of explicit respect towards indigenous worldviews and traditions of knowledge.

REFERENCES

Alivizatou, Marilena (2007): "Intangible Cultural Heritage: A New Universal Museological Discourse?" (= Lecture at the ICOM General Conference in Vienna 2007).

Beier-de Haan, Rosmarie (2007): "Einige Anmerkungen zum 'Intangible Heritage'", in: UNESCO Heute 1/2007, pp. 55-57.

Bräunlein, Peter (2004/1): "'Zurück zu den Sachen!' – Religionswissenschaft vor dem Objekt. Zur Einleitung", in: Peter Bräunlein (ed.), Religion und Museum: Zur visuellen Repräsentation/en im öffentlichen Raum, Bielefeld: transcript, pp. 7-54.

_____ (2004/2): "Shiva und der Teufel – Museale Vermittlung von Religion als religionswissenschaftliche Herausforderung", in: Peter Bräunlein (ed.), Religion und Museum: Zur visuellen Repräsentation/en im öffentlichen Raum, Bielefeld: transcript, pp. 55-76.

Bredekamp, Horst (2009): "Von der Kunstkammer zum Museum", in: Ausstellungsführer "Anders zur Welt kommen" – Das Humboldt-Forum im Schloss. Ein Werkstattblick, Berlin: Ed. Stiftung Preussischer Kulturbesitz [a.o.], pp. 26-31.

Hanna, Judith Lynne (1987): To Dance is Human. A Theory of Nonverbal Communication, Chicago: Chicago University Press.

Hoffmann, Hilmar (1979): Kultur für alle, Frankfurt am Main: S. Fischer.

Hornbacher, Annette (2005): Zuschreibung und Befremden. Postmoderne Repräsentationskrise und verkörpertes Wissen im Balinesischen Tanz, Berlin: Reimer.

Huschka, Sabine (ed.) (2009): Wissenskultur Tanz. Historische und zeitgenössische Vermittlungsakte zwischen Praktiken und Diskursen, Bielefeld: transcript.

Köstering, Susanne (2003): Natur zum Anschauen. Das Naturkundemuseum des Deutschen Kaiserreichs, 1871-1914, Cologne [a.o.]: Böhlau.

Kuhnt-Saptodewo, Sri (2006): Getanzte Geschichte. Tanz, Religion und Geschichte auf Java. (= Veröffentlichung zum Archiv für Völkerkunde Band 11), Münster [a.o.]: LIT.

Laukötter, Anja (2008): Vom Alltags- zum Wissensort. Zur Transformation von Gegenständen in Völkerkundemuseen im beginnenden 20. Jahrhundert. Themenportal Europäische Geschichte, http://www.europa.clio-online.de/site/lang__de/ItemID__290/mid__11428/40208214/default.aspx (March 21, 2010).

_____ (2010): "Kultur in Vitrinen. Zur Bedeutung der Völkerkundemuseen im beginnenden 20. Jahrhundert", in: Georg-Kolbe-Museum (ed.), Wilde Welten. Aneignung des Fremden in der Moderne, Berlin: Koehler & Amelang, pp. 109-126.

Meijer-van Mensch, Leontine (2009): "Vom Besucher zum Benutzer. Chefsache Bildung", in: Museumskunde, Volume 74, Number 2, pp. 20-26.

Pazzini, Karl Josef (1989): "Tod im Museum. Über eine gewisse Nähe von Pädagogik, Museum und Tod", in: Hans-Hermann Groppe/Frank Jürgensen (eds.), Gegenstände der Fremdheit. Museale Grenzgänge, Marburg: Jonas, pp. 124-136.

Raabe, Eva Charlotte (ed.) (2008): Reisen und Entdecken. Vom Sepik an den Main. Hintergründe einer Ausstellung, Frankfurt am Main: Museum der Weltkulturen.

Rein, Anette (1994): Tempeltanz auf Bali: Rejang – der Tanz der Reisseelen, Münster [a.o.]: LIT.

_____ (2000/1): Der gedoppelte Mensch. Performative Grenzüberschreitungen auf Bali, in: Sociologus, Volume 50, Number 2, pp. 175-198.

_____ (2000/2): Die Präsentation der Reisgötting Sri im Tanz: Zur Performanz balinesischer Rituale, in: Klaus-Peter Köpping/Ursula Rao (eds.), Im Rausch des Rituals, Münster [a.o.]: LIT, pp. 72-86.

_____ (2009): "Schlösser, Speere, Perlenstickerei – die Vielfalt des Weltkulturerbes", in: World Heritage and Arts Education, http://groups.uni-paderborn.de/stroeter-bender/medien/whae/WHAE_1.pdf (March 21, 2010).

_____ (2010): "One Object – Many Voices. The Museum is no 'neutral' Place", in: Museum Aktuell 165, pp. 9-18.

Seyppel, Marcel (2007): "Wie wird das UNESCO-Übereinkommen zum immateriellen Kulturerbe umgesetzt? Facts & Figures", in: UNESCO 1/2007, pp. 77-79.

van Elsbergen, Antje (1998): "Von der Bühne zur Vitrine und zurück. Das musealisierte Drama einer Maske", in: Bettina E. Schmidt/Mark Münzel (eds.): Ethnologie und Inszenierung, Marburg: Curupira, pp. 537-554.

van Gennep, Arnold (1909): Les rites de passage, Paris.

WEBSITES

Deutscher Museumsbund: Fachgruppen und Arbeitskreise, http://www.museumsbund.de/de/fachgruppen_arbeitskreise/ (March 16, 2010).

Museum der Weltkulturen, http://www.mdw-frankfurt.de/Deutsch/ (March 21, 2010).

The Bluff of Contemporary Dance

MONIKA GINTERSDORFER in conversation with GABRIELE KLEIN

GABRIELE KLEIN: Today, on April 7, 2011, the Ivorian president Laurent Ghagbo barricaded himself in the bunker under his residency in Abidjan. He insists on his right to presidency although he has been voted out of office and he is fighting against the elected president Ouattara and the Ivorian people. You have many close contacts with the Ivory Coast and work a lot with Ivorian dancers ...

MONIKA GINTERSDORFER: Yes, it is interesting to see how we already anticipated the current political situation in a piece that we developed a year ago with Franck Edmond Yao. In this production, he dances the role of a typical nightclub-goer fighting for space in front of the mirror in a disco. "It is all about defending one's place. It doesn't matter what for. This place is my place and that is exactly how it is in politics" says Frank E. Yao and attempts to take up as much space as possible by moving his arms and legs, kicking and beating the floor. In the piece, he directly shifts over from narcissistic clubber to a western scene in which two political rivals stand facing each other just like Gbabgo himself formulated it in foresight. In a combination of movements and text – a style, which has now become typical for our work – theories become physical reality and the physical turns back into language.

GABRIELE KLEIN: You are a theater director, who also develops choreographic pieces with dancers, such as the *Logobi* series[1].

---

1   *Logobi 01* (2009, with: Gotta Depri, Hauke Heumann), *Logobi 02* (2009, with: Gotta Depri, Gudrun Lange), *Logobi 03* (2009, with: Laurent Chétouane, Franck Edmond Yao), *Logobi 04* (2009, with: Jochen Roller, Franck Edmond Yao), *Logobi 05*

MONIKA GINTERSDORFER: I know nothing about contemporary dance nor have I ever claimed that my work is about dance. We[2] created the *Logobi* series, because I had been working with dancers from the Ivory Coast for years, but I did so as a theater director. The working principle behind *Logobi* is no more specifically dance-oriented than in our other creations, where we also already worked with movement. They are however always about the relationship of language and movement. If I weren't able to work with language, I would be lost in working with movement. In other words, yes, I use dance elements, but I only do so in order to accomplish other things and not as a reflection of dance itself. Ultimately, I've always exploited movement in order to make theater.

GABRIELE KLEIN: How did the *Logobi* series begin?

MONIKA GINTERSDORFER: Gotta Depri, a dancer from the Ivory Coast, who I've known for a very long time, said he'd like to live in Hamburg. But there's no dance scene for him here, nobody knows him and as an Ivorian dancer with a different dance culture, he's marginalized. He received his training in traditional dance and in the contemporary urban dances of the Ivory Coast. In *Logobi 01*, he shows what he has danced so far. In contrast to European dances, which we appreciate abstractly, the dances from the Ivory Coast are readable for all, just not for a European audience. This is also why we explain the movements during the dancing. It was a research project for Gotta Depri, Franck Edmond Yao and myself, because for all of us – them as African dancers and myself as a theater director – European dance or what is here commonly considered contemporary dance, for example in respect to technique, is something we are not familiar with.

GABRIELE KLEIN: What does *Logobi* mean?

(2010/11, with: Richard Siegal or Paula Sachez, Franck Edmond Yao), directed by: Gintersdorfer/Klaßen

2   Theater director Monika Gintersdorfer, Ivorian dancer Franck Edmond Yao and visual artist Knut Klaßen began working together in 2005. With a German-African team of performers, they have produced pieces in independent venues and theaters, in galleries and museums, as well as in the public sphere in the field of theater, dance and performance. They have participated with their work in festivals in Abidjan, Ivory Coast and in Europe and received numerous prizes, e.g. Impulse Prize of the Jury 2009, George Tabori Prize 2010, Dance Company of the Year 2010, Faust Prize for Richard Siegal in *Logobi 05* 2010.

MONIKA GINTERSDORFER: *Logobi* is the name of an urban dance form, a street dance from the Ivory Coast. Initially, it was primarily danced by very muscular men: doormen, bouncers, tough guys. Then the dance became sleeker, more elegant, no longer so male-agressive. It became a dance that anyone can dance, a woman, a little girl. Nowadays everyone dances *Logobi*.

GABRIELE KLEIN: Does *Logobi* have a special dance technique?

MONIKA GINTERSDORFER: *Logobi* has a canon of movements. The movements are actually quite provocative. They say: look at me. I am a strong, handsome guy and perhaps I'll be a real star some day. If you want, come compete with me. But you may get your ass kicked.

GABRIELE KLEIN: It sounds similar to the battle culture of hip hop.

MONIKA GINTERSDORFER: Yes, *Logobi* is glamorous and a very gestural dance. The movements are meant to tell stories, imitate language. Unlike hip hop, *Logobi* is also a very beautiful and sleek dance and not necessarily purely about confrontation. *Ziguei* was more aggressive. There were even cases, in which it caused other dancers to leave the dance floor. But anyone can dance *Logobi* and people often dance it in front of the mirror. It is a kind of self-reflection that serves as a form of self-confirmation. *Logobi* is not really a dance, danced with a partner. Everyone dances in row facing the mirror. So you have to fight for a good place in front of the mirror and then defend this spot.

GABRIELE KLEIN: Where do they dance *Logobi* in the Ivory Coast?

MONIKA GINTERSDORFER: In clubs, discos. Abidjan is the economic capital. That is where most people live. That is also where most of the new urban dances are created and where all the important clubs are. New trends spill outwards from there over into the countryside or into the smaller cities. Urban dances also serve to immediately translate current events. At the moment, for example, there is a curfew and as soon as they can, everyone crowds into the clubs. You will find all ethnicities gathered together in the clubs. Ethnic differences aren't as important there. The only thing that counts is style.

GABRIELE KLEIN: Is *Logobi* also a dance spread with the help of visual media, as e.g. in the case of *b-boying* or *video clip dancing*?

Monika Gintersdorfer: *Logobi* first and foremost developed in the streets. Meanwhile, there are a lot of video clips about *Logobi*, but in the beginning, it was purely street and club performance culture.

Gabriele Klein: How and where did you develop an interest in dance?

Monika Gintersdorfer: I first encountered *Logobi*, when I was commissioned to film a *Coupé Décalé*[3]-Show in Hamburg. As a performance, I found this system to be very strong: to call out certain words and immediately perform them. In the process, the sequence of the texts produced new meaning, a non-narrative content. It was very crazy craziness and to a large degree contained much freedom: to constantly re-formulate new combinations and to design a kind of reality through performance, which provides the performer with status as subject. In Abidjan, club dance is not just amusement. Instead, the participants take what they have created in the performance into their everyday lives and thus transform accordingly. *Coupé Décalé* was created by the group *Jet Set*[4]. I filmed several of

---

3 Douk Saga (1975-2006), called the 'President', Lino Versace, Solo Béton, Boro Sanguy and the other members of the self-proclaimed *Jet Set* created *Coupé Décalé* in 2003 in the milieu of the Ivorian diaspora in Paris. Developed in a period of crisis and impoverishment in the Ivory Coast, *Coupé Décalé* provides space for a parallel world between Paris and Abidjan, which allows individual existences to become expressions of an assertive play with codes and clichés in a mixture of subversive self-affirmation, dandyism and glamour. With breathtaking speed, this music, dance and lifestyle genre soon spread through the clubs of Abidjan to then become a massive success in West and Central Africa, the Caribbean and Europe. *Coupé Décalé* reached such popularity that Douk Saga's funeral even took on the form of a real ceremony of state for a true president of Abidjan. *Coupé* is street slang in Abidjan for 'doing mischief or being drunk'. In the Parisian reality of the Ivorians, the term transformed its meaning into 'to cheat, to bluff, to make a cut', followed by *décalé* and *travaillé*, running away and working. However, this modern term for working actually means declaring a hedonistic lifestyle with expensive cars, brand-name clothes, champagne and Cuban cigars and the earning and spending of a fast buck out of hand to be a true profession.

4 The *Jet Set* combine artistic expertise and glamour with precarious living conditions, problems with the law and money, in other words common everyday life as experienced by those migrants living in the banlieues of Paris. As self-proclaimed stars, they keep their battles with the police, the courts and their fluctuation of solvency as invisible as possible, while asserting the status of fame, glamour and wealth. Theatrical presentation, exclusive designer fashion and the creation of ever-

their performances. These performances are not about embodying certain roles and contrasting them with mundane everyday life. On the contrary, the performers give themselves names such as 'Le President', 'Le Bankier', without associating these roles with specific gestures, facial expressions or movements. But they are always and everywhere 'Le President' and everyone call them by that name. In this respect something created in the performance, which has an effect on life itself. From this perspective, life itself a performance: we perform what we want to be.

GABRIELE KLEIN: How did you translate that into a theatrical concept?

MONIKA GINTERSDORFER: We used the system that these shows have, combining text with movement, but without the music, which normally also plays a part. We formed teams in which dancers worked with actors. The language had to be translated, German-French and French-English. Initially, we chose simple movements loosely connected to what is being said. The movements could be dance movements or more athletic or look like working motions. At first, the movements were there in order to create something similar to a group identity: one person does a movement, which the others can immediately join in on. And we kept it so simple, because we wanted to keep audience inhibition as low as possible, when we were performing outside. We performed in places, such as the banlieues of Paris, where the audience has a lot of knowledge about and experience with movement. The audience was the experts and we wanted to integrate them.

GABRIELE KLEIN: What role does the audience play?

MONIKA GINTERSDORFER: For us, it's not about: here are the artists and superstars and you can just sit and watch. We do not build stages when we play in the streets in order to stand level with the audience. Eye to eye and not elevated. As a performer, this makes you very vulnerable. The audience reaches out to touch

---

new dance forms are indispensable elements of this concept. In accordance with the principles of reevaluation and exaggeration, a parallel society is created. The members of this society meet in the suburbs of Paris, in the Ritz, the Atlantis or along the Rue Princess, the party strip of Abidjan the *Jet Set* sets the stage, not vice versa. In the clubs, DJs sing stories of a Jet-Set world, in which the migrants occupy the higher positions, become bankers, ambassadors or presidents. The political mixes with irony, amusement and show.

you, push you. By making the movements simple, anyone can immediately join in. If you are talking while you are dancing, you have to think and formulate at the same time as well. And when you take a pause from speaking and the movement continues, it's no problem at all.

GABRIELE KLEIN: What kind of texts did you use?

MONIKA GINTERSDORFER: One of our first pieces was *Verlieren* (*Losing*) (2006). *Verlieren* was a mix of outdoor performances. We went out onto the streets and visited Ivorian artists in their homes in Paris, Marseille and Hamburg. These were, in other words, people who also had the status of migrants. This double life as artists and migrants of color is something we wanted to make visible in the performances and in a film.

We also showed it in La Courneuve, which is the banlieue in Paris, where journalists made those pictures of burning cars that went around the world. It was also a period of intensified conflict between France and the Ivory Coast, a conflict, which also greatly changed the lives of Ivorians in France. The texts that we used also referred to the political situation of the migrants.

The performances featured, for example, DJ Arafat, Maga Din Din or Zike, as well as people, who are well-known in show business and nevertheless still live in the banlieues. We developed scenes with them and filmed them in their apartments. So actually it was more like 10 to 12 people, who performed in the film.

GABRIELE KLEIN: What is your typical working process, for example, in *Logobi*?

MONIKA GINTERSDORFER: *Logobi 01* was about the situation of Gotta Depri. And from *Logobi 02* onwards, we asked people, who are not part of our team, to collaborate for a short space of time. We didn't want to rehearse *Logobi* longer than a week.

GABRIELE KLEIN: Why?

MONIKA GINTERSDORFER: First of all, Ivorian dancers work rather quickly. They don't want to repeat and rehash what they are doing for 4 weeks. And we don't want anyone to act as if they are watching something that they have already seen 10 times before. Ideally, they should watch as attentively as if they were seeing it for the first or second time. In *Logobi 04*, we worked with Jochen Roller, in

Logobi 05 with Richard Siegal – in order to have any chance at working with these very busy dancers, you have to keep the rehearsal periods short.

GABRIELE KLEIN: How would you describe the work on *Logobi 04* with Jochen Roller, for example? What was your role as director therein?

MONIKA GINTERSDORFER: The dancers, Jochen and Franck, and I spoke with each other, even before entering the rehearsal space. We also showed each other things. It was a constant back and forth – a system of demonstration – from talking to performing to talking, from table to stage to table. Later, I disappeared from the stage. Because I've known Franck Edmond and Gotta Depri for so long and also actually know Ivorian dance pretty well by now, I can easily say which movements are interesting to present.

GABRIELE KLEIN: And then there's the moment of choreographic decision-making. Who makes them and which decisions?

MONIKA GINTERSDORFER: It depends. *Logobi 01*, *02* and *04* have a fixed order, i.e. I select the order of the performance out of the material that was created over a period of 5 days. For example: we begin with the funeral dance, then do the rain dance and from this, we move on to the first urban dance. In *Logobi*, it is up to the performers whether something is fixed or not. In *Logobi 05* with Richard Siegal, nothing is fixed, absolutely nothing. Richard didn't want to provoke any form of repetition.

GABRIELE KLEIN: Neither did you, right?

MONIKA GINTERSDORFER: Yes. In *Logobi 05*, I wrote a list during rehearsals. Half an hour before the performance I went to Richard and said to him: if you could get to this point sometime during the performance – that would be nice. And he said: Monica, you told me, you don't like repetition. And I said, yes, but that was really very good and then I threw away my list. In other words, in *Logobi 05*, our goal is to never repeat anything and the structure between the two dancers has to be found anew every evening. *Logobi 05* therefore has very different performances. When I send out a DVD, it's never clear whether the presenter will really get the performance that's on it.

GABRIELE KLEIN: I see a difference: *Logobi 01* and *02* seem to be more about representation and *Logobi 05* more about the performative. From this perspective: Is *Logobi 01* more a piece and *Logobi 05* more a process?

MONIKA GINTERSDORFER: The method is the same. The way we approach rehearsals and ask questions: why could such a movement be successful? Or why would such a movement be accepted in one cultural system and not in another? In *Logobi 01* and *02*, we explored Gotta Depri's question of whether contemporary dance is no more than a bluff.

GABRIELE KLEIN: Is this a politically, a post-colonially motivated question?

MONIKA GINTERSDORFER: In my opinion, it is not particularly political to make politics an issue. It is political, when you try to change the personal circumstances of people through your work. We did *Logobi*, for example, because Franck and Gotta Depri had no contact yet with the European dance scene. To get to know contemporary dance, or what the Europeans define as such, by performing and not by reading books or watching films. Through and in performance, real change takes place. Before the performances, they were dancers, who performed in Europe in a specific dance milieu, which had no connections whatsoever to the European dance scene. I wanted to lift this separation between their dance community and European dance. That is why I did *Logobi*. And things have changed as a result. Richard Siegal has invited Franck to take part in his next piece, for example. *Logobi 05* was invited to the German Dance Platform 2010 and Franck and Gotta Depri are now dancers in the contemporary dance context.

GABRIELE KLEIN: It changes the circumstances of individual lives.

MONIKA GINTERSDORFER: Yes, it is always quite concrete. In our collaborations with African dancers, it is always also about visas, about receiving permission to move. Until 2009, I invited the dancers at my own risk and with a lot of administrative expenses. That was not without problems, for if one of them had not gone back, I would never have been allowed to invite anyone ever again. Later, I received support from institutions such as the House of World Cultures in Berlin. They organized the invitations and also assumed responsibility and liability. That was a relief, but much has changed due to the current political situation. Our work is currently about providing support for people in the Ivory Coast and trying to get them out of a country on the verge of a civil war. That is currently our main project.

GABRIELE KLEIN: We can differentiate here between three concepts of inter-culturalism. The first concept pursues an early modernist idea of dance, which says: dance is a universal language. You can see this in ballet: ballet is a European, courtly, i.e. class-specific dance culture, which follows a certain concept of gender and translates feudal structures of power into choreography. Ballet today is a globalized language, disseminated worldwide through colonialization and imperialism, among other things. As a globalized language, ballet disseminates, one could say, the post-colonial myth that anyone can understand dance and choreography, that anyone can read it. This concept of dance as a universal language is something you clearly did not choose. The second concept is that of cultural difference. That dance can be understood as a cultural technique and that its identity is located in a specific culture. Inter-culturalism here means: accepting the 'Other', striving towards an understanding between cultures. The third concept is the deconstructivist idea of constant cultural translation. Here there is no source or target culture; dance cultures are always 'in between', interstitial, on a journey.

MONIKA GINTERSDORFER: Yes, the last one interests us a lot at the moment. The first *Logobis* were about cultural differences and about making these recognizable. *Logobi 05* was about the transformation of movements. Here cultural identities were more than just starting points, transcultural formations were the process. Whether transformation can take place or not, also depends on the dancers and their dance biographies. Some move more intensely in a system, have a distinct identity.

GABRIELE KLEIN: Transcending cultural identities is quite an ambivalent process ...

MONIKA GINTERSDORFER: For an Ivorian dancer, that which emerges from this 'in-between' space is extremely dangerous. There is the danger of *n'importe quoi* – of no longer being able to recognize anything at all. That it no longer stands for and doesn't relate to anything. In the Ivory Coast, every dance has to have its own name. If someone just simply does something, they are accused of *n'importe quoi*. Just doing something or another, producing a bastard. It was therefore clear that the principle of transformation had to be distinct. How do we manage to not create a *n'importe quoi* in the process of transformation?

ART WORLDS

Transcription – Materiality – Signature. Dancing and Writing between Resistance and Excess

GABRIELE BRANDSTETTER

Dance and *Schrift*[1], i.e. writing, are engaged in a dynamic relationship – and have been so in various respects over a long historical period of time. How can we explore these dynamics, this love-hate relationship? In current dance discourse, opposing as well as connecting positions have been, so it seems, clearly adopted in theory and practice. To exemplify these positions, I would like to quote two statements from the field of dance practice: in response to a question on the relationship of dance and *Schrift*, choreographer Thomas Lehmen stated that they are "completely different domains. Dancing and *Schrift* are simply not the same. There is no linguistic equivalent to what is being danced. There is no such thing." (Klementz/Cramer 2004: 21) Curator Heike Albrecht represents the opposite point of view – a commitment to the communicability of language/*Schrift* and dance:

"Nevertheless, I still see the process of reading dance through language as decisive. The act of repetition, of recognition is also one of reflection, the reflection of one's own positi-on […]. A cognitive process is set in motion and this is where the articulation of ideas through dance and language come face to face." (Id.)

---

1 Translator's note: The German terms *Schrift* and *Schreiben* both translate as writing in English. *Schrift* stands for the material side of writing, i.e. text (typeface, font, script, etc.). We have chosen to retain the German term in italics throughout the text to differentiate it from *Schreiben*, which is the actual physical act of writing.

The following paper seeks to explore the relationship of dance and *Schrift* in a way that examines their differences and conjunctions beyond the usual well-known oppositions – the oppositions of orality/corporeality and texuality, presence and absence, performativity and semiotics, ephemerality and traces.

This requires ignoring a large part of the relationship between dance and *Schrift* – a field, which is, after all, widely discussed in the area of cultural studies. In the case of *Schrift*, I am first of all referring to the broad range of discourses covering the history and presentation of dance and choreography and which are, in fact, inseparable from their creation: discourses, such as those expressed in concept papers, written project applications, program notes, reviews as well as essays and historical analyses. In addition, I will also ignore the highly varied 'forms of dance notation' with their intricate intertwining of *Schrift* and movement and their historic transformations. And finally, this is also not the place to examine 'dance' and '*Schrift* as cultural techniques', although this is also an important aspect.[2]

Instead, I would like to concentrate on a perspective that focuses on the performativity – of dance, as well as *Schrift*. Instead of speaking of dance and *Schrift* in a 'general' sense, I would like to approach it from the perspective of movement and its corporeality – and examine both forms of expression, dancing and writing, as movement phenomena. So, instead of speaking of dance and *Schrift* – i.e. writing as text, it will be dancing/choreographing and *Schreiben*[3] – i.e. writing as a physical act. This will bring to our attention other similarities and disparities.

In philosophy – especially in phenomenologically accentuated philosophy – the issues of dancing-writing are examined primarily from the body's point of view. Jean-Luc Nancy, for example, approaches the subject of "writing the body" (cf. Nancy 2008) from the perspective of the gesture of addressing. Writing here means "not the monstration, the demonstration of a signification, but a

---

2   On dance as a cultural technique (the theory of Marcel Mauss) cf. Inge Baxmann: *The Body as Archive. On the Difficult Relationship between Movement and History* (2007); as representative of the extensive literature on *Schrift* cf. Gernot Grube/Werner Kogge/Sybille Krämer (eds.): *Schrift. Kulturtechnik zwischen Auge, Hand und Maschine* (2005). On the debate between *Schrift* and performance cf. e.g. Waltraud Wiethölter/Hans Georg Pott/Alfred Messerli (eds.): *Stimme und Schrift. Zur Geschichte und Systematik sekundärer Oralität* (2008), as well as Davide Giuriato/Stephan Kammer (eds.): *Bilder der Handschrift. Die graphische Dimension der Literatur* (2006).

3   See footnote 1.

gesture toward touching upon sense" (id. 2008: 17). The 'body' is thus always already in itself different:

"Hence the impossibility of writing *to* or of writing *the* body without ruptures, reversals, discontinuities (discreteness) or trivialities, contradictions and displacements of discourse within itself." (Id. 2008: 19)

But finally, it is precisely here – in this contingent 'body writing' – where resistance, the excess of the corporeal becomes apparent: "the ongoing protest of bodies in-against-writing" (id. 2008: 21).

Even writing itself, as a physical act of movement, should be included in this approach. Roland Barthes has pointed out that this aspect of writing has largely been neglected in the theory of poststructuralism: the sensual, physical act that writing can be (aside from the semiotic production of meaningful signs): "[...] *scription*, the moving, the muscular act of writing" (Barthes 2002: 983-984).

In the following, I would like to examine these intersections and differences of 'dancing-writing' and their performative manifestations from three perspectives: 1. transcriptions and transmissions; 2. materiality; and 3. signature.

A literary episode from literature on understanding dancing and writing will provide insight into the fundamental difference between these processes.

The author Robert Walser has discovered a unique form of writing in his 'micrograms'. He permits himself to 'digress' in his *Räuber* novel in order to keep the quill moving, as he calls it. He comments on this as follows: "Maybe this is one of the secrets of better authorship, i.e. there simply has to be something impulsive entering the writing." (Kammer 2008: 195)[4] Walser's poetological reflections repeatedly revolve around the execution and limitations of writing. He observes and comments the scribbling, the sweep of the pen and the application of the pencil. It is about the performance of writing, the complexity of this 'action' as a movement of the body as a graphic act. In an essay on Robert Walser, Walter Benjamin reflects precisely on this aspect of performative writing: "To write and to never correct what has been written is the ultimate penetration of unintentionality and greatest intent." (Benjamin 1977: 325) For the act of writing, this type of performance is highly unusual: to write – for example when creating a poetic text – almost always means moving forward and back again. As a production of text, writing doesn't take place in a single, dynamic movement. Instead, writing is 'roughened' by interruption, deletion, erasure,

---

4 I am grateful to an excellent essay by Stephan Kammer for pointing out this passage in the text.

overwriting – by those processes of stratified graphé, which, for example, editors are confronted with in the archeology of text generation.

Conversely, this is precisely the distinguishing feature of the performance of dance when presented – namely moving in a single motion, without interruption, without re-vision or correction. If writing reveals itself as performative in the act of putting something (down) *into* writing, then dance does the same during live performance. The difference in 'showing oneself' in each action is characteristic: in its self-recursivity and its self-interruptions, writing already brings its own transformation, modification, re-scription into the performative act. In dance as performance, the reverse is usually the case: the act is unique, irreversible, and cannot be retrieved again nor later corrected. William Forsythe sums up this quality of dance in the words:

"The choreographic idea traditionally materializes in a chain of bodily action with the moments of its performance being the first, last and only instances of a particular interpretation." (Forsythe 2008: 6)

We have here a substantiation of ideas in movement that "cannot be repeated in the totality of its dimensions by any other means" (id.).

This difference between the singularity of performing dance and the self-interruption in performing writing coincides with another aspect of dancing/ writing and performativity. It is the aspect of showing and showing-oneself in the act of movement. In the act of performance, dance shows (manifests itself) and shows itself (points to itself). In contrast, writing as movement – and this has as yet been little reflected upon as an aspect of the performativity of writing (Kammer 2008: 201ff) – eludes observation by an audience. The physical co-presence of actor/performer and observer, constitutive to the presentation of dance, is only of conditional relevance for the act of writing. Instead, the unobserved nature of this act is characteristic for writing. Writing, unless it is done in experimental situations, is a performance that doesn't present itself and is not subjugated to the regime of observation through an audience. All the more complex, however, are the scenes of self-observation in the performance of writing – and here writing and dancing see eye to eye. The 'showing-itself' and 'reading-itself' in the act of writing is a staggered process: by reading what I have written, I see the 'have-written', I see myself as writer. I observe myself in the act of writing-reading. A dancer does not read himself or herself, i.e. the traces of what his or her movement in space has 'written'. Nevertheless, in a temporal dimension that reaches backwards and forwards in time, the multiplicity of self-perception is comparable.

Elizabeth Waterhouse, a Forsythe Company dancer, formulates this self-perception in the following way:

"I have learned to spread my awareness throughout my body [...] to maintain a large proprioceptive awareness that extends from fingertips to toes. I have learned to multitask my concentration into observing/feedback and anticipating/feedforward. [...] Dancing [...] is a skilful activity that binds analyzing and acting." (Waterhouse 2010: 153-181)

This side of an elaborated self-perception in the act of dancing, writing – in a complex temporal structure of remembering and "intuiting" (cf. Walter Benjamin) – seems to me an aspect of performing writing and dancing that deserves further discussion.

TRANSCRIPTIONS AND TRANSMISSIONS BETWEEN DANCE AND SCRIPT

One possibility for examining the relationship between dance and *Schrift* is the aspect of transmission/transcription. Of course, direct translation between dancing and writing isn't possible. Nevertheless, transmissions of a kind do take place – in various discourse scenarios: from dance into texts about dance and choreography, reviews, descriptions, scientific analyses. And, *vice versa*, from writing – from myths, stories, linguistic imagery or theoretical texts – *into* choreography and dance. It is this process in which the ambivalences, attractions and repulsions between dance and text occur – an ongoing process that creates friction. How should we imagine transmissions between disparate elements? And how should we proceed to act upon them? We are thus constantly confronted with the topos of 'untranslatability'. Merce Cunningham, for example, repeatedly emphasized the 'untranslatability' not only of dance, but also of music and other arts.[5]

This emphasizes a side of intransigence, which describes a peculiar quality of the art form of dance – a 'presentation of difference' and action that occurs nowhere else in a similar fashion. In Thomas Lehmen's words: "In working with dance, I (already) see a space in which things can be said in a different manner than with language" (Klementz/Cramer 2004: 21) – a statement, which *mutatis*

---

5   Susan Foster made a critical reference to this debate on 'untranslatability' in her reflections on methodological problems, while however still assuming that the integrity of dance allows for transmission into other media (cf. Foster 1986: 187).

mutandis also applies to other art forms. In the theory of translation – from Charles Peirce, Roman Jacobson, Walter Benjamin to Umberto Eco – there is an almost irresolvable argument about if and how something is lost or whether something is gained – a surplus of sense and sensuality – in the process of transmission or transcription (from one language to another, from one art form to another). In his – broad – concept of translation, Roman Jacobson refers to the work of semiotician Charles Peirce and praises his theory for stating that in "translation, the element that is to be interpreted is always enriched in a creative way" (Eco 2006: 271). In other words, there is an excess of alternatives of meaning and comprehension in such a process. The shifts, detours as well as the gaps and permanent obstacles in what is to be transmitted open up a creative dimension. Disfigurement and similarity are in a state of friction – and it is precisely here that the potential of a third element, *between* dance and *Schrift*, could reveal itself: a similarity without an original. This is why Walter Benjamin speaks of "translatability" and not of (a complete) translation (cf. Benjamin 1972)[6]. Given such reflections on the openness of and the shifts in the translation process, the question 'where is the primary and where the secondary?' seems obsolete. In the process of translation, the intransigency of an artwork becomes apparent – its untranslatablility into language or other media. When dancers and choreographers insist on this chasm between dance and *Schrift* (of translation), they highlight a crucial aspect of the aesthetic experience. They point out the openness of meaning in choreographic work – as does William Forsythe, when he emphasizes the resistance of a choreographic performance to objectifying, unequivocal interpretation: the space-time experience, as succinct as it may be, is ephemeral and evades examination "from the position that language offers the sciences and other branches of arts, that leave up synchronic artifacts for detailed inspection" (Forsythe 2008: 7). Once again, the familiar topos of ephemerality, which makes an act of dance inaccessible and resistant, is invoked to resist the fixation/transcription into *Schrift*. At the same time, there has always been an exchange between *Schrift* and dance, between body and language – especially in the choreographies/performances of William Forsythe. Thomas Lehmen himself points this out when establishing that language and *Schrift* represent media for the conceptualization and interpretation/reading of dance movements on the one hand, but on the other, also constitute elements of the choreographic process:

---

6   On Benjamin's theory of translation: cf. Jacques Derrida: *Babylonische Türme. Wege, Umwege, Abwege* (1997) and *Theologie der Übersetzung* (1997) as well as Paul de Man: *Schlußfolgerungen: Walter Benjamins 'Die Aufgabe des Übersetzers'* (1997).

"In a ballet by William Forsythe," Lehmen says, "it's about graphic elements, about letters, so to say [...] about words that appear again and again. But they have no assigned meanings. They enter a space in which we can't and shouldn't say what a specific element concretely means, although they are articulated in a super clear way. That is simply the space of art." (Klementz/Cramer 2004: 21)

In his *Schreibstück*, Thomas Lehmen himself started an experiment in the space between writing/*Schrift* and choreography. What does it mean to base a choreography on a book, to start from a piece of writing? This implies that the idea already includes a process of transcription. "The idea was," Thomas Lehmen says, "to write a 'dance piece as a book'. Choreographers, dancers and producers were supposed to communicate about the idea and with one another in order to perform the piece." (id. 2004: 20) In a series of performances, three choreographers each showed their version, i.e.: their implementation of the 'plans' outlined in the text and the attached 'boxes'. The transcriptions – into body movement, into dance – are implemented on the basis of an act of writing; they are staggered in time like a musical canon and visible in the same space: as realizations of the infinite possible number of transcriptions in the "simultaneity of corporeal reality" (cf. Lehmen 2002: n.p.)[7]. Each implementation of *Schreibstück* and its respective choreographic re-writing simultaneously refers to what is not being implemented. In the process of transcription and showing the transmitted, it becomes transparent how choreographers work: in the juxtaposition, we behold the processes of decision-making, freedom and reduction contained in the creative process. And what becomes clear is that there is no original version that an author (in the traditional sense of the term) could be responsible for. It is evident that the dynamic relationship of text and body, of writing and dancing is situated in the open field of translatability: as a never-ending process of transcriptivity. Ludwig Jäger applies the concept of transcriptivity from a linguistic perspective and relates it to basal processes of transcriptive adaptation in language: speech (its performance) as an 'ante-script' of the scriptural. – A reflection/the application of this theoretical model for the relationship of dance/choreography and *Schrift* seems self-evident (cf. Jäger 2002).

---

7   On Thomas Lehmen's *Schreibstück* cf. Pirkko Husemann: *Choreographie als kritische Praxis. Arbeitsweisen bei Xavier Le Roy und Thomas Lehmen* (2009).

MATERIALITY: RESISTANT WRITING/DANCING

Apart from Roland Barthes' books on the theory of writing, the theory of *Schrift* has only recently turned its attention to the intrinsic value of the materiality of *Schrift* and writing: its visual and haptic materiality, the concreteness, dynamics and corporeal nature of writing (cf. Greber/Ehlich/Müller 2002). To describe the relationship of this physical act (in contrast to *Schrift* as documentation), Jean-Luc Nancy uses a term derived from Roland Barthes' concept of "dysgraphia": "exscription".

"There is only exscription through writing, but what's exscribed remains this other edge that inscription, though signifying on an edge obstinately continues to indicate as its own-other edge. Thus, for every writing, a body is own-other edge […]." (Nancy 2008: 87)

According to Nancy, writing/reading is not primarily a visual act of deciphering, but rather "touching and being touched": "writing, reading, a matter of tact" (id.). The materiality of writing is, thus, fundamentally linked to the experience of resistance. Not only do the 'figures' of movement – writing/dancing – describe the complex structure of the space-time matrix. Their materiality[8] reveals itself instead in the 'flow' of the movement, which makes the exertion directed at the resistant material tangible. Roland Barthes mentioned that the line and the flow of inscription testifies to a power, to work – an 'energon' that appears as a gesture of exhaustion. "The line is a visible action." (Barthes 1991: 170) Is the other side of resistance contained in this act, even if it is not perceivable on the surface? Not just the materiality of the carrier of inscription, but also that of the body, in the resistance of practice, rejection and omission of movement?

The resistance of writing and dancing does not however only mean the friction of the materiality of movement, but also the aesthetic and political dimension of a movement *out* of resistance: writing-dancing as resistance! Contemporary artists from various cultures stage the inscribing motion of the body as a gesture of protest, as an act of resistance against political violence. William Forsythe did so in his choreography *Human Writes* (2005), as did Taysir Batnij in his *Photographic Fragments* (2001) in which he wrote on the walls and entranceways of houses in Gaza: he painted graffiti and scratched names, numbers and drawings into the walls as a protest against the violation of human

---

8 On the subject – concerning cultural techniques of communication – cf. Hans Ulrich Gumbrecht/K. Ludwig Pfeiffer (eds.): *Materialität der Kommunikation* (1988).

dignity.[9] These are gestures that write against the denigration and expropriation of human rights. William Forsythe's choreographic installation *Human Writes* attempts to make the denied corporeal traces of a resistant writing visible as movement (cf. Brandstetter 2008). The project follows a trail that – beyond any perfection of writing/dancing – leads to a victims' perspective on this power of writing. It travels to the very edge of writing, the underground areas and cracks in the movements demarcate the other side of good and beautiful writing, of good and beautiful dancing: "dysgraphia" (Barthes 1991: 173).

Forsythe's *Human Writes* deals with writing as action:

"Writing is always also movement. I consider my choreographic practice to be spatial writing. The dancers' movements should leave traces. In *Human Writes* they have to be good in order to deal with hindrances as best they can to be able to at least reproduce a few letters." (Forsythe 2006: n.p.)

However, the act of reproduction becomes an act of "exscription", of "dysgraphia". The performance is about re-writing individual sentences from the *Declaration of Human Rights*. Dancers and non-dancers/audience members move around desks, 'writing tables'. The rule governing the writing action is that 'no line or letter' is to be created directly. Writing "must be accompanied by a physical limitation, a resistance" (id.). Thus every gesture, every learned movement is broken down and beset with hindrances. Smooth, unobstructed writing – the mastery of movement and thus the performance of writing – is distorted and disfigured. These limiting acts, which the audience participates in as co-writers, are so far from any school of familiar writing/dancing that they become an extreme challenge to movement coordination. Thus these resistances permit something to become visible and tangible in every move, which is hidden in the official text of the *Declaration of Human Rights*: the violence *in* the *Schrift* of the statute. Paradoxically, we are dealing here with a text that postulates the physical and political 'integrity' of the individual body over the power of the state and judiciary. The constitutive paradox that "humanity is still filled with inhumanity" (id.) here becomes evident in the process of writing – even *where* politics acts in the name of *Human Rights*. The white sheets of paper, painstakingly written on, preserve the traces of writing. They are witness to this protest against a disposability of the body, which is defined by politics, economics and the media.

---

9   See the exhibition *TASWIR – Islamische Bildwelten und Moderne* in the Martin-Gropius-Bau, Berlin 2009, as well as Gabriele Brandstetter: *Forsythes Human Writes: Vom widerständigen Schreiben* (2009).

SIGNATURE: WRITING/DANCING AS AN ACT OF SIGNING

Finally, I would like to turn to a specific aspect of writing that is related to dancing: the signature. Is there such a thing as signing dance, signing *as* dancing? What could it consist of? In the unique, non-reproducible movement of a dancer? Then *every* dance would be a signing – inseparable from the individual act of movement. Or is the subsequent *trace* of a movement its signature? This presumes that movement is reproducible and transferable – a figuration of dance that refers to the absence of the body. Is the character of a signature the recognizable handwriting of a dancer, a choreographer – in terms of "style" (Foster 1986: 76ff)? What would such an identity consist of? And who or which 'reader'-witness would attest to such a signature?

Who signs (for) dance? And how does dance (counter)sign?

Signing – in terms of signing one's name – is a special act of writing. It refers to (coming from *signatura* = official seal, signature) an artifact, a legal text, a creation or object provided by a sign, name or artist's mark (cf. Macho 2005). Signature is closely tied to the history of authority and authorship, to ratification and authentication. This relationship between authorship and signature is equally important for dance – though far more complicated than in the fields of law, politics and art. I don't want to review here the historically and theoretically difficult issues of dance, 'authorship' and the concept of artistic oeuvre, which are closely linked to the meaning of 'signature' (cf. Brandstetter 2010). This relationship – especially the subject of 'authorship' – is often also the topic of conceptual reflection in many dance pieces by contemporary performers.[10]

The defining aspect of these pieces is an approach to choreography/dance that is not focused on a 'product', but rather on triggering a process of experience. Signature in dance thus does not consist of fixing and preserving an intention behind the movement. Instead it opens up a space for an encounter with the audience in which the choreographic *Schrift* delineates a "neutral, composite, oblique space where our subject slips away, the negative where all identity is lost, starting with the very identity of the body writing" (cf. Barthes 1977). Tino Sehgal's work, for example, of which there is no written or visual documentation of any kind, is a radical experiment on the question of whether and how signing can still occur if all discourse about a performance and its documentation is

---

10 The post-structural discourse on authorship – Roland Barthes' *La Mort de l'auteur* (1968) and Michel Foucault's *Qu'est-ce qu'un Auteur?* (1969) – form the matrix of performances by numerous contemporary dancers and choreographers, among them Jérôme Bel, Xavier Le Roy, deufert&plischke.

circumvented. Wherein lies the production, the 'signing', of the performative 'sculpture' in Sehgal's concept installations? Does the viewer – in this co-production – become a co-author of the performance's re-signing? Is it the museum visitors, who assume the act of signing as soon as they enter the museum space that a Sehgal sculpture fills (cf. von Hantelmann 2007)?

The dynamic relationship between author-performer and choreographer-dancer has been dissolved in various concepts underlying postmodern and contemporary productions. This includes the process of removing hierarchies, in which more and more collective forms of production seem to circumvent the rules of (author) representation and the economic rules of commercial exploitation. If these processes of cooperative production as contained in different forms of collective 'working methods' (as Pirkko Husemann has shown) today characterize choreographing-performing: wherein then lies the signing? Choreographers such as Jérôme Bel, Xavier Le Roy and Thomas Lehmen represent a *different* form of (counter)signing *in* dance: for example, the form of 'negotiating' decisions and actions as in Xavier Le Roy's *Projekt* (2003) (Husemann 2009: 140ff).

In connection with issues surrounding the relationship between signing and authorship in dance (which has only been touched upon here), I would finally like to examine the subject of signature from another perspective: can dancing(-writing) be regarded as choreographic signing via the body? Sketching the performance with the 'body-stylo' (to modify a term used in film for the 'auteur'-camera)? Signature and signing are characterized by an irresolvable ambivalence: a signature attests to the signer's identity and the originality of this act of writing; at the same time, it also signifies the absence of the signer. We could thus ask in Jacques Derrida's words: "Does the absolute singularity of an event of the signature ever occur? Are there signatures?" (Derrida 1971: 17) In order to function, "a signature must have a reproducible, iterable, imitable form" (id.). A signature can only be read as a *seal, if* repeatable. Bearing this in mind, can dance be signed? For on the one hand, the movement of writing-dancing is unique and cannot be repeated; on the other, its (*Schrift*/signature) motion comes from a repetition, a re-citation. In his thoughts on the "choreographic act" (Forsythe 2008: 6), William Forsythe emphasizes the "irretrievability of choreographic enactment" (id. 2008: 7). All the same, 'repetition' does take place – albeit as ongoing displacement; in this sense, signing would be repetition as a re-citation of the unrepeatable. If we regard 'signing' in dance *not* as a sign of authorship (not as the signet of a product), then we can look at another facet of signing as writing/dancing: signing as poetic practice. This practice is realized with significant differences in different media. Benoît Lachambre's performance

Is you me //// Par B.Leux (2008) is characterized by 'inscription' as a process of incessant signing. In the piece, video artist Laurent Goldring's simultaneous graffiti and Benoît Lachambre's movement actions are inscribed into the performance space, laid out as a 'white cube', as a permanent superimposition.[11] For the audience, the flatness of the quick drawings and their projection on the rear wall of the stage are translated into the physicality of the dancer, who, in a state of permanent transformation, merges with the graphics like a manga or comic book animation. A prominent characteristic of this 'graphing' are the acts of deleting, overwriting and (colorfully) superimposing the writing-motions. Processes, which apply to the processing of computer fonts as well as the editing of text, namely the central operations of 'substitute' and 'delete', are here presented and named as part of the proceedings.[12] Yet: who is responsible for these processes? Who is signing? Who applies the blood-red welt-lines to the performer's bare back? It is like an alien signature critically examining the ethical dimension of 'inscription' in light of its endless virtual manipulability.

By comparison, dancing and inscription can enter into complex poetic and media relationships in other ways, the dynamics of which produce a game of excess – a transformative, kinaesthetic experience that transcends dancing and writing. Trisha Brown thus describes her drawings as "dancing on the paper" (Brown/Teicher 1998: 25). Her "dancegrams" appear neither as documentary nor as prescriptive notations, but rather as a medium that describes the surroundings ("they sculpt space", id. 1998: 15). The drawings open up an in-between space; they are like a "word", "that sits in the air between me and the dancers" (id. 1998: 21). Dancing and writing: both are processes that do *not* represent. In an interview with Hendel Teicher, Trisha Brown remarks that before she began drawing, she used language to describe dances and movement. But her type of choreographic thinking led her to begin drawing, because, as she adds, "my personal language of movement was polydirectional" (id. 1998: 13). Here, dance-writing becomes visual poetry, which – in the style of its markings, the rhythm of its lines and their orientation – is itself choreographically conceived. "For instance, the pyramid on graph paper was a dance for three people, and I wanted them to be able to understand the notion of accumulating and de-accumulating." (Id. 1998: 14)

---

11 Because of illness, the performances in Berlin (Tanz im August) on August 17/18, 2009, took place without the second performer, Louise Lecavalier.

12 This vocabulary is repeatedly used in the 'rap' text of the audio installation.

Illustration 1: Trisha Brown: Untitled, 1975.

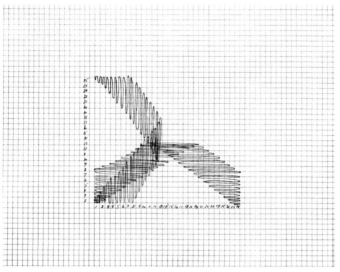

Photo: D. James Dee

Illustration 2: Trisha Brown: Untitled, 1975.

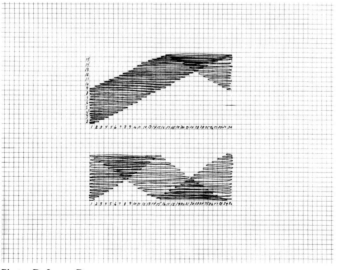

Photo: D. James Dee

Dance (de)scription as 'graph' thus gains analytical potential for the choreography of spatial relationships. Drawing lines on paper is simultaneously also a strategy of designing and a laboratory of ideas in search of movements that are surprising (also to oneself). This is, so Trisha Brown, "a quietly explosive moment". "A drawing? I don't know where it comes from and I can't control it and that's thrilling, so that's the pleasure. The rare simultaneity of intention, action, result, timing." (id. 1998: 32) "Drawing" thus becomes a method of exploration, with which to investigate the limitations of the body and of movement.

Another example is Amos Hetz's choreography, *I am drawing you are dancing. You are drawing I am dancing* (Tel Aviv, 2007).[13] The performance oscillates between two fields of drawing: the 'graph' of writing – a piece with large, dynamic brushstrokes – and the physical movements of dancing. The dancer/illustrator alternates between both fields of writing-signing. For both movement scenarios – for the brushstroke and the physical action – the style, the dynamics of the movement impulse, the positioning and release of the gesture are significant. Amos Hetz explains his choreography:

"Two actions of the moving body: the first isolated to the hand and arm. The other following with the whole body. [...] This meandering between action and waiting, between the gesture, drawing the disappearing image, still haunts me." (Brandstetter 2010: 53)

It could be that this drawing, in perceiving the gap between the hand and body, between writing and dancing, is no signing in the sense of authorship. It is not about (counter)signing/naming a piece. What is revealed here is the trace which precedes the act of signing as a gesture: a *paraphieren*, (to place one's initials)[14], in the sense of a provisional (counter)signing. To *paraphe*, to furnish with an idiosyncratic name, stands for a provisional signature; an act that does not yet imply the form of a (legally) binding text/signature. It is a form of writing-dancing in which the border between body and binding signature is open: a movement by the *Schrift* as well as the dance, which unfolds even *before* the code. On this wavering line of indeterminacy, signing(-dancing) is a poetic game in which – to quote Amos Hetz – "images from the unknown emerge onto the page

---

13 In the first version, the piece was performed as a dialogue between Amos Hetz and dancer Yael Cnaani. In a second version (that I am referring to here), Amos Hetz showed the piece as a solo (Berlin 2007, Academy of the Arts).

14 Translator's Note: The German term paraphe is descended from the Greek παραγράφειν and stands for name stamps or shorthand symbols as often used in the signing of several page long contracts, so that individual pages cannot later be replaced unknown. While also used for name stamps or shorthand symbols, the English term initial lacks this legal implication.

and into the core of dancing" (Brandstetter 2010: 53). It is a space in which writing and dancing do not exclude one another, but instead meet in a dynamic encounter.

REFERENCES

Barthes, Roland (1968): La mort de l'auteur, in: Manteia 1968, pp. 12-17.

_____ (1977): "The Death of the Author", http://www.deathofthe-author.com (January 18, 2011).

_____ (1991): "Cy Twombly: Works on Paper", in: Roland Barthes, The Responsibility of Forms, trans. by Richard Howard, Berkeley/Los Angeles: University of California Press, pp. 157-194.

_____ (2002): "Ecrire", in: Roland Barthes, Œuvres complètes, ed. by Eric Marty, Volume 4 (1972-1976), Paris: Seuil, pp. 983-984.

Baxmann, Inge (2007): "The Body as Archive. Of the Difficult Relationship between Movement and History", in: Sabine Gehm/Pirkko Husemann/Katharina von Wilcke (eds.), Knowledge in Motion, Bielefeld: transcript, pp. 207-218.

Benjamin, Walter (1972): "Die Aufgabe des Übersetzers", in: Walter Benjamin, Gesammelte Werke, ed. by Tillman Rexroth, Volume IV/1, Frankfurt am Main: Suhrkamp, pp. 474-508.

_____ (1977): "Robert Walser", in: Walter Benjamin, Gesammelte Schriften, ed. by Rolf Tiedemann and Hermann Schweppenhäuser, Volume II/1, Frankfurt am Main: Suhrkamp, pp. 324-328.

Brandstetter, Gabriele (2008): "Un/Sichtbarkeit: Blindheit und Schrift. Peter Turrinis 'Alpenglühen' und William Forsythes 'Human Writes'", in: Henri Schoenmakers/Stefan Bläske/Kay Kirchmann/Jens Ruchaz (eds.), Theater und Medien, Bielefeld: transcript, pp. 85-97.

_____ (2009): "Forsythes 'Human Writes': Vom widerständigen Schreiben", in: Almut Sh. Bruckstein Çoruh/Hendrik Budde (eds.), TASWIR – Islamische Bildwelten und Moderne, Katalog zur Ausstellung im Martin-Gropius-Bau, Berlin: Nicolai, pp. 98-100.

_____ (2010): "Signatur des Tanzens. Autorschaft und Zeichnung der Bewegung – mit einer Performance von Amos Hetz: 'I am Drawing You are Dancing. You are Drawing I am Dancing'", in: Nicole Haitzinger (ed.), Denkfiguren. Performatives zwischen Bewegen, Schreiben und Erfinden, Munich: epodium, pp. 38-53.

Brown, Trisha/Teicher, Hendel (1998): "Danse et Dessin/Dancing and Drawing", in: Corinne Diserens (ed.), Danse, précis de liberté, Catalogue de l'exposition du 20 Juillet au 27 Septembre 1998, Centre de la Vieille Charité Marseille, Marseille: Rmn, pp. 13-33.

de Man, Paul (1997): "Schlußfolgerungen: Walter Benjamins 'Die Aufgabe des Übersetzers'", in: Alfred Hirsch (ed.), Übersetzung und Dekonstruktion, Frankfurt am Main: Suhrkamp, pp. 183-228.

Derrida, Jacques (1997): "Babylonische Türme. Wege, Umwege, Abwege" in: Alfred Hirsch (ed.), Übersetzung und Dekonstruktion, Frankfurt am Main: Suhrkamp, pp. 119-165.

_____ (1997): "Theologie der Übersetzung", in: Alfred Hirsch (ed.), Übersetzung und Dekonstruktion, Frankfurt am Main: Suhrkamp, pp. 15-36.

_____ (1971): "Signature, Event, Context", http://pdflibrary.files.wordpress.com/2008/02/derrida-signature.pdf (January 18, 2011).

Eco, Umberto (2006): Quasi dasselbe mit anderen Worten. Über das Übersetzen, Munich: Hanser.

Forsythe, William (2006): Program Booklet of the Performance in Hellerau, September 15, 2006.

_____ (2008): "Choreographic Objects", in: William Forsythe, Suspense, ed. by Markus Weisbeck, Zurich: Jrp Ringier Kunstverlag, pp. 5-7.

Foster, Susan Leigh (1986): Reading Dancing: Bodies and Subjects in Contemporary American Dance, Berkeley/Los Angeles/London: University of California Press.

Foucault, Michel (1969): "Qu'est-ce qu'un auteur?", in: Bulletin de la société française de philosophie, Volume 63, Number 3, pp. 73-104.

Giuriato, Davide/Kammer, Stephan (eds.) (2006): Bilder der Handschrift. Die graphische Dimension der Literatur, Frankfurt am Main/Basel: Stroemfeld.

Greber, Erika/Ehlich, Konrad/Müller, Jan Dirk (2002): Materialität und Medialität von Schrift, Bielefeld: Aisthesis.

Grube, Gernot/Kogge, Werner/Krämer, Sybille (eds.) (2005): Schrift. Kulturtechnik zwischen Auge, Hand und Maschine, Munich: Fink.

Gumbrecht, Hans Ulrich/Pfeiffer, K. Ludwig (1988): Materialität der Kommunikation, Frankfurt am Main: Suhrkamp.

Hirsch, Alfred (1997): Übersetzung und Dekonstruktion, Frankfurt am Main: Suhrkamp.

Husemann, Pirkko (2009): Choreographie als kritische Praxis. Arbeitsweisen bei Xavier Le Roy und Thomas Lehmen, Bielefeld: transcript.

Jäger, Ludwig (2002): "Transkriptivität. Zur medialen Logik der kulturellen Semantik", in: Ludwig Jäger/Georg Stanitzek (eds.), Transkribieren. Medien/Lektüre, Munich: Fink, pp. 19-41.

Kammer, Stephan (2008): "Redende Federn. Schreibgeräusch und Stimme der Schrift", in: Waltraud Wiethölter/Hans Georg Pott/Alfred Messerli (eds.), Stimme und Schrift. Zur Geschichte und Systematik sekundärer Oralität, Munich: Fink, pp. 195-215.

Klementz, Constanze/Cramer, Franz Anton (2004): "Die große Verantwortung gibt es nicht. Constanze Klementz und Franz Anton Cramer im Gespräch mit Heike Albrecht und Thomas Lehmen", in: Theater der Zeit 12/2004, pp. 19-21.

Lehmen, Thomas (2002): Schreibstück, Berlin: Thomas Lehmen.

Macho, Thomas (2005): "Handschrift – Schriftbild. Analysen zu einer Geschichte der Unterschrift", in: Gernot Grube/Werner Kogge/Sybille Krämer (eds.), Schrift. Kulturtechnik zwischen Auge, Hand und Maschine, Munich: Fink, pp. 413-423.

Nancy, Jean-Luc (2008): Corpus, trans. by Richard A. Rand, New York: Fordham University Press.

Von Hantelmann, Dorothee (2007): How to Do Things with Art. Zur Bedeutsamkeit der Performativität von Kunst, Zurich/Berlin: diaphanes, pp. 147-192.

Waterhouse, Elizabeth (2010): "Dancing Amidst The Forsythe Company. Space, Enactment, and Identity", in: Gabriele Brandstetter/Birgit Wiens (eds.), Theatre without Vanishing Points. The Legacy of Adolphe Appia: Scenography and Chorography in Contemporary Theatre, Berlin: Alexander, pp. 153-181.

Wiethölter, Waltraud/Pott, Hans Georg/Messerli, Alfred (eds.) (2008): Stimme und Schrift. Zur Geschichte und Systematik sekundärer Oralität, Munich: Fink.

Autobiography and the *Coulisses*: Narrator, Dancer, Spectator

Julie Townsend

When we approach the question of dance as a historical question, we necessarily rely on visual and textual artifacts. A perusal of journalistic, critical, and literary writing about *danseuses* in 19th century France reveals that images of dance, and specifically of *danseuses*, are embedded with highly charged narratives of desire. The figure of the *danseuse* and the trajectories of desire that frame her in this period have been studied quite extensively in both dance and literary studies (cf. Foster 1996; Townsend 2010). One of the difficulties of uncoupling the desire for the dancer from the desire that might be expressed by the dancer is the dearth of literature written by women dancers before the turn of the century. If the terms of the relationship between dance and desire in the 19th century are largely shaped by the literary, critical, and visual production of men, then how can we begin to approach the question of desire from the position of the dancer? By considering the structures of desire that framed the dancer, and then juxtaposing those structures with representations created by dancers in the early 20th century, we can use the artifacts created by dancers, that is, autobiographies to analyze dancers' own relationships to dance, the role of the dancer in her cultural context, and the relationship of the dancer to spectators. When the dancer, having been the object of desire for so long, takes up the narrative position, she reconfigures the trajectories of desire that have come to characterize her.

COULISSES LITERATURE

The vast majority of 19th century publicly circulated documents about dancers, be they critical, journalistic, literary, or visual, are produced by men with limited training in dance. In my research of the literature that characterized the figure of the *danseuse* in 19th century France, I found almost no documents by women – or women dancers – but did find a wealth of materials that presented the *danseuse* from the perspective of the desiring male spectator or reader. From fictional memoirs, to novels, to manuals and encyclopedias of the Opéra de Paris, this literature of the "coulisses" or the theatre wings and backstage constitutes a veritable genre of 19th century literature.[1]

In his study of ballet under the Second Empire, Ivor Guest attributes the following quip to an 1859 article in *Le Figaro*:

"What a paltry opinion novelists have of the ballet girl's virtue. There is not one Parisian novel which does not introduce a banker or a man of fashion who keeps a ballet girl of the *Opéra*. But the *Académie de Musique* barely contains thirty *danseuses*, so that even if the *rats* and supers were included, there would be at least a thousand happy admirers for each of them." (Guest 1974: 20)

This quote appears, as well, as the opening passage of an 1887 text entitled *Les Coulisses*.[2] By the late 19th century, the mockery or critique of male desire of the *danseuse* became itself a pretext for representing such desire. Whether in Émile Zola's critique of the bourgeois's desire for Nana, Edgar Degas's implicit critique of the male spectator of the dancer in his series, or Huysmans's hyperframed discussion of Gustave Moreau's Salomé paintings in *A Rebours*, there appear to be layers upon layers of representations of the *danseuse* insofar as she functions as the object of desire for the male spectator. So, in fact, these representations might be read not as representations of dance or of the dancer but of, collectively, a representational landscape of masculine heterosexual desire for the *danseuse*.

If the voices of dancers, specifically female dancers, are largely absent in the 19th century literature, the contrasting proliferation of dancer's autobiographies in the early 20th century points to a radical shift in women's ability, through available artistic outlets, to circulate their visions as women, as dancers, and as artists. The period from the turn of the century and the decades that follow offer myriad representations of desire from the position of the dancer her-

---

1   A few examples of these popular *coulisses* publications include: Un Vieil Abonné: *Ces Demoiselles de l'Opéra* (1887), Joachim Duflot: *Les Secrets des coulisses des théâtres de Paris: Mystères, mœurs, usages, anecdotes* (1865), Aurélien Scholl: *Les Coulisses* (1887).

2   See footnote 1.

self. These examples arise in a variety of circumstances. We have autobiographical writing from a variety of early modern dancers, including Isadora Duncan, Loïe Fuller, Ruth St. Denis, Josephine Baker, Maud Allen, and others. These accompany the choreography of these dancers and add an archival dimension to our ability to read and interpret their relationships to earlier representations of dance and of the dancer. Theorizing these autobiographical materials may not be an obvious critical task. It is often clear that the autobiography functions more as a form of self-promotion than as a thoughtful reflection on the work of the artist; however, the genre of autobiography, I argue, reconfigures the historically male narrator of the female dancer and thus does important ideological work with respect to gender, narrative authority, and the performer/spectator configuration.

The dancer's autobiography or memoir, which, in the early 20th century, became a mainstay of major dancers' careers might then be read as a sub-genre of *coulisses* literature.[3] As such, we can interpret them both as self-representation and as a voice contributing to a larger cultural and aesthetic discussion about dance. The move to add writing to choreography and performance is one regularly taken up by 20th century dancers. My reading will consider the ways in which dancers deliver certain expected moves even while they supplement, transgress, or deviate from the conventions of the theatre literature. That is, these choreographer-dancer-writers function within the category of *coulisses* literature while they engage in polemics about the aesthetics of dance; and, through their aesthetics, they reach outside the world of performance and into broader socio-cultural and aesthetic arenas. As such, writing by dancers often developed a critical standpoint by which to reconfigure the relationship of performer to spectator. These works, to a greater or lesser degree, comprise some genre standards: early experiences of dance, the discovery of oneself as a dancer, an articulation of one's aesthetic principles, and anecdotes of famous persons and venues. What lies beneath the surface, however, is a desire to represent oneself and one's art, especially insofar as female dancers had been represented – and often idealized or degraded – in such an over-determined way by male artists and writers in the previous decades. The autobiography offers dancers the opportunity to articulate their own stories, to define the aesthetic terms of their art form, and to theorize the relevance of their art in the world. The role of dance critic being largely the

---

3   Better known autobiographies by early 20th century dancers include: Loïe Fuller: *Quinze ans de ma vie* (1908), Isadora Duncan: *My Life* (1927), Ruth St. Denis: *An Unfinished Life* (1939), Josephine Baker's two co-written autobiographies with Marcel Sauvage: *Les Mémoires de Joséphine Baker* (1927) and *Voyages et Aventures* (1931).

purview of men, women found ways of engaging in aesthetic debates through popular memoirs, autobiographies, or novels. My examples suggest that these texts put forth aesthetic arguments about dance and that they reach out to a broader cultural or artistic landscape in order to articulate sociological, cultural, and political critiques.

SUBVERTING THE GENRE

Amidst the personal anecdotes of Loïe Fuller's autobiography, *Quinze ans de ma vie* (1908) or *Fifteen Years of a Dancer's Life* (1913), the reader finds a narrator who apologizes, sincerely or not, for writing about matters of aesthetics. Fuller's autobiography first appeared at a time of crisis in her career, and its publication was most certainly motivated by the economic pressures of starting a dance school as well as her own transition from performer to teacher. But among the anecdotes of childhood struggles, hard won theatrical successes, and encounters with famous personages from intellectual and artistic milieus, Fuller inserts *Light and the Dance*, a chapter on her aesthetics, which she prefaces with the following:

"Since it is generally agreed that I have created something new, something composed of light, colour, music, and the dance, more especially of light and the dance, it seems to me that it would perhaps be appropriate, after having considered my creation from the anecdotal and picturesque standpoint, to explain, in more serious terms, just what my ideas are relative to my art, and how I conceive it both independently and in its relationship to the other arts. If I appear to be to serious, I apologise in advance." (Fuller 1908: 62)

Most striking in this passage, is of course the extent to which Fuller either is uncomfortable writing as an authority on her own artistic practice or takes the rhetorical position of being uncomfortable with such a treatise on aesthetics. This also tells us something about Fuller's expectations of her readership who might be less interested in her theories of dance than in anecdotes of celebrity. Fuller delivers titillating anecdotes, but by embedding a chapter on her aesthetics and artistic process, she proposes a different performer-spectator relationship through her narration, which feigns an apology only to present an authoritative discourse on her theory of art. What is most interesting to me, though, is that way in which Fuller critiques, albeit subtly, the 'anecdotal' and 'picturesque' aspects of the autobiographical genre in favor of a more 'serious' treatment of the subject of innovation in dance, light, and color as well as the ways in which this innovation engages a relationship to the other arts. Later in this chapter, she offers a broad critique of cultural knowledge of motion:

"Our knowledge of motion is nearly as primitive as our knowledge of colour. We say 'prostrated by grief', but, in reality, we pay attention only to the grief; 'transported by joy', but we observe only the joy; 'weighted down by chagrin', but we consider only the chagrin. Throughout, we place no value on the movement that expresses the thought. We are not taught to do so, and we never think of it. Who of us has not been pained by a movement of impatience, a lifting of the eyebrows, a shaking of the head, the sudden withdrawal of a hand. We are far from knowing that there is as much harmony in motion as in music and colour. We do not grasp the facts of motion." (Id. 1908: 67)

Fuller's critique of our lack of attention to motion, via a linguistic example, signals not only a limit in the general study of motion, but also a more specific problem in terms of the ability to theorize dance. Without a body of knowledge from which to draw, she presents herself, throughout the autobiography, as a kind of experimenter who discovers hitherto unknown relationships between motion, color, and light. Her aesthetic theories, then, emerge out of a kind of scientific-spiritual journey of discovery; and Fuller measures the aesthetic value of her work by evaluating the audience reactions. Fuller characterizes her artistic intention and its relationship to the spectator:

"To impress an idea I endeavour, by my motions, to *cause its birth* in the spectator's mind, to *awaken his imagination*, that it may be prepared to *receive the image*. Thus we are able, I do not say to understand, but to feel within ourselves as an impulse an indefinable and wavering force, which urges and dominates us. Well, I can express this force which is indefinable but certain in its impact. I have motion." (Id. 1908: 71)

Fuller presents her art as an impregnation of the spectator's mind and then interprets the impact of her dance through a reading – a spectatorship – of her motion's domination over the spectator. Fuller, in a sense, turns the tables on the gendered relationship of the spectator to the performer and presents herself as the wielder of a dominating aesthetic power. Her authorship, apologetic as it may seem in the beginning of the chapter, presents the spectator-performer relationship from the authorial position of the dancer.

Fuller's narration challenges a century of writing on *danseuses* that situates the spectator as the authority on the dancer, and in the later-19th century, situates the male narrator as arbiter of the dancer-spectator relationship. In the 19th cen-

tury, to deploy the figure of the *danseuse* in literature or the visual arts constituted a kind of culturally and aesthetically elite position. The poetics of dance, as
it is expressed by novelists, poets, painters and filmmakers, often employed
narrative and perspectival strategies that rendered the dancer's body an available
commodity to the artist who then seems to withhold or deliver the body to the
reader or spectator. Fuller's writing resists the narrative power of the spectator,
especially the male spectator, with an aesthetic that draws upon her experimentation rather than an existing body of knowledge. She thus opens up a variety of
positions from which the dancer might engage in discourse about her art, sexuality, and gender. The narrative position, when taken up by the performer – particularly by a female dancer – disturbs the performer-spectator dynamic and the
desires implicit in that relationship.

RECOVERING THE *DANSEUSE*

While the autobiographies of better known and studied dancers such as Fuller
are in wide circulation (though often out of print), I'll turn now to two autobiographical novels that have had little or no critical attention. Both are written by
women dancers of the early 20th century, and both use the genre of the dancer's
autobiography as a platform by which to address broader sociological issues,
hence situating dance, and representations of the *danseuse*, as part of a broader
cultural discussion. By recovering narratives written by dancers, we gain access
to a part of the conversation about dance that is frequently absent from critical or
theoretical work. Like Fuller's autobiography, these two novels, one by an Armenian dancer who performed in Paris in the 1910s and 1920s and another by a
French dancer who was quite popular in the music halls in the 20s and 30s, offer
dancers' viewpoints on the representation of dance and on the role of the dancer-
choreographer in a broader artistic and cultural landscape.

The first example is Armenian dancer Armen Ohanian's *La Danseuse de
Shamakha* (1918). The novel begins with an account of Ohanian's childhood in
Armenia, the displacement of her family due to an earthquake, and her arranged
– and failed – marriage to a Persian Christian. After the dissolution of her marriage, Ohanian lives with a group of Muslim women and learns to dance. She
becomes a celebrated performer. Through her travels, and as a dancer, she develops a comparative perspective that allows her the role of diplomat in certain
instances. In others though, Ohanian is pointed in her criticism, especially in her
comments on European spectators of the Orient. As the book comes to a close,
and Ohanian gets closer to Europe, she sharpens her critical voice vis-à-vis colonialism and tourism. As she travels to Egypt, her sense of a clash of cultures be-

gins to magnify. Not only is she critical of the new Cairo and of its European in-
habitants and visitors, but she similarly clashes with Middle Eastern men who
take her for a prostitute. In a sense, Egypt becomes a site of conflict where she
must do more than dance; she must make a political stand through her dance.

Visiting the sites in Egypt, Ohanian is struck by the lack of gravity with
which the tourists travel – the English, in tennis outfits, climbing to the summit
of the pyramids and the American tourists calmly savoring their sandwiches.
Dance, for Ohanian, becomes a complex figure of negotiation between Europe
and Asia:

"Far from my Persia and my Caucasus, I was drawn more closely to them by a profound
nostalgia. And having set aside my pride and my prejudices against the dancers, I clung
more and more to Asiatic dances. When with half-closed eyes, to the sound of the stringed
instruments, I drew with my naked feet the arabesques of our dances upon the Persian car-
pets, I would forget that I was very far from the dear walls of our gardens. My dancing
was also a mute but eloquent language by which I said to those who treated us with con-
tempt that, although humble in our inferiority to Europeans, we nevertheless have a little
grace and tenderness, and that even in our dreaminess there is the strange splendor of hur-
ricanes. In my illusion I thought that the watching demi-gods would mingle with their disdain for us also a little understanding and respect. But the more I knew of these gods and
their Europe, the more I withdrew within myself, burying jealously in my secret depths all
that was sensitive and poetic. Thus I was wounded less. But … it's difficult to run away
from all that you love, to struggle against your own heart and to exhaust yourself in vain
attempts to resemble others." (Ohanian 1918: 336-337)[4]

The bitter irony of this passage marks a radical change from the narration until this point in the autobiographical novel. Having presented the reader with a
portrait of an educated, worldly performer, Ohanian mock-humbles herself in
front of the European spectators and readers. Thus, she illustrates the exploita-
tive nature of colonial tourism and suggests a complex inter-cultural communication between performer and spectator as well as between writer and reader.
Through her encounters with colonialism, she goes from cultural diplomat to
cultural critic. This passage functions as a double allegory: first, for the voice of
the colonized body in the face of colonial power; and, second, it represents the
silence of the dancer in the face of so much male narration of her body. Cairo is,
for Ohanian, a revelation of the commodification and manipulation of history,

---

4   Translations are adapted from: Ohanian, Armen (1923): The Dancer of Shamahka,
     trans. by Rose Wilder Lane, New York: Dutton, pp. 260-61.

culture, and art. Dance becomes a mode of narration and of translation across seemingly un-navigable straits. She ends the novel embarking to Europe to dance in the music-hall. Ohanian's autobiography ends early – she has, in fact, not yet acquired the language in which she will write. It is not until *Les Griffes de la Civilisation*, published three years later, that we hear of her experiences in London and Paris. *La Danseuse de Shamakha* does not reveal any of her European exploits; it allows the reader to speculate on how Ohanian will encounter Europe, just as we are familiar with how so many Europeans have encountered the Orient. Finally, *La Danseuse de Shamakha* elaborates, through its narrative, a perspective on the position of dance in a broader socio-cultural context.

Ohanian's text is largely about travelling to different contexts and observing how to engage in her new reality but it is also an Orientalist text that critiques Orientalism. She learns throughout the novel how to be errant, how to be home when one cannot be home. In her autobiography, Ohanian becomes both a performer and critical spectator of cultural difference. The conventionality of her writing is contrasted by her exceptional story and the development of a critical voice that engages in broad cultural commentary. The figure of dance as an expression of emotion, a narrative, a religious ritual, or an ambassador across cultures becomes an eloquent language with which to challenge authority. Desire, in this text, finally resides in the notion that dance might speak; or, perhaps provide an alternative representational discourse to European Orientalism.

Though her cultural and artistic position is entirely different from Ohanian, Colette Andris also formulates cultural critique through the *coulisses* genre, and she seeks to reconfigure the trajectories of desire between dancer and spectator through a layered, multiple narration that persistently undercuts the notion of authenticity even while it claims to be the voice of lived experience. Andris has a geographic center, but her movement like Ohanian's involves coming into a new world – that of music-hall –, seeing how it works, and then effecting change through the development of her aesthetic. Her second novel, *Une Danseuse Nue* (1933), begins with a disclaimer about the fictional nature of the novel. Based on my research of press clippings, it appears that the story of Miss Nocturne is at least loosely based on Colette Andris's own life (cf. Andris 1933/1). However, Andris insists that:

"Miss Nocturne, *danseuse nue*, is, you may well suspect, a fictional character. Nevertheless, as to the facts of her career, I've invented nothing: why then? I gathered so many secrets, witnessed so many little dramas, and I myself have so many personal memories! I could have simply given you the autobiography of a *danseuse nue*? But, then I would have told you that which I was and not that which I would have liked to be, and it seemed to me that my modest personality was of less interest than the character of whom I wanted to draw a type: that of the ideal *danseuse nue*." (Andris 1933/2: 4)

Just as she disavows the autobiographical nature of the novel, she reinforces the authenticity of her own experience and thus secures herself both the authority of an autobiography and the freedom of a novel. Andris breaks away from the convention of dancers' autobiographies and opens up a space for literary experimentation through complex narrative approaches and the blending of autobiography and fiction. Through her hybrid narration, she sets up a viewpoint that both reproduces and critiques the standards of *coulisses* literature: make-up and costuming, dramatic scenes between performers backstage, lesbian love scenes, Orientalist motifs, and more.

Before launching into the story of her protagonist, Andris takes time to define a *danseuse nue* for readers:

"What we call a danseuse nue is an already protected body, defended, dressed, by a layer of grease and by a layer of powder; and then, some flowers, a jewel or a bit of lace come to constitute the [...] obligatory triangle, which must be superimposed over that of Mother Nature; finally, accessories, sandals, wig, necklaces, an immense veil, an immense fan, who knows what other immense items! And so, just as you might think, the 'costume' of a danseuse nue does not fit in a handbag." (Id. 1933/2: 8)

According to Andris, to name the dancer, is to mistake her for something other than she is; the name misrepresents her because it fails to take into account her performance. Andris presents the dancer as a series of layers. While nude may imply the absence of clothing, this *danseuse nue* is not only made-up, as it were, and adorned with any number of accoutrements, but she is "protected" and "defended" from an implied audience – and from the implied narrator, the namer, writer. The 'triangle obligatoire', the *cache-sexe*, which is a double costume in that it re-covers what Mother Nature has already covered is the costume that constitutes the thing just as the make-up and accessories constitute the *danseuse nue*. The costume, like the name, lead the audience and the reader entirely astray, or so argues Colette Andris.

DESIRE AND THE DANCER'S VOICE

The literature of the *coulisses* in some sense suggests a narrative striptease; it tantalizes readers with a promise of access to a backstage or an interiority that goes beyond the performance. Of course these narratives, written by spectators, gossips, or performers are an extension of the performance into a narrative realm. While the representation of dancers was largely the purview of men during the 19th century, women – especially women dancers – wrote the most compelling *coulisses* literature of the early 20th century. These dancers turn the reader's desires away from the established trajectory from spectator to dancer and instead complicate the dancer-spectator relationship by introducing a dancer-narrator.

Women's *coulisses* literature participated in a whole variety of cultural, sociological, and aesthetic discourses, the terms of which had been established in the previous century. The conventions of *coulisses* literature and of the performer's autobiography offered women choreographer-dancers an opportunity not only for publicity but for contributing to the discussion of dance aesthetics. The popularity of the dancer's autobiography comes out of the 19th century fascination with the dancer's life, her association with prostitution, and the extent to which access to the dancer's body was a literary and visual trope for masculine artistic prowess. The audience provoked by this less than artistic interest in the dancer opened up the space for the dancer's memoir and, as such, many dancer-choreographers engaged this genre.

As we continue to develop ways of theorizing dance, especially historical dance, we are often dependent on representations, be they visual or literary that take a particular ideological position vis-à-vis the dancer. These works give us insight into the reception of dance, the cultural fascination with dancers, and the role that dancers play in the representational landscape of the period. The importance of the figure of the *danseuse* in 19th and early 20th century literary and visual arts suggests that we ought to take seriously dancers' own representations of their aesthetics, practices, and the implications of their work. Although these might be available only through autobiography or memoir – genres often looked upon with suspicion in academic circles. We ought to read against the grain and allow these choreographer-dancer-writers to help us think through the relationship of dance to writing, of performer to spectator, and to acknowledge the historical development of the complex desires that circulate between the text and the body – language and motion.

REFERENCES

Andris, Colette (1933/1): Une Danseuse Nue, Paris: Flammerion (= Press Clippings from the Bibliothèque de l'Arsenal, Collection Rondel, 11859).

_____ (1933/2): Une Danseuse Nue, roman, Paris: Flammerion.

Baker, Josephine (1927): Les Mémoires de Joséphine Baker, Vol. I, Paris: Kra.

_____ (1931): Voyages et Aventures de Joséphine Baker (with Marcel Sauvage), Vol. II, Paris: M. Seheur.

Duflot, Joachim (1865): Les Secrets des coulisses des théâtres de Paris: Mystères, mœurs, usages, anecdotes, Paris: Lévy.

Duncan, Isadora (1927): My Life, New York: Boni and Liveright.

Foster, Susan Leigh (1996): Choreography and Narrative: Ballet's Staging of Story and Desire, Bloomington: Indiana University Press.

Fuller, Loïe (1908): Quinze ans de ma vie, Paris: Librairie Félix Juven.

_____ (1913): Fifteen Years of a Dancer's Life: With Some Account of Her Distinguished Friends, Boston: Small.

Guest, Ivor (1974): The Ballet of the Second Empire, London: Pitman Publishing.

Townsend, Julie (2010): The Choreography of Modernism in France: La Danseuse, 1830-1930, Oxford: Legenda Press.

Ohanian, Armen (1918): La Danseuse de Shamakha, Paris: Grasset.

_____ (1923): The Dancer of Shamahka, trans. by Rose Wilder Lane, New York: Dutton.

Scholl, Aurélien (1887): Les Coulisses, Paris: Victor-Harvard.

St. Denis, Ruth (1939): *An Unfinished Life,* New York: Harper and Brothers.

Un Vieil Abonné (1887): Ces Demoiselles de l'Opéra, Paris: Tresse.

Dance Images.
Dance Films as an Example of the
Representation and Production of Movement

KNUT HICKETHIER

Movement and emotion are central categories for dance and choreography – as well as other time-based media, especially film. Film takes aspects of physical movement in space and sets them into relationship to its own potential for creating movement, visualizing and simultaneously recording them and so thus making them reproducible.

In the following paper I will discuss these points based on the example of dance in film. The discussion will focus neither on video performance, nor experimental film or avant-garde mixtures of dance and film. Instead I will focus on 'popular' or 'mainstream' film and within this field more specifically on fictional, in other words, feature films. Mainstream films are produced both for movie theaters as well as for television. 'Mainstream film' here means: the films are intended for a broad general audience and therefore rely on conventional norms of representation and their universal comprehensibility. We are therefore looking at films that are ascribed to popular culture in the widest sense, not special artistic artifacts, which may provide new concepts, new possibilities for the further aesthetic development of dance for the stage. The question that I will address here is thus how popular film handles physical action and dance. I would like to begin with some basic remarks on the subject of 'Movement and Film'.

FILM AS MOVEMENT-IMAGE

Gilles Deleuze called film the "medium of movement-images" (cf. Deleuze 1986) and by doing so only formulated what has already been widely accepted in film theory since the 1910s: that the mediality of film is essentially determined by movement as image. This movement is achieved through the impression of movement. A series of still images is shown in quick succession, each image capturing a single phase of the movement. The impression of continuous movement is created by projecting the images at a rate of at least 16 images per second or to produce a stable flow of images without flickering: a minimum of 24 images per second. This effect is not because our eyes are too lazy to follow a quick succession of individual images, but because the human brain simplifies the process and creates continuous movement under certain conditions out of a succession of images and the transitions from one image to the next. In film, we are therefore not dealing with ontologically stated movement, but always only with an individual spectator's impression of movement. This will be important for further definitions of movement later.

Movements in film are above all movements by living creatures or objects in front of a camera, which then records and stores single images of these movements on photographic material (cf. Hickethier 2007: 59). The camera records that which it sees and hands it over to the spectator – the camera's point of view thus becomes the spectator's point of view. It shows him what he sees. Film supports this form of total identification, but the spectator nevertheless is always free to take his eyes off the film image and look elsewhere (for example at the woman sitting next to him in the movie theater). Again, this means that film makes the spectator a certain offering of what he can look at – and ultimately the spectator is aware of this, even though he is usually happy to go along and identify with the camera's point of view.

Movement in film is therefore always connected to the gaze, first that of the camera and then that of the spectator. *Movements in film are thus observed movements.*

In film, the action in front of the camera is called 'mise en scène', or simply movement in front of the camera. The camera itself is however also capable of moving and can therefore bring about changes in the depiction of what is happening in front of the camera lens. These changes are not caused by the object being filmed, but by the camera itself, which can also be said to have authority over the gaze. These movements are movements by the camera in the space surrounding it, especially in the space in front of it, which is thus constantly in flux (contracting, expanding, or offering the spectator new spatial perspectives). The spectator experiences these movements through his perception of the continuous changes in the spatial composition of the image, not through visible movements of the camera itself. The camera as the determining figure remains invisible throughout – it is never seen in the image. If there is a camera visible in the image, it is not the one whose image we, the spectators, are seeing.

So what does this mean for the perception of dance in film? We are dealing with three different actors or rather authorities: the characters acting in front of the camera, the camera itself, and the spectator as observer.

These three have different scopes of action available:

In spite of being the most important of the three – as addressee of all actions by the dancers or characters in front of the camera, as well as of the camera itself – the spectator has the fewest possibilities for action at his disposal: he is stuck in the situation as recipient, unable to leave what the filmic products provides him with: the world of images. He is unable to interact with what is depicted, not even in a limited way, as is the case with video games. He basically remains 'immobile'; the actions he experiences are the actions of others, whose movements can only be conveyed inductively (for example, in car chases, falls from great heights and so on, which have the spectator holding on to his seat as he physically has the impression of also chasing, also falling, for example in films such as Steven Spielberg's *Duel* [1971] and his *Indiana Jones*-series, in particular *Indiana Jones and the Temple of Doom* [1984]).

The camera has distinctly greater range of action. Since its gaze and range of movement are of a technical nature, changes in the technical apparatus open up numerous possibilities. Moreover, editing and montage are able to create and suggest movement that has never actually happened in front of a camera. This opens up new filmic possibilities that far exceed the physicality of human movement. In the image itself, these technically produced or cinematographically induced movements are not recognizable as technical, but they seem to place the actors in front of the camera in a new context and give the spectator the impression that they themselves are also capable of completely different movements.

The actors in front of the camera have to rely on their own physical abilities to create movement, but these can be improved with periphery technical equipment. In the case of especially complex or fast movements, this can mean that the actor is moving in a car, a train, a plane, on horseback, or in any other kind of movement apparatus. The imagination knows no bounds and digital film production is able to create human or humanoid movements never seen before with the help of digital enhancement or modification (for example in films such as *Matrix* [1999] or *Avatar* [2009]). Within these movement processes and constellations, which are often linked to the narrative, dance appears as specifically choreographed movement that is integrated into the film as part of a broader ensemble of movements and dynamics.

THE ISOLATION OF DANCE IN FILM REALITY

In order to be able to locate the specific quality of choreographed dance movement in the context of film, I will first introduce a few more characteristics of film.

First of all: film sees itself, and is also seen as such by its users, as a medium for rendering reality. As Siegfried Kracauer wrote, film is a medium for "saving exterior reality" (cf. Kracauer 1964) and what we see on screen is a medium that depicts reality and thus produces a new – filmic – kind of reality. The spectators are guided by an appearance of reality created by the film. Film theory therefore refers to the reality effect that occurs when we watch a photographic film. This reality effect is the result of the 'dispositif' of cinema, in other words the medial structure of perception, which fundamentally influences how we watch films.

The appearance of reality is further strengthened by the audiovisual quality of the film, as the images are accompanied by sound, by language, and by music. Silent movements appear artificial, not real. The bodies seem to lack a grip on reality; the illusion of being present in a moment of real movement disintegrates. That is why images in sound films and also in television are always accompanied by sound, be it only atmospheric sounds, the so-called 'atmo', which is however what truly makes the images come to life. This audiophonic accompaniment of the visual in popular film means that the action and therefore also the movement are strongly orient themselves towards the spoken action.

Action that largely manages to do without language is therefore rare in popular film. As a result, the physical actions of the film characters are also strongly dominated by the spoken word and therefore also by the narrative of the story.

When language is not used and movements are presented without the accompaniment of language, physical movement is forced to replace language, in other words movements must evoke meaning for the spectator.

Usually, this pantomime-like type of performance does not at first appear 'realistic', but is alienating instead. In the early days of silent movies, Max Reinhardt made such a pantomime type of film with *Sumurun* (1910). The actors used theatrical pantomime to give the actions of the characters a dreamlike quality; they seemed to float through the cinematic space. The actions therefore appeared to convey something unreal. However, this form did not catch on as a basis for arranging movement and creating cinematic meaning. Film aesthetics went down a different path and relied on silent speaking. Experienced spectators were able to read the meaning of what was being said from the actors' lips; written text (intertitles) conveyed the meaning to all others. The characters' movements were not exaggerated through pantomime, but were modeled more closely on the physical movements of every-day life. Only their meaning was made more explicit and pronounced if needed (cf. Hickethier 1986: 11-42). Such physical and silent performances were therefore often employed in the field of film comedy.

Jacques Tati's films are good examples of the effects of performed movement. In *Play Time* (1967), there is a scene in which we see the protagonist (Tati himself as Monsiour Hulot) in a modern office building in Paris, waiting to be admitted. The film leaves a lot of space for Tati's movements; the spectators are able to follow the protagonist's movements in long shots as he leads them through a flight of rooms. Tati's movements and the camera eye behind him visually enter and travel through the rooms in the film. The comic moment is triggered on the one hand by the protagonist's movements, which are evidently inappropriate for the exploration of a building, but also gradually appear more and more natural to the spectator, while the modern architectural setting with its automatic doors, lamps, and glass room partitions, which don't really bring transparency into the space, appear less and less suitable for human movement.

The film accentuates the arrangement of the rooms through editing and montage, creating new spatial perspectives and thus constantly confronting both the protagonist and the spectator with new rooms and new situations. This provides a stage for the protagonist to act on – a special sphere of action. This impression is underlined by the fact that the character is often shown from head to toe, thus also directing the spectators' gaze towards proxemic movements.

However, mainstream films usually operate differently from Tati's film *Play Time*, which mainly used long shots and wide angles. In mainstream film, a long shot is often employed to give an overview of the scene or used as a symbolic angle (to show something of general meaning, which is not conducive to the action). Here, the camera is often very close to the characters and alternates between a socially accepted distance (1,20 to 3,50 m) and a personal distance (less than 1,20 m). This also has an effect on the presentation of movement. In mainstream film, movements recorded by the camera are usually accentuated by frequent shifts between the positions of various observers and their various distances to the action.

Unlike Tati in his films, the actor usually is not 'master of his movements'. The film makes the selection, often only showing parts of the body and only for a very short space of time. The body and the movements are thus fragmented; the fragments are reassembled and synthesized. The film accentuates and underlines this. An arm movement may be continued by or confronted with an eye movement. This is then followed by the image of an upper body turning, followed by the position of a pair of feet. The montage usually depends on whether the plausibility of events is familiar enough to the spectator – a probability deduced from the knowledge of everyday movements. This can also produce new physical movements, constituted by film itself, and new sequences of movement, which are no longer identical with the movements of the actor or actress in front of the camera.

FRAMING AND ORNAMENTATION

As far as dance in film is concerned, we can now say for the time being that dance challenges the claim to reality posited by the cinematic narrative. Dance elements must therefore be specially legitimized in the film's plot. In short, dance is here a movement made by the body, which expresses a meaning that cannot always be put into words, but can stand for itself as a genuine form of physical expression. For the film and its own claim to reality, dance is thus usually a special, not necessarily natural form of physical movement, a special event. Dance in film is often framed by specific accentuations or markers. The frame also emphasizes the distinctiveness of the dancing.

In Sergio Leone's film *Once Upon a Time in America* from 1984, the hero Noodles (Robert de Niro) returns to New York after many years. He left the city in the 1930s after having been cheated in some prohibition deals and in danger of being murdered by rival gangs. He has now become a respectable elderly citizen. Returning to the bar of his youth to find an old friend and in search of those responsible for cheating him in the past, he goes into the back room of the bar. There, he climbs onto the toilet seat and peers through a small window into a storage room. And sees – a girl dancing.

It is an image from his memory, and it provides the starting point for the subsequent story of his childhood and youth. The dancing is framed as an anomaly in several ways: the film changes color and becomes sepia-toned. As spectators, we therefore now know that we are in a different, past age. The dancing takes place on a stage, in the storage room of the bar. The girl is the bar owner's daughter practicing for her ballet class; we have already been told that she went on to become a famous star. And the scene introduces as observer, the older

Noodles, whose gaze we see and which is then replaced by the gaze of the younger Noodles, thus marking the scene as a starting point for a flashback.

The spectator's point of view is close to that of the observer, whose gaze is returned by the gaze of the small dancer – he, who thought himself invisible in his viewing post is recognized and himself observed – while the spectator in turn observes this exchange of gazes from a third position. The camera repeatedly takes him into the storage room, but he always remains at a greater distance from the dancer than from the observing Noodles. We have here a multiple combination of different characters and their actions, accompanied by, what is now, leitmotif music. This becomes a choreographed movement – the girl's dancing transforms into the mental movement of the observer Noodles, which in turn becomes the (e)motion of the spectator.

The result of this kind of framing of dance in a plot that lays claim to filmic reality, is that, since the 1920s, 'dance in film' has manifested mainly in a specific group of films, a genre or sub-genre, which we call 'Dance Film'.

Dance in mainstream movies is generally dance supported by music. Therefore these films are also referred to as music films, revue films, musical films, etc. Here too, dance usually occurs in framed situations, in other words, a specific space is created for the dancing in the plot of the film, a dance floor, often a clearly defined space in the cinematic image, which is itself defined by a frame and therefore presents the action within this frame as a composed unit – with various emphases, balancing surfaces and forms, and not just simply as dance.

One of the most important examples in film history is from 1934, when sound movies were just emerging. In *Wonder Bar*, the mere depiction of a dance is cinematically enhanced by camera technique and a montage of images and angles, as well as stage machinery and film architecture. The film goes beyond simply framing the dance space and does what it is good at and what has become its main principle: the enhancement of space into a cinematically altered and structured space. Still, all this remains in the realm of physical dance.

The director and screenwriter (Lloyd Bacon) as well as the performers (Ricardo Cortez and Dolores Del Rio) never achieved wide recognition, unlike the film's choreographer: Busby Berkeley. He drove the producers mad with his choreographies and the staging of his dance pieces, but his films set a precedent worldwide and in the end inspired Siegfried Kracauer's famous formula of the "ornament of the masses" (cf. Kracauer 1963).

In *Wonder Bar* (other Busby Berkeley films later resumed this motif), the camera shows a small dance club, a round dance floor surrounded by tables, a host, a small orchestra, a singer. A male and a female dancer enter. Applause. They begin to dance along to the singing and the music: a ballroom dance. The camera follows their movements. Then it slowly withdraws up to a higher position, so that the dancers move to the bottom end of the image. Suddenly a staggered line of singers moves in front of the dancing couple, they turn around, and taper open, leaving the stage visible again. The two dancers draw back a curtain, a new stage opens up; the dancing couples multiply between the pillars into numerous different formations. They move between the pillars, the space is shown in ever new variations, multiplied by various mirrors. The camera moves to an overhead position: the dancers form circular ornaments and the space keeps changing accompanied by indulgent music: first a mirror cabinet, then the vanishing points dissolve and finally the space itself is multiplied. The cinematic realm acquires a fantastic quality. A female dancer runs away and deliberately loses a shoe, the male dancer follows her, they find each other under leaves moving in the breeze, become leaves themselves by using masks, then break away. As they say at the end of the dance sequence: "Oh, if only this dream would never end."

The focus here is not on the dancers, but on the spectators. It is they, who are supposed to be drawn into the movements to experience the whirlwind of emotions. These music revue films were the starting point for the history of dance film. It is not possible to give a complete overview here, but I will sketch the most significant aspects.

THE RHYTHMIZATION OF CINEMATIC ACTION

An important characteristic is the rhythmization of cinematic action. This can be seen in a German music film, which incorporated dance elements in the depiction of cinematic reality at roughly the same time as Busby Berkeley's reinvention of the revue film in Hollywood. The film in question was made by Reinold Schünzel – a director of various comedies in Germany – who was forced to leave the country after 1933 because he was regarded 'half-Jewish'. One of his masterpieces was the revue film *Viktor and Viktoria*, made in 1933: The unemployed comedian Victor Hempel (Hermann Thimig) has caught a bad cold and is therefore unable to perform in a female role at a Kaschemme (pub), a job that would earn him 10 Deutschmark per show. So he asks a female colleague (Renate Müller in one of her best performances), whom he met at his agency, to stand in for him. Her subsequent performance – she thus plays a man playing a woman – is so successful that she is discovered by a theatre agent and goes on to perform in big theatres, always accompanied by her co-partner Viktor Hempel. She tours across half of Europe to adoring audiences before her bluff is called and she ends up marrying a rich husband. Gender crossing therefore takes place on multiple levels, and the film draws its fascination from the constant mix-ups and ambiguity.

The film deals with the production of dynamics and rhythm in cinematic reality – outside of the stage performances, as for example, in the following film scene accompanied by music: Viktor Hempel is leaving the agent's office and meets the young Susanne Rohr (Müller) on the stairs. She is a young actress dreaming of a stage career. The physical acting of the two is totally different in spite of the underlying rhythm: her physical expression makes her a prototype of what is natural on film – while he becomes a prototype of what appears theatrical, not natural on film, exaggerated and therefore funny. Rhythmically, they walk down the stairs, their body movements becoming more and more aligned. Their movements pointedly refer to one another, and the exaggeration and slightly hammy gestures of the one are counteracted by the more reserved, seemingly 'natural' gestures of the other. Their walk down the stairs is crucial as a rhythmically structured process, which simultaneously unfolds the exposition of the narrative, laying the groundwork for their relationship. The movements are not allowed to fully destroy the impression of cinematic reality, even though they are structured and transformed into a dance element.

THE CAMERA AS OBSERVER AND CO-ACTOR

A rhythmization of the cinematic action can also be achieved by moving the dance action away from the enclosed stage, the specifically marked area, into the reality of every-day life, into the streets. Backyards and street corners are now the spaces in which the performance takes place, the dance action turning them into dance spaces: ad hoc – only to immediately lose this status as soon as the dancing ends.

In this kind of film, we are thus dealing with a ballet choreographed to music, which only bit by bit reveals itself to us as such. The world is expressed through dance.

First, we have an almost documentary view of New York City. The dancing is introduced little by little. Robert Wise's *West Side Story*, made in 1961 (choreography by Jerome Robbins) based on music by Leonard Bernstein, combines documentary images of inner city life with the space manifesting itself through dance.

The main theme is introduced through and in the dance: a fight between rival youth gangs. The camera is involved as a co-actor: the scene begins with the skyline of New York. Then the camera travels along the houses, picking up the music that can now be heard. It wanders through the streets and ends up zooming in on some backyard where two gangs, The Jets and The Sharks, clash, provoking and fighting each other, to escape and pursue each other. A danced duel. The dancers constantly form new constellations, break apart, come together again, all the while continuously producing new images of dance movement. The film setting remains the same throughout; it only changes when the camera eye opens up new perspectives and passageways.

The spectators are invited to move through the streets and backyards of New York along with the characters, they are often directly the 'target' of the dancers' movements and are addressed head-on, although ultimately they are only observers after all. The movement sequences are designed in such a way that they are quickly recognizable and identifiable.

There is no underlying irritation of perception, as Busby Berkeley created to some extent. The spectators are meant to be involved; this involvement is achieved through the interaction of the camera eye and the dance movements of the actors in front of the camera. The film musicalizes and rhythmizes the characters' sphere of action, as well as the urban space, and makes the city vibrate and move. The dance fights between the gangs translate the aggression of battle into dance steps, choreographies, which become more and more recognizable as such in the film and increasingly correspond to theatrical conventions. However, they are thus also simply steps, which solidify their theme's claim to reality and thereby consistently separate the dance movements as anomalies from the non-dance movements.

Despite the impressive choreography framed by conventional comprehensibility, what remains with us is: that even in the face of all rhythmization, the order of the world is not overturned.

A more recent example of rhythmization in film and a certain type of audience involvement is *Moulin Rouge* by Baz Luhrmann from 2001, which attempts to create cascades of movement, involving the spectators in a frenzy of movement. Here the separation of the dance scene from the cinematic world with its claim to reality, the definition of the dance as something set apart and different from reality, often depicting feelings and emotions, is largely abolished. In the beginning *Moulin Rouge* also presents the dance scenes in a space set apart from the every-day realm of the film's reality – the cabaret theater that gives the film its name. However, the outside and inside worlds soon begin to mingle, blurring the boundaries between the two. This blurring and overstepping of boundaries is however not achieved by the dancers and their dance movements, but by the movement of the camera, through montage, and the high frequency of fast-paced cuts.

What is therefore important here is how the dance is presented. In contrast to the almost contemplative treatment of the dance action in *Wonder Bar*, the movements in *Moulin Rouge* are totally fragmentized and re-synthesized in a fast montage of different points of view. The determining factor is the rhythm of the music: the performance becomes an almost frantic whirl of bodies, which is directed straight at the audience and attempts to overwhelm them.

In one scene, about half-way through the film, the young writer and artistic nobody Christian meets the star of the show, the dancer Sadine, and falls in love with her and her dancing. He becomes involved in the action (and with him the spectator in an illusionary way) through a cancan of film characters and cinematic perspectives, which increasingly pick up speed. Here the dance space within the film is no longer clearly separated from the rest of the action. Scenes from the inside of the building, of the stage, and of the dancers are mixed with exterior scenes; the actors seem to be here and there, constantly on the move. The cinematic space is shaped by the 'dance' of the camera, the excessive montage. The bodies of the dancers are disembodied, become visual ciphers, which alternate, disappear and reform in staccato. The film itself and its sequences of camera perspectives and images becomes a frenzy of movement. Singular dance movements become indistinguishable, as everything dissolves in a whirlwind of movement.

The rhythmization of the entire cinematic action abolishes the framing of the dance within the cinematic reality, as has by now become the convention in most mainstream movies. The spectator is invited to abandon his contemplative gaze, his observation post in the distance. He is involved with the help of superficial visual stimuli that are not only founded in the physical movements of the actors, but in all optical tricks that film has to offer. His senses are so overwhelmed that he is hardly able to distinguish single movement sequences and he experiences a rush of excitement. The film therefore focuses on itself and its presentation of the world (and not on dance as an art form in its own right set apart within the film). In doing so, film – especially mainstream movies – has thus returned to its carnivalesque beginnings as spectacle. However, as far as dance in film is concerned, it comes close to what Luuk Utrecht has called "Postmodernism-Dance" (Utrecht 1987: 442), with its tendencies of depersonalization and dehumanization in dance and with parallels to developments in other artistic genres.

CONCLUSION

As far as dance in popular mainstream film is concerned, we can conclude that:

Film and dance are related in that they both focus on movement, the body, and rhythmization.

Due to its nature as a technical medium, film makes other forms of presenting physical movement possible; it fragmentizes movement and re-synthesizes it in new and different ways. It accelerates human movement, enhances it and mechanizes it.

Film lays claim to the representation and depiction of reality. In its presentation, it usually separates dance from the depicted reality by framing it in order to avoid dance threatening its claim to reality.

Film uses dance to create special moods, characterize situations and open up particular narrative spaces.

Film can also integrate dance as an element of rhythm in its depiction of reality and use dance to structure its cinematic reality. This, however, means that the cinematic reality becomes subject as a whole to the mode of a depiction of the world through dance.

REFERENCES

Deleuze, Gilles (1986): Cinema 1: The Movement-Image, Minneapolis: University of Minnesota Press.

Hickethier, Knut (ed.) (1986): Grenzgänger zwischen Theater und Kino. Schauspielerporträts aus dem Berlin der Zwanziger Jahre, Berlin: Ästhetik und Kommunikation.

_____ (2007): Film- und Fernsehanalyse, Stuttgart: Metzler.

Kracauer, Siegfried (1963): Das Ornament der Masse, Frankfurt am Main: Suhrkamp.

_____ (1964): Theorie des Films. Die Errettung der äußeren Wirklichkeit, Frankfurt am Main: Suhrkamp.

Utrecht, Luuk (1987): "Postmoderne-Tanz", in: Dietmar Kamper/Willem van Reijen (eds.), Die unvollendete Vernunft. Moderne versus Postmoderne, Frankfurt am Main: Suhrkamp, pp. 427-445.

FILMS

Avatar (2009) (USA, D: James Cameron)
Duel (1971) (USA, D: Steven Spielberg)
Indiana Jones and the Temple of Doom (1984) (USA, D: Steven Spielberg)
Matrix (1999) (USA, D: Andy Wachowski/Lana Wachowski)
Moulin Rouge (2001) (USA/AU, D: Baz Luhrmann)
Once Upon a Time in America (1984) (USA/I, D: Sergio Leone)
Play Time (1967) (F/I, D: Jaques Tati)
Sumurun (1910) (DE, D: Max Reinhardt)
Viktor and Viktoria (1933) (DE, D: Reinhold Schünzel)
West Side Story (1961) (USA, D: Jerome Robbins/Robert Wise)
Wonder Bar (1934) (USA, D: Lloyd Bacon)

Against the Beat.
Music, Dance and the Image in
Michelangelo Antonioni's *Blow-Up*

MICHAEL DIERS

> Editing is similar to dancing – the finished film
> is a kind of crystallized dance.[1]

Antonioni's *Blow-Up* (1966) is neither a music nor a dance film. Dance, theater
and music do, however, play a prominent role in the richly faceted panorama of
mid-sixties Swinging London, which the film unfurls.[2] This is especially the case
if we define dance in a less restrictive and more broad and open way, the way recent dance theory does[3] – not least as a reaction to the radical artistic advances of
choreographers such as Pina Bausch, Susanne Linke and Johann Kresnik since
the mid-seventies. Dance *is* – or, depending on the point of view, *can be* – simp-

---

1 Cf. Walter Murch: *Ein Lidschlag, ein Schnitt. Die Kunst der Filmmontage* (2004).
   I am indebted to Ulrike Schilfert, Berlin for suggesting the motto.
2 From the vast amount of literature, I only wish to list those general titles that were the
   most helpful for this essay: Sandra Wake: *Blow-Up. A Film by Michelangelo
   Antonioni* (1971), Roy Huss: *Focus on Blow-Up* (1971), Roland Barthes, Jean-Luc
   Godard, Wolfgang Jacobsen a.o. *Michelangelo Antonioni* (= Reihe Film Nr. 31)
   (1984), Ted Perry and Rene Prieto: *Michelangelo Antonioni. A Guide to References
   and Resources* (1986), Bernhard Kock: *Michelangelo Antonionis Bilderwelt. Eine
   phänomenologische Studie* (1994), Peter Brunette: *The Films of Michelangelo Antonioni* (1998), Uwe Müller: *Der intime Realismus des Michelangelo Antonioni* (2004).
3 See also the motto of the Dance Congress 2009 (Kampnagel Hamburg): "No Step
   Without Movement".

ly anything, which, in an everyday or artistic act of reflection from the perspective of theatrical representation, focuses on a moving or immobile body.

In his movie – which takes place in the milieu of a fashion, i.e. 'body' photographer, Antonioni not only reflects the differences and rivalry between the central media of photography and film, but also simultaneously gives center stage (marginally) to the visual arts and (centrally) to the performing arts, thus adding multiple dimensions to the general discussion of the subject of image and movements – moving images and movements of the body on film, especially in terms of a conditioning of the gaze and perception.

I.

To begin with I will quickly summarize the plot to then present in detail a number of select episodes in which theatrical dance play a central role.[4] *Blow-Up* is about a young, very successful fashion photographer, who has tired of the world of glamour and thus occupies himself with a documentary reportage in his spare time – a project meant to culminate in a socio-critical photo book about the British metropolis (illustration 1). The planned book is largely finished; Thomas, the hero's name according to the script, has taken his second-to-last pictures last night in a doss house. The last photos – a scene of lovers in a park – are shot the next morning on precisely the same Saturday in June, of which the film now tells the tale (illustration 2).

---

4   There are 11 dance/theater/performance-related scenes altogether (central scenes are written in italics): 1. *Introductory credits* – dancer, audience and photographer [music]; 2. *Opening* – drive-in/appearance of the pantomimes [sound, atmosphere]; 3. *Photo shooting* – I and II with Verushka [music]; 4. Dance of the models (warming up) [music in the background]; 5. *Models on stage* – photo shooting I and II [music]; 6. Thomas' jump in the park/jump [without music/ sound]; 7. The lovers swaying in the park [with a parallel pan of the camera in a swinging motion]; 8. *Against the beat* (the girl/Jane); 9. *Struggle and strip scene* (the blonde/the brunette plus photographer as an audience member, later participant) [screenplay: "I'll put you in a ring together…"]; 10. *Yardbirds concert* – frozen/liberated public [music]; 11. *Pantomimes' tennis game* (appearance and disappearance of the hero) [without music/sound]; see also: decelerated, 'paralyzed' movement of stoned people (party guests) [slow motion]; dead man in the park; classical dance figure made of porcelain in the antique shop.

Illustration 1: A scene from the homeless shelter[5]

Illustration 2: Scene in the park

While the pictures from the shelter depict social misery via images of 'deformed' male bodies, the photos of the park emphasize the idyll of mankind and nature. But the idyll is a delusion. As our hero will discover upon examining his photos more closely, death lurks in its wake (*Et in Arcadia ego*). Thomas sees himself compelled to study more intensely what on the surface seems to be no more than innocent photos, after the young woman/Jane, who he had photographed unasked with her lover apparently *in flagranti delicto*, confronts him and insists with all her might that he hand over the photos. However, Thomas does not yield and insists on his right to documentation. Back at the studio, he

---

5   All film stills are taken from the *Blow-Up* DVD published in the *Cinemathek* edition of the *Süddeutsche Zeitung*, Munich 2005.

immediately tries to unravel the secret by quickly developing and analyzing the pictures. By blowing the pictures up and comparing the individual photos in a complicated procedure, he believes to have come across a murder case. In the thick of the bushes, he first recognizes the murderer's shape, then his weapon, and then, in the last picture of the series, a dead man lying on the ground. However, the crime case immediately vanishes again into thin air, as first the photos, then the young woman and, in the end, even the corpse disappears. Just one single photo, a highly magnified detail of the corpse under the bush, remains with Thomas. But the coarse-grained image doesn't suffice to document a murder; only someone versed in 'reading clouds' could identify the profile of a lying form. In the end, the photographer is left behind perplex with a photo in his hands that proves nothing of what he had witnessed by recording it on camera during the day and thought to have seen deep into the night.

Opening credits or 'All the world's a stage'

The stage and its concept of presentation are elementary motifs in the film, which it exploits in its ambitious forays into a theory of the image and of art. In the opening credits (illustration 3) the viewer peers through a lattice of letters onto a scene in which a young woman in a bikini is dancing on the roof of a shed observed by a diffuse group of onlookers and photographed by a wildly gesticulating man in the foreground. Bit by bit, the camera zooms in on the dancer, so that her face is finally revealed in close-up in the empty spaces between the individual letters and occasionally her eyes looks out of this kaleidoscopically fragmented window or mirror towards the audience.[6] The images and words fit together in so far as that the movement behind the text, with its presentation and study of the female body, announces one of the main topics of the film. In addition, the dolly shot of the camera in the dance scene and the parallel zooming out of the BLOW-UP text block causes the title itself to be cinematically explicated. *Blow-up*, so the message of this composition of words and image in the introductory credits, means magnifying and viewing something up close. However, the

---

6   The interaction shown here between text and images is reminiscent of figure alphabets from the Late Middle Ages in which the surfaces of the letters are adorned with figures and even small scenes, as if to suffuse the mute letters with life (cf. Debes 1968). But it is different from the many cases in which medieval calligraphy and miniature painting consciously forewent bringing the written word and the image embedded in its shape into direct association; a biblical text could thus easily be accompanied by profane drolleries.

viewer, who would like to read *and* peer through the letters at the same time to see what precisely is being shown, is quickly overwhelmed. Either he concentrates on the words and reads, or he directs his attention towards the action and thus ignores the list of names. The direct superposition of stationary writing and moving images as well as the film-in-film modus provide the viewer with a initial borderline media experience, making it clear from the onset that it can sometimes be difficult to decipher interfering optical information.[7] The seemingly exhibitionistic dance scene, witnessed as if through a keyhole, simultaneously exposes a first theatrical situation complete with audience and photojournalist.

Illustration 3: 'Dance scene' in the opening credits

II.

The film's actual beginning also creates a theatrical situation. The opening is dedicated to a performance of mimes. The first take is of a loud and wildly gesticulating group of young people who, like clowns, are wearing colorful clothes and white make-up and carry donation boxes in their hands. They arrive in a convertible four-by-four on an empty square between high-rises[8], turn a few

---

7 Script as a signifier and image will continue to play a role in the numerous advertising signs throughout the course of the film.

8 According to the *World Guide to Movie Locations*, it is the Economist Plaza, West End, "a hidden courtyard immediately north of Ryder Street, off Piccadilly in London's West End", www.movie-locations.com/movies/b/blowup.html (January 30, 2011).

rounds and finally leave their vehicle. In great haste, they dash down a flight of stairs in the direction of the street, where they begin their wild task of collecting donations (illustration 4). This playful scene with 'traveling folk', who operate in public spaces and turn pedestrians into accomplices was not something Antonioni had to invent on his own; instead, he could take inspiration from the *rag week*: a kind of carnival for charity that takes place in London every spring.[9] The protagonists of this event draw attention to themselves by making noise, playing small tricks and simultaneously demanding a donation from the public. All this is already inherently contained in the word *rag*, which means prank, bedlam and shenanigan, but it also means stuff, garbage and trumpery. Thus the name of this bizarre spectacle, which aims at alleviating poverty, is also closely associated with social awareness, as beggars often appear in rags.[10]

Illustration 4: Rag week scene

Antonioni continues this train of thought in the next scene by shifting in an abrupt transition to a scene of homeless people leaving a shelter. Once again, we have a group stepping out onto the street, but in this case in perfect silence and with non-descript clothing and behavior. The contrast is then again emphasized by jumping back from London's Southbank district to the West End and dramaturgically finally cementing the impression by portraying the hero, who has just stepped out of the group of homeless people, as a 'go-between' for both milieus. After having climbed into his Rolls Royce cabriolet close to the shelter, where he spent the night for his reportage, he heads downtown and passes the group of

---

9 As well as in other English university towns.

10 See also the beggar behind Thomas' car after dealing with the pantomimes.

mimes, who ask him for a donation. At first, the director lets both scenes run parallel, only to then intertwine them thematically with the same characters. The protagonist returns to his daily life as a successful fashion photographer; he is still wearing his beggar's clothes, but he's already back in his luxury car, which socially places him worlds apart from his previous night's companions. Back in the studio, he gives his beggar's garb to an assistant so that it can be thrown away.

III.

Here super model Verushka, cowering in a corner, has been waiting impatiently for quite some time. In the wink of an eye, the shooting begins and proceeds in two phases: first, with music running, Verushka poses in front of a paper backdrop, facing a fixed camera on a tripod (illustration 5); then Thomas switches cameras (and the music) and a kind of *pas de deux* unfolds between photographer and model. He literally 'gets on top' of her (illustration 6) capturing head and details, instead of her entire body, as he had done previously. Now that the previous distance between them has been overcome, the act of photography becomes something more equivalent to a sexual act, maybe even that of an animal trainer, and in the end it leaves both partners exhausted.

Illustration 5: Photographer and model (Verushka)

Illustration 6: Photographer and model (Verushka)

The film camera confidently follows the events and visibly establishes itself as narrator, as, for example, when it is placed directly behind the photo camera in the Verushka sequence and then moves upward as Thomas enters the frame.

"In this take, the film camera traverses the entire space one full time on a vertical plane; the background hardly changes. Thus the main action in this scene relates to the relationship between the recording apparatuses, and only then to the theatrical act itself." (Schulz 2008: n.p.)

We, as observers, never get to see the pictures that the photographer is taking. One lens dominates the other; precedence is given to the moving image produced by an anonymous and autonomous observer, who presents the scene as an act of dressage.

This ambitious, as well as eccentric version of a photo shoot is answered two scenes later by the routine of a magazine photographer. We see him arranging a group of models into tableaux vivants in order to photograph them – in other words, choreograph them (illustration 7). As a strict dance master, Thomas summons the young women, who have previously been loosening up their bodies to music, and lets them take their places in the prepared set. As Thomas is tired and irritated, and moreover bored by the job, the project has to be interrupted and the models called in again at a later point in time.

Illustration 7: Photographer and models ('birdies')

IV.

To recover from the night's exertions, but also from his work in the studio, Thomas goes out into the park, to go search for an appropriate, i.e., conciliatory and idyllic final image for his book (illustration 2). The park is portrayed as an alternative to the studio on the one hand, and to the city, on the other – a reference to the classical model of *rus in urbe*. Here calm and vast, open spaces abound in place of labyrinthine narrowness and hectic; here the reign of green-in-green nature versus garish color, and instead of angular concrete, meadows and softly rolling hills. It's a humble paradise with a uniformed park attendant and her garbage-collecting spear standing guard at the entrance.[11] As though transformed, Thomas now moves forward in high spirits into the slightly hilly terrain and even jumps into the air like a jaunty child. This physical act clearly breaks with the dominant 'choreographic' mode of the studio.[12] It feels like an act of liberation from the normative and stylized atelier situation. This exuberance is likewise an obeisance to the medium film, which knows how to present the little scene with the young man in the green vest with pleasure – with such happiness,

---

11 Antonioni apparently had the white houses in the background especially built, see *World Guide to Movie Locations* (see footnote 8); he also had the asphalt spray-painted grey and the lawn colored green.

12 Incidentally there are numerous photographs showing people jumping on the walls of Thomas' studio.

in fact, that the montage immediately following the scene seems in its technique to imitate the heel-knocking jump. From jump to cut (illustration 8).

Illustration 8: The jump in the park

Similarly, in the next scene, the film camera gently flirts with the swaying lovers that Thomas is observing and taking photos of. With a slight camera pan from left to right and back again, Carlo di Palma's camera once again comments on the scene by accompanying the couple and playing the role of an autonomous teammate, a real co-dancer (see illustration 2).

Later, in the atelier, Thomas has to deal with the woman from the park/Jane, who, no matter what the price, demands that he hand over the photos he took of her and her lover. First he treats her like a model – *deformation professionelle* – and casually rehearses positions and poses with her, later offering her a seat and asking her join him for a drink and a joint. Suddenly aware of the jazz music (Herbie Hancock) coming from the record player, he tells her to stop hectically moving to the rhythm, but to calmly work against it: finally, the young woman willingly obeys his insistent "Slowly, slowly. Against the beat" (illustration 9). Once again the photographer is a kind of choreographer, now also coordinating everyday movements to background music.

Illustration 9: Studio scene 'against the beat'

V.

At first glance, one of the most turbulent scenes in the film – things are all topsy-turvy, so to speak – seems to have nothing to do with dance and theater; neither does music play a role. But it still has an important function in terms of contrasting comparison. Incidentally, it takes place on precisely the same studio floor, on which the models and the super model also had their appearances. And this gives the scene its *tertium comparationis*, providing a contrasting image to the two model sequences mentioned above.

Two young women (Jane Birkin and Gillian Hills) appear unexpectedly at Thomas' studio and want him to photograph them. At first, he sends them away again; later, he lets them enter, but only to make fun of them. The two young women, who both dream of careers as models, use an unobserved moment to take a look at the clothes hanging within easy reach on a stand. Upon Thomas' return, one of the most turbulent (and provocative) film scenes in the movie begins. It features a wild tussle; first, between the two girls and then with the photographer. It is a sequence in which both fashion and photography are forgotten as professions and only naked skin and the erotic struggle between the sexes reign; it ends in a kind of 'battle for the (panty)hose' and thus, in a playful way, references the classic *topos* of the female catfight (illustration 10). Antonioni lets his hero frolic, in the words of the moral authorities and censors of that time, 'excessively and lasciviously' with the two teenagers around the photographer's set, which is usually the backdrop for fashion photos (cf. DVDBeaver.com). It is the only important scene of the film in which the photo camera, which the hero is rarely ever seen without, plays absolutely no role whatsoever. Instead, all is ruled by the film camera, whose medial demands are met to the maximum with plenty of movement and powerful and fashionable colorfulness. It triumphs in the studio, as photography, its related décor and even the clothes are pushed aside. In an about-face, quite libertine for the times, Antonioni intertwines the most important subjects of the film – photography, fashion, silence – by boiling them down to nothing and, in their place, demonstratively and with relish replacing them with alternatives – the moving image, nudity and screaming. Instead of the photographer, it is now the film director shooting portraits of the two wannabe models, who have intruded into the studio like a Shakespearian *buffo* pair to suspend the existing order of things and ignore customary norms and boundaries – those of photography, as well as those of fashion and the 'measured step'. On the one hand, this scene teaches the audience a lesson on promiscuity and voyeurism; on the other, a lesson about the explosive potential of physical-playful actions based on temperament and an excess of strength, which is wantonly wasted. Here play acts as an alternative to pretended and posed action and takes their place.

Illustration 10: The photographer and the two teenage models

VI.

In search of the young woman from the park, who stole the pictures from his studio and who is the only person that can shed some light on the mysterious events, Thomas strays, among other things, into a beat club (Ricky Tick Club), where the Yardbirds are playing. With the exception of a single dancing couple, the audience is standing mysteriously still, almost turned to stone, in front of a stage on which the musicians are playing their song *Stroll On*. An amplifier begins buzzing and one of the two guitarists (Jeff Beck) unsuccessfully tries to fix the problem by repeatedly smashing his instrument against the speaker. Frustrated, he throws his guitar on the floor, destroying it with his hands and feet, then throwing the splintered neck of the guitar into the audience (illustration 11). As if waiting for a sign, the people in the audience suddenly awaken from their stupor and try to take possession of the fragment.[13] Thomas joins the battle just for fun and wins. He quickly leaves the room carrying the trophy. Having arrived out on the street, he casts one last glance at the object he has just won and then simply throws it away. A passerby finds it – this former object of collective desire – and lifts it up, only to likewise immediately let it fall again; for him, it is also just a useless and meaningless thing, a piece of trash.

Illustration 11: In the Ricky Tick Club: the guitar neck flies into the audience

Paradigmatically, this scene demonstrates the 'genesis' and role of a classic fetish. By first presenting the audience as paralyzed and soon afterwards as if electrified, i.e. by shifting from immobility to movement, or even frenzy, Antonioni demonstrates the mechanics of such a magically charged object, which has attained cult status. Only now does that musical energy truly appear to be released, which moments before, for whatever reason, was encapsulated.

---

13 Cf. as a prototype for the scene in which the guitar gets destroyed, the spectacular performances and actions of Pete Townshend, member of the rock band The Who, who has destroyed innumerous guitars on stage and has cited, as his intellectual background, Gustav Metzger's auto-destructive art that he encountered at Ealing Art College where Metzger taught. Cf. in general Justin Hoffmann's *Destruktionskunst. Der Mythos der Zerstörung in der Kunst der frühen sechziger Jahre* (1995).

The film audience is at first alienated by the initial, totally atypical immobility of the concertgoers. Why don't they submit to the rhythm of the music and dance? And why are they only then released from their stasis, when offered such a simultaneously concrete and symbolic prize from the stage? Antonioni uses the scene to compare the two spaces of spectatorship: the rock and roll palace on the one hand, and the movie theater, on the other. The immobile music audience represents the spectator in the movie theater, who similarly paralyzed sit in their seats and stare spellbound, as if in a trance, at the hustle and bustle on the screen.

The guitar neck serves as a fetish in the context of the fan club and, beyond that, as a kind of media-theoretical sensor, which seeks to awaken awareness of the audience for itself. In the live concert moment, both public spheres merge – the one *in* as well as the one *in front of* the film; the acoustic irritation that provokes the destruction (and awakens the destructive powers) makes itself known to both public spheres in a similar way. Therefore, the instrument-fetish is also a tool to wake up the film audience. At any rate, what communicates itself to the film audience, when the fetish-meteorite lands among the concertgoers, is not just a disturbing noise, but also a little moment of shock. As music as well as silence play a decisive dramaturgic role in *Blow-Up* on a diegetic, as well as extradiegetic level, this is one comparison among many that easily and by way of association not only explicates and comments on the relationship between paralysis/stasis and life/kinesis in reference to dance, but also in reference to the medium of film and the institution of movie theaters. It is a strategy that the director pursues systematically.

In addition, Antonioni uses this etude to draw his audience's attention indirectly to the fundamental opposition of immobility and movement as it is dealt with continually in the comparison of the two different media photography and film. The stationary (black and white) photographic images that the film camera previously paid tribute to via the protagonist's investigative detective work interrupt the familiar continual flow of images by asserting their contrary nature and, like a *freeze frame*, upsetting the film's customary form. This is one of the moments in which the film reflects back on itself – and the audience, awakened from its dream, is called upon to join in this reflection.

VII.

The pantomimes appear both in the first and last scene of the film, as counterparts to the image-obsessed, iconodule hero (illustration 12). While the group is shown in the beginning as participants of the student *rag week*, in the end of the film, they perform a tennis pantomime (*pas de deux*) on a court in the park, watched attentively not only by the other members of the group, but also by Thomas. Pantomime is a genre that uses gestures to imitate reality. In order to be successful, the performance is forced to appeal to our imagination for its elliptical, deficient images to be completed via association. That this appeal even touches a skeptic like Thomas is somewhat of a theatrical turn and demonstrates a triumph of art and its ability to liberate reality from immediacy and transcend it poetically in an instant of insight. The spectator is needed as collaborator; as is concretely the case for the nameless Thomas. As the imaginary ball suddenly leaves the stage – the playing court – and rolls to the feet of the film's protagonist, he is invited to actively join in (illustration 13). By picking up the ball, he is accepting and legitimizing the rules of a game that in its performances has to make do without tangible objects and tools and be satisfied with silent hints. This departure from concrete material reality and the emphasis on gestural language is a systematic counterpart to the marked object fetishism of photography, which composes everything that openly appears before its camera lens into an image.

Illustration 12: Pantomimes appear in the park

Illustration 13: The photographer and the imaginary tennis ball

In the end, the pantomimes prevail; even the camera follows their make-believe flight paths, simulates them, and – as a last consequence – finally magically lets the hero disappear (illustration 14). Visibility is simultaneously a symptom and a syndrome of an image-obsessed, iconodule world, which has completely lost sight of reality under the flood of images.

Illustration 14: The photographer disappears from the screen

Blow-Up is a film that explicates creative and skeptical thoughts on the subject of the image, the body and media. Its director uses the intermedial, self-referential and historic interdependencies of the visual and performing arts for a fundamental reflection on stationary and moving pictures, the inter-mediality of genres and the theatricality of physical movement.

It is tempting to use the accommodating term of *Gesamtkunstwerk* (total work of art) to categorize Antonioni's film due to how it apostrophizes the many named art forms – but it is far from being a synthesis in terms of a harmonious summary. On the contrary: the differences between the art forms and media are not meant to be smoothed over or overruled, but rather exposed, thus letting the film negotiate contrast and confrontation, as well as the possibility of comparison and the reflection of aesthetic and artistic, and not least of all political boundaries and differences.

In the field of dance studies, Gabriele Brandstetter has pointed out that on a more general level the "perspective on the body, the image and temporal structures in postmodern dance and choreography [...] can only be considered in relation to a gaze modeled by photo and film technology" (Brandstetter 2005: 68). Antonioni's film also suggests an inverse point of view. Film and photography can indeed be contemplated in relation to a gaze and events shaped by dance theater by correlating and comparing (and thus not least of all revealing the deficiancies) of motion and immobility, as options of the 'new' technical media, with those of the classical performing arts and their patterns of perception.[14]

REFERENCES

Brandstetter, Gabriele (2005): Bild-Sprung. TanzTheaterBewegung im Wechsel der Medien, Berlin: Theater der Zeit.

Brunette, Peter (1998): The Films of Michelangelo Antonioni, Cambridge: Cambridge University Press.

Debes, Dietmar (1968): Das Figurenalphabet, Munich-Pullach: Verlag Dokumentation.

Diers, Michael (2010): "Mode im Bild, Modus des Bildes", in: Philipp Zitzlsperger (ed.), Kleid und Bild. Zur Ikonologie dargestellter Gewandung, Berlin: Edition Imorde, pp. 195-211.

---

14 This text is closely related to a current research project in preparation by the author and devoted to the media-reflexive aspects of Antonioni's *Blow-Up*; please also see the following essays by the author: *Mode im Bild, Modus des Bildes* (2010), as well as *Der Fetisch und sein (Kunst)Charakter in Michelangelo Anto-nionis 'Blow-Up'* (2010). I would like to thank the participants of the seminar *Blow-Up or Art History and Film* at the Institut für Kunst- und Bildgeschichte of the Humboldt University, Berlin in the summer semester of 2008 for their nu-merous suggestions, in particular Ulrike Schilfert, Florian Unger and Tobias Weißmann.

_____ (2010): "Der Fetisch und sein (Kunst)Charakter in Michelangelo Antonionis 'Blow-Up'", in: Hartmut Böhme/Johannes Endres (eds.), Der Code der Leidenschaften. Fetischismus in den Künsten, Munich: Wilhelm Fink, pp. 270-289.

Hoffmann, Justin (1995): Destruktionskunst. Der Mythos der Zerstörung in der Kunst der frühen sechziger Jahre, Munich: Schreiber.

Huss, Roy (ed.) (1971): Focus on Blow-Up, Englewood Cliffs, NJ: Prentice Hall.

Jansen, Peter W./Schütte, Wolfram (eds.) (1984): Michelangelo Antonioni (= Reihe Film Nr. 31), Munich/Vienna: Hanser.

Kock, Bernhard (1994): Michelangelo Antonionis Bilderwelt. Eine phänomenologische Studie, Munich: Schaudig und Ledig.

Müller, Uwe (2004): Der intime Realismus des Michelangelo Antonioni, Norderstedt: Books on Demand.

Murch, Walter (2004): Ein Lidschlag, ein Schnitt. Die Kunst der Filmmontage, Berlin: Alexander.

Perry, Ted/Prieto, Rene (1986): Michelangelo Antonioni. A Guide to References and Resources, Boston: G.K. Hall.

Schultz, Sonja (2008): BLOW-UP: Einige filmwissenschaftliche und kameratechnische Anmerkungen, unpublished manuscript.

Wake, Sandra (ed.) (1971): Blow-Up. A Film by Michelangelo Antonioni (= Modern Film Scripts), New York: Simon and Schuster.

FILM

Blow-Up (1966) (UK/IT/USA, D: Michelangelo Antonioni)

WEBSITES

Film Locations for Blow Up: www.movie-locations.com/movies/b/blowup.html (January 30, 2011).

Is Blowup Censored?: www.dvdbeaver.com/film/DVDCompare6/blowup-censored.htm (January 30, 2010).

DIGITAL WORLDS – PROCESSING BODIES

Gesture Capture: Paradigms in Interactive Music/ Dance Systems

FRÉDÉRIC BEVILACQUA, NORBERT SCHNELL, SARAH FDILI ALAOUI

INTRODUCTION

Electronic or digital interactive systems have been experimented with in dance for more than fifty years. The piece *Variations V* by Merce Cunningham and John Cage, performed in 1965 with dancers interacting with analog electronic sound systems, is one such groundbreaking case (cf. Miller 2001). The use of interactive digital technology grew in importance in the 1990s with the advent of affordable sensor technologies and software dedicated to motion tracking, such as *Eycon*, *EyesWeb*, *BigEye*, and *softVNS*, which were developed for artistic use. The first decade of the 21st century showed a steady increase of new experimentation and usage of media technologies in various dance contexts and aesthetics, including performances and installations.

This text gives some idea of the wide range of currently available technological tools used to sense gesture and movement. Most importantly, we would like to emphasize that the current discourse on interactive systems has moved away from 'experimenting' with technology, which is nowadays ubiquitous, to more fundamental questions on the description and notation of gesture and movement (cf. deLahunta/Bevilacqua 2007), and what transmission these systems could provide or facilitate. Several choreographers and dance companies have built ambitious interdisciplinary research projects (cf. InsideMovement Knowledge.net; SynchronousObjects.osu.edu) involved with such questions. These initiatives reflect the converging interests of different disciplines – dance, music, engineering and cognitive sciences – towards gesture research. For example, research on sensorimotor learning has influenced the Human Computer Interaction field, where the role of action and gesture has increased significantly (cf. Dourish 2001; Leman 2007).

Working in such an interdisciplinary context at IRCAM (Institut de Recherche et Coordination Acoustique/Musique)[1], we have developed, in collaboration with choreographers/composers/media artists, computer based gesture analysis and interactive audio processing systems that allows performers to control or interact with digital media – sound or video (cf. Bevilacqua 2007). At the Dance Congress 2009, we presented a lecture/demonstration of these tools and explained paradigms that are central to these applications. Summarizing key elements of our presentation here, we will first categorize the different sensing systems typically found in dance contexts, in order to clarify what the term 'gesture capture' can encompass. In the second part, we will provide examples of gesture sound controls often found in interactive dance performances.

SENSING FOR INTERACTING

It is possible to argue that in any interactive dance system, the technical constraints related to the chosen gesture capture apparatus influences the choreographic work. Therefore, it is generally useful to describe technical constraints that might inform some aspects of the work. Nevertheless, we wish to emphasize here the interaction paradigms that are associated with gesture technology instead of simply describing the technical features of specific systems. For this reason, we propose to classify the different approaches for sensing gesture as used in dance performances or installations using three main categories, 'body', 'space', and 'time'. This classification helps to clarify the metaphors implicitly or explicitly related to interactive systems. Obviously, these categories should not be considered absolute, or their limits as definite: most interactive systems will generally include more than one of these categories.

---

1 IRCAM is one of the largest public research centers dedicated to both musical expression and scientific research. This article relates specifically to research performed by the Real Time Musical Interaction and the Performing Arts Technology Research Teams, which have been collaborating regularly with various choreographers since 2003, developing interactive systems for the performing arts, such as the *gesture follower* and audio processing tools.

Body

Although it is clear that physical movement is largely used in interactive systems, we first also want to call to mind that numerous other types of body-centered interaction are possible by using, for example, physiological signals.

Physiological signals

All kinds of measurements of physiological parameters can be utilized in interactive systems. Technically these systems are generally adapted from technology developed for biofeedback. Mechanisms such as muscle activation, for example, can be measured in form of electrical activity with sensors that are put in contact with the skin (electromyography). Such systems have been incorporated in dance performances (cf. Palindrome.de) or music performance (cf. Tanaka/Knapp 2002). Interestingly, these techniques can also be sensitive to 'pre-movements' or muscle tension even if there is no significant visible movement.

Other types of physiological quantities have also been used in media performance including breathing[2], the heartbeat, and even brain waves. Skin contact between two people, or between the skin and an (electrically conductive) object can also be easily measured thanks to the skin's electrical conductivity. This property allows for the design of 'touch sensitive' objects.[3] Performances have also been designed that take advantage of this effect, sonifying skin contact between performers and even the public (cf. Woudi-Tat.org).

Body posture and movement

Different types of technological systems enable the measurement of body posture and motion. First, sensors can be attached to the body as illustrated in Figure 1. Miniature accelerometers and gyroscopes are, for example, sensitive to inclination, rotation and acceleration (note: these later types of sensors are now found

---

2 Myriam Gourfink, for example, used a breathing sensor in her piece *This is my House*, along with other motion sensors, http://myriam-gourfink.com/thisIsMyHouse.htm (April 5, 2010).

3 The crackle box invented by Michel Waisvisz is a historic musical example, http://www.crackle.org (April 5, 2010).

for example in gaming interfaces such as the *Wiimote*); bending sensors measure joint angles.[4] Generally, the sensors are connected to wireless data emitters.

Second, video systems are efficient in capturing postures and movements of the entire body remotely. For example, a single camera system can track the dancer's silhouette, as shown in Figure 2, taken from the *Double Skin/Double Mind* installation (cf. InsideMovementKnowledge.net).

A large number of computer programs characterize body movement by tracking the whole silhouette or specific body parts. The *EyesWeb* software, for example, computes parameters such as 'quantity of motion', 'direction', and 'stability' among several others (cf. Camurri/Mazzarino/Volpe 2004). This software was recently used to automatically annotate short videos of a web dance database (cf. Tardieu/Chessini et al. 2009).

In single camera systems, the measurement of the movement highly depends on the position of the dancer relative to the camera. To avoid such problems, multiple cameras are required. Typically, 3D optical motion-capture systems, initially developed for biomechanic studies or for animation, allow for the 3D reconstruction of a simplified skeleton. Nevertheless, they require the use of small reflective markers on the body and are generally complex to handle in real-time and in performance situations. Dance performances using such systems have been relatively rare, with few notable exceptions such as two pieces by Bill T. Jones and Trisha Brown, developed at the Arizona State University, in collaboration with the OpenEndedGroup (cf. Downie 2005).

Figure 1: Sensors for breathing and acceleration measurements

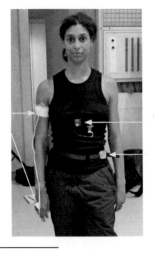

accelerometers

breathing sensor

wireless emitter

4　See the *mini dancer*, http://www.troikaranch.org (April 5, 2010).

Figure 2: Video tracking of the dancer silhouette and analysis of the size of different parts of the silhouette (from the Double Skin/Double Mind installation).

Photography: Thomas Lenden

Space

We refer here to paradigms where some properties of the space are explicitly included in the interaction. This can, for example, imply defining particular zones of the space, in which the presence of the user triggers specific electronic events. This type of paradigm is among one of the first implemented historically, using either light barriers or camera systems. In the experimental piece *Variations V* mentioned earlier, proximity to sensors (Theremin antenna) were placed on particular spots on stage and reacted to dancers approaching these particular spots.

Generally, space-based interaction implies structuring the space, and associating audio/video processes with specific spatial location. Commons paradigms are, for example: body presence/absence, crossing borders, entering/leaving zones. Obviously, motion can also be naturally associated with these interactions, for example, by measuring the 'quantity of motion' in a particular spatial zone. Nevertheless, we would like to point out that in these cases the motion remains referenced to absolute spatial locations, and not relative to the body itself as described in the previous section.

Time

At first, it might seem unclear how 'time' can be referred to a category of interaction. We argue that 'temporal interaction' can be put forward in a similar fashion as spatial interaction (cf. Bevilacqua 2007). Similar to spatial limits or zones, one can define time limits and time moments. Moreover, interaction can be based on synchronizing specific dance gestures and sound/visual processes. In other words, interaction can be driven by temporal events, time sequences and synchronization mechanisms.

Generally, this interaction paradigm relies on software that is designed to analyze temporal data, i.e. a sequence of events or postures. Our research currently aims at taking into account gesture data as 'time processes'. This implies considering basic elements such as 'phrases' and 'transitions' (as opposed to 'postures') in relationship to time-based media such as sound or video (we will describe in more detail possible interaction models in the next section). Note that this approach was motivated in part by collaboration with choreographers, who pointed out the necessity of considering gestures as continuous time-related processes.

EXAMPLES OF GESTURE CONTROLLED SOUND INTERACTION

Digital sound processes can be controlled or altered using the different types of gesture parameters we have described in the previous section. Establishing the relationship between gesture parameters and the actual sound properties is a central task when building any interactive system. Such a procedure is often referred as a gesture-to-sound "mapping" (cf. Wanderley 2002; Bevilacqua/Muller/Schnell 2005).

In the following, we will describe concrete examples ranging from relatively simple mappings to more elaborate scenarios working with complex gestures analysis and audio-visual processes. In the first two sections below, we will define simple relationships between gesture and sound rendering, corresponding to explicit interaction metaphors. By defining this relationship, we can create a sort of 'musical instrument' that can be 'played' by the dancer. In the last two sections, we will introduce the possibility of handling complex phrases in the interaction design, which can lead to more abstract relationships between gesture and sound.

Triggering sound events

Triggering is one of the most simple and common processes used in interactive systems. As an introductory example, we can show that 'percussive' gesture (i.e. strokes measured with 'accelerometers') can directly trigger percussive sound events. The gesture 'intensity' can furthermore affect the volume and characteristics of the sound.

An application of this paradigm is the sequential triggering of discrete recorded sound events. For example: the dancer selects, in a preliminary step, particular sound events in a recording. Then, each sound event can be played one by one by the dancer using percussive gestures. The dancer can also control the tempo and rhythm of the sequence of the recorded sound. Experiments generally show that the clarity of this interaction allows for a rapid appropriation of the sound control by the dance movements. Nevertheless, this influences performers towards performing discrete strokes or accents. Continuous sound control appears then as a natural extension, as explained in the next section.

Continuous control of sound grains

Continuous movement parameters, e.g. inclination or velocity, can naturally be 'mapped' to continuous sound parameters. Examples based on granular synthesis techniques, which have been widely used in dance/music systems, were among the many techniques that we demonstrated during the workshop. Granular synthesis is based on segmenting sound recordings in small 'sound grains' and then playing them in such as way as to create sound textures. The original sound characteristics can be either preserved or radically altered.

We experimented in particular with sound recordings related to natural, human or mechanical movements, sounds of liquid pouring, rolling/rotating objects, human beat boxing and machines. These sounds can be easily decomposed into very short elementary elements (i.e. sound grains) and recomposed according to gestural input (cf. Schnell/Borghesi et al. 2005; Schnell/Röbel et al. 2009). In simple cases, dynamic movement parameters such as 'energy' can be directly used to control the intensity of rendered sound textures.

More complex relationships make use of an intermediate model mediating specific behaviors between gesture input and sound responses. A compelling example is based on the rainstick metaphor.[5] In detail, the sound rendering can si-

---

5   Such a paradigm was used in the installation *Grainstick* by Pierre Jodlowski, see: http://agora2010.ircam.fr/935.html?event=887&L=1 (April 5, 2010).

mulate the sound of various materials (water, stones or abstract sound textures) as if agitated and moved from one side to the other of an object, according to the inclination of the object. By holding a real object containing an inclination sensor, dancers therefore control the sound of various virtual 'sound grains' pouring from one side to the other side of the object. By directly holding the inclinometer sensor to their body, dancers can even directly embody the sound object, 'pouring sound grains' by bending their body.

Gesture recognition for media control

Gesture recognition systems are particularly useful where interpretation of sensor parameters becomes complex, leading to cumbersome programming. Even simple gestures and body movements may in fact generate a very large number of movement parameters and complex data patterns.

Using a gesture recognition system can simplify the setting of the interaction and offers possibilities of using longer choreographed movements. A first step is to define 'phrases', i.e. gestures units, that the computer system must learn in a first phase in order to be able to recognize them automatically in a second phase. Interestingly, this approach lets the dancer define a gesture 'vocabulary' and thus work on a symbolic level. Over the past years, we have developed a system at IRCAM called the *gesture follower* that can be used for gesture recognition of complex postures, phrases or trajectories (cf. Bevilacqua/Guédy et al. 2007; Bevilacqua/Zamborlin et al. 2009). The *gesture follower* has been used in dance performances (cf. TheBakery.org), interactive installations (cf. if-then-installed.leprojet.net) and in music pedagogy (cf. Bevilacqua/Guédy et al. 2007). To use the *gesture follower*, the dancer first records phrases, using sensors or video systems, to define a vocabulary. The control of audio processes (triggering, synchronization and continuous sound control) can then be built on the basis of this vocabulary.

In the case of the *Double Skin/Double Mind* installation motion parameters were fed into the analyzing system, which was in this case especially tuned to movements principles defined by the Emio Greco | PC. The results of the analysis could either be connected to sounds or visual feedback.

In the case of a collaboration with Richard Siegal, we developed another application of the *gesture follower* for an installation (cf. If-then-installed. leprojet.net) and a multimedia dance performance. In *Homo Ludens* (cf. TheBakery.org), Richard Siegal improvises at the beginning of the piece with a set of dance phrases that are recognized in real-time by the systems (he wore motion sensors on his wrists). When recognized, pre-recorded videos of theses phrases were displayed, creating a sort of dialog between the dancer and the videos.

Beyond recognizing phrases, the *gesture follower* allows for the synchronization of arbitrary gestures and movements to time-based media, such as audio and video recordings. Once a particular dance phrase and recording have been entered in the system, it can control in real-time the synchronized rendering of the recording according to the gesture variations. More precisely, the system can continuously control the pace and mix of digital media (rather than just triggering start/stop). In other words, the dancer can continuously control the choices and the temporality (i.e. tempo, rhythm, order) of recording rendered by her/his performance. Therefore, the interaction paradigm enabled by the *gesture follower* equals intrinsically translating the 'temporal' unfolding of gestures to the 'temporal' unfolding of digital media.

CONCLUSION

In this paper we have given examples of sensing techniques for dance-music interactive systems. We proposed to categorize the different paradigms as 'body'-, 'space'- or 'time'-related. The combination of these different paradigms can lead to different layers of computer-mediated interaction between dance and sound/visual processes. The combination of both simple interaction paradigms with recent advances on gesture recognition and following currently gives rise to the novel experiments that we are pursuing. Important challenges lie now in the use of interactive systems with coherent gesture descriptions that could be shared by dancers, musicians and engineers. Recent productions (e.g. *If/Then Installed*) and research projects (e.g. *Inside Movement Knowledge*) that we have participated in are very promising in this regard. Furthermore, we will continue to pursue research on notions such as 'quality of movements' that could be derived from gesture capture system. We believe that such analysis should further enrich interaction paradigms with new media.

We acknowledge partial support of the following projects: *EarToy* and *Interlude* (ANR – French National Research Agency) and *SAME* (EU – ICT). We thank all the members of the Real-Time Musical Interactions Team at IRCAM.

REFERENCES

Bevilacqua, Frédéric/Muller, Rémy/Schnell, Norbert (2005): "Mnm: a Max/msp Mapping Toolbox", in: NIME 05: Proceedings of The 2005 International Conference on New Interfaces for Musical Expression, Vancouver, pp. 85-88.

_____ (2007): "Momentary Notes on Capturing Gestures", in: Emio Greco | PC and the Amsterdam School of the Arts (eds.), (Capturing Intentions), Amsterdam: Emio Greco | PC and the Amsterdam School of the Arts, pp. 26-31.

_____/Guédy, Fabrice/Schnell, Norbert et al. (2007): "Wireless Sensor Interface and Gesture-follower for Music Pedagogy", in: NIME 07: Proceedings of The Seventh International Conference on New Interfaces for Musical Expression, New York, pp. 124-129.

_____/Zamborlin, Bruno/Sypniewski, Anthony et al. (2009): "Continuous Realtime Gesture Following and Recognition", in: Lecture Notes in Computer Science, Volume 5934, Berlin/Heidelberg: Springer, pp. 73-84.

Camurri, Antonio/Mazzarino, Barbara/Volpe, Gaultiero (2004): "Analysis of Expressive Gesture: The Eyesweb Expressive Gesture Processing Library", in: Antonio Camurri/Gaultiero Volpe (eds.), Gesture-Based Communication in Human-Computer Interaction (= LNAI 2915), Berlin [a.o.]: Springer, pp. 460-467.

deLahunta, Scott/Bevilacqua, Frédéric (2007): "Sharing Descriptions of Movement", in: International Journal of Performance and Digital Media, Volume 3, Number 1, pp. 3-16.

Dourish, Paul (2001): Where The Action Is: The Foundations of Embodied Interaction, Cambridge, MA: MIT Press.

Downie, Marc (2005): Choreographing the Digital Agent: Live Performance Graphics for Dance Theater, Cambridge, MA: MIT PhD thesis.

Emio Greco | PC and the Amsterdam School of Arts (eds.) (2007): (Capturing Intentions), Amsterdam: Emio Greco | PC and the Amsterdam School of Arts.

Leman, Marc (2007): Embodied Music Cognition and Mediation Technology, Cambridge, MA: MIT Press.

Miller, Leta E. (2001): "Cage, Cunningham, and Collaborators: The Odyssey of Variations V", in: The Music Quarterly, Volume 85, Number 3, pp. 545-567.

Schnell, Norbert/Borghesi, Riccardo/Schwarz, Diemo et al. (2005): "Ftm – Complex Data Structures for Max", proceedings of the International Computer Music Conference (ICMC), Barcelona, Spain, September 2005.

Schnell, Norbert/ Röbel, Axel/ Schwarz, Diemo et al. (2009): Assembling Tools for Content-based Real-time Interactive Audio Processing in Max/msp, Proceedings of the International Computer Music Conference (ICMC), Montreal, Canada, August 2009.

Tardieu, Damien/Chessini, Ricardo/ Dubois, Julien et al. (2009): Video Navigation Tool: Application to Browsing a Database of Sancers' Performances, QPSR of the Numediart Research Program, Volume 2, Number 3, September 2009.

Tanaka, Atau/Knapp, Benjamin R. (2002): "Multimodal Interaction in Music Using the Electromyogram and Relative Position Sensing", in: Proceedings of the 2002 Conference on New Interfaces for Musical Expression, Dublin, Ireland, May 24-26, 2002, pp. 43-48.

Wanderley, Marcelo (ed.) (2002): Mapping Strategies in Real-Time Computer Music (= Organised Sound 7/02), Cambridge: Cambrigde University Press.

WEBSITES

Agora 2010: http://agora2010.ircam.fr/935.html?event=887&L=1 (April 5, 2010).

Crackle: http://www.crackle.org/ (April 5, 2010).

If Then Installed: http://if-then-installed.leprojet.net/ (April 5, 2010).

Inside Movement Knowledge: http://insidemovementknowledge.net/ (April 5, 2010).

Myriam Gourfink: http://www.myriam-gourfink.com/thisIsMyHouse.htm (April 5, 2010).

Palindrome Inter.media Performance Group: http://www.palindrome.de/ (April 5, 2010).

Synchronous Objects: http://synchronousobjects.osu.edu/ (April 5, 2010).

The Bakery: http://www.thebakery.org/index02.html (April 5, 2010).

The OpenEnded Group: http://openendedgroup.com/ (April 5, 2010).

Troika Ranch: http://www.troikaranch.org (April 5, 2010).

Woudi-Tat: http://www.woudi-tat.org/ (April 5, 2010).

Tables of Weights and Measures: Architecture and the *Synchronous Objects* Project

STEPHEN TURK

Writing about a topic outside one's own discipline forces at the most basic level a resituating of standard disciplinary assumptions so that they can be positioned in a meaningful way to the broadest of audiences. This is all the more true in a case such as what I write about today which concerns my work for the *Synchronous Objects* project. This project was a multidisciplinary research effort centered at the Ohio State University which focused on the implications of the complex organizational strategies and conceptual systems found within William Forsythe's celebrated choreographic work *One Flat Thing, reproduced* (2000). The intention of the project was to bring together a group of scholars from various disciplines to explore the possible ramifications of this compelling work for their specific fields; to see whether certain concepts relative to choreographic thinking might cross between disciplinary boundaries. To begin a discussion of the architectural contribution to the project, I would like to briefly revisit certain fundamental aspects of the relationship between the human figure and frame within architecture as a way of situating the architectural component of the *Synchronous Objects* project. The idea of measurement implicit within Forsythe's work and what we saw as an architectural affinity with the issue of frame to body within the dance were central features of the project that I and a pair of student assistants developed. Our project therefore drew upon both our analysis of Forsythe's choreography and the multidisciplinary effort of *Synchronous Objects* project itself.

Architecture has over the last couple of decades rediscovered its connection to the immediate, temporal, and material world of behaviors and effects. So too has it sought to make its own logics of organization and assembly performative. That is, to make systems that behave not so much as abstract linguistic objects but rather responsive organisms which react to the forces of the world. In this sense there is some parallel movement between what is happening in architecture and the goals of the *Synchronous Objects* project, albeit perhaps in different planes of understanding. Architecture has moved from an obsession with the notion of the describable architectural object as a discrete and knowable thing to the environmental notion of architecture as a result of an extended field of forces and flows; a condition where 'architecture' loses itself first in the landscape and then in a generalized array of the global ecological, economic, logistical and informational forces in the world. Architecture is therefore, to paraphrase the architectural theorist Bernard Tschumi, not so much an event of construction but is the construction of events.

FURNISHING INTERVAL AND POSITIONING GROUND

From a layman's point of view *One Flat Thing, reproduced* seems an unconventional piece of choreography. This judgment emerges for many reasons but perhaps central among these is the fact that its staging is dominated by the creation of an artificial 'ground' upon, under and around which the dance is performed. Forsythe's furnishing of the performance space with an array of tables unbalances the conventional understanding of ground by providing a new surface datum which acts perceptually on the figure of the dancers as their bodies are effectively bisected, sectioned and measured by the plane of the tables. The dancers no longer gracefully spring from the surface of a stable earth in this work but rather must negotiate the shifting planes of a newly mobile and fluid set of surfaces, an artificial and somewhat uncanny horizon. They are in a sense partially buried or floating in an unstable world. These playful and surprising juxtapositions between pieces of furniture and performers are perhaps not so surprising when one considers the historical relationship between the words furnishing and performance.

Linguistically these words are nearly identical having at their core the Latin root *fournir*, which means to furnish, to provide, or supply in full. Performance is simply the compound meaning through, during, or by the agency of which something is provided. Performers supply or furnish something; they are a kind of agent or vector of logistics. In this sense Forsythe's dance is furnished by this table array, as it provides the field for a new expressive world to unfold. To the architectural interpreter, the spatial, organizational, structural and tactile armature provided by the array of tables plays a central role in the conceptual and symbolic understanding of the meaning of the dance. Their presence remind us of the intimate and archaic connection between architecture and dance by reiterating fundamental conditions in all architectural phenomena, the most central on which is the relationship of the mobile occupant to an envelope or enclosure.

The tables provide us with a perceptual field through which to understand interval, distance, unit and number, the conditions that join the temporal art of dance to the spatial art of architecture. So too can the work be read as an allegorical exploration of the relationship between the human figure and the frames established by society; frames which whether registered through the regulating grid of cities, or the systems of demarcation in mathematics and science, are the cultural legacy of ideas of measurement.

THE CHORA AND THE EMERGENCE OF THE FIGURE

To understand the relationship between architectural notions of spatiality, ideas of measure and choreography that I am developing here, it might be useful to briefly review the classical relationship between the Greek *chora* (situated space, place, position in order) and *choros* (round dance, open dancing ground, enclosure). Both are related to the Indo-European roots *gher-* (to grasp, to bind, to enclose) and *ghe-* (to release, to go, to abandon). *Chora* is quite simply: the place that is made through the going.

This oppositional pairing, to bind and to release, points to a fundamental set of beliefs in classical Greece concerning the possibility of rhythmic interval as the prior condition to the establishment of space. The very possibility of movement is the necessary property for the emergence of measurable and occupiable dimensions. *Chora* is the vessel or receptacle of enclosure, a mold through which this emergence is made possible. The *chora* is quite literally a matrix, a mothering structure, which gives rise to being by providing room for the performance of movement, the interval for becoming in time. In this sense the space of the *chora* precedes and underlies the process of figuration.

Forsythe's *One Flat Thing, reproduced* literalizes this process in the sense that the array of tables is positioned in a grid-like matrix; a coordinate set, a 'table' of intervals and positions, or weights and measures, which both engenders space and sponsors the becoming of a new kind of figure, a cloud-like field of subjectivity. The *Noise Void Tool* from the *Synchronous Objects* project neatly encapsulates this idea, where the statistical sampling of movement variation is captured through the device of what might be called visual absence or in architectural terms *the figural void*. The void presented by this tool is the registration of the differences and accelerations of movement; it is in a very real sense a digital registration of the ancient idea of *chora*.

TABULATING MEASURE

Forsythe's *One Flat Thing, reproduced* can be read as exploring contemporary notions of ideas of measure in an era when measurement is understood to be probabilistic and statistical rather than fixed and ideal. The work can also be seen as mobilizing a Deleuzian concept of 'duration'; an interest in temporal and qualitative conditions in opposition to a transcendental and absolute notion of quantitative analysis. In a somewhat Duchampian sense in which scientific principles are mobilized to describe ironic or non-scientific qualities, Forsythe's *Synchronous Objects* project is actively pursuing the problems of mapping and measuring of distributed flows within a contemporary scientific framework. Certain illustrations from the sciences such as the statistical mapping of *Brownian motion* (the small and apparently random movements of particles suspended in fluids) metaphorically echo the entire graphic ambitions of the *Synchronous Objects* project. The emphasis here seems to be less about mapping in the transcendental sense but rather is in my view an attempt to situate the embodied knowledge of dance as a mediator between the now dispersed disciplinary fields of contemporary aesthetic and scientific cultures.

Forsythe, through *One Flat Thing, reproduced*, might be said to be situating these ideas as a central feature of a post-humanist system of knowledge whose salient figure of study is the manifestation of a new type of statistical or probabilistic identity. This is an identity that is not an ideal humanist centered singularity (a self in the classic sense) but rather one that is conditioned by and constituted out of the flows of modern society; a society in which individual identity is increasingly distributed across electronic networks and broad ecologies. The 'table' in this system is not the physical object but the conceptual representation, a system of 'tabulation', the matrix of columns and rows of a database chart or a cross-reference of associations. This is embodied most closely perhaps in those foundational charts entitled 'Tables of Weights and Measures', the charts which outline the units of measure that underlie experimental technique. This idea was at a certain point in history embodied in actual objects. Tables of weights and measure were literally quite common in the ancient world.

The *mensa ponderaria*, the weigh table from the forum market of Pompeii is a salient example. To ponder in Latin is to weigh; to metaphorically measure and evaluate the burden of various possibilities and it is interesting to note the importance of the table as the site of this action.

Mensuration in contemporary physics is as is well known subject to the limitations of the uncertainty principle. This is an acknowledgement of the effects produced by the act of observation and measurement itself on the state of any particle. The quantum reality of objects exists in a kind of state of superimposition or probabilistic potentiality. From this point of view, Forsythe's piece can be seen as an allegorical elaboration of the problems and dilemmas of contemporary notions of physical reality relative to human perception and subjectivity. The work can be seen as a rumination on the fact that culture in the West has long since moved past the centrality of the body as a measure of reality, a state which was classically evoked by the dual inverted poles of dance and architecture; mirror disciplines which have acted as cultural embodiments of ideas of measure.

Dance and architecture were those arts in the past that ancient man used to symbolically demarcate his space in the universe, to position and circumscribe a sacred precinct. For the ancients these two arts were symbolic models of how the universe was structured, they were maps of reality based upon both the relative scale of the singular body (building, temple, house, dance) and the collective scale of the people (the theater, processional, city). One might look to the idea of pediment sculpture to see this played out in the most direct sense in ancient architecture. Allegorical sculptures of gods and heroes were traditionally positioned on the entablature of temples as were anthropometric figures used in the codification of ancient measuring systems.

The word entablature is of course referring to an idea of a kind of visual table; a ground for a scene to unfold. These groupings were essentially didactic tableaux enacting various foundation and cosmological events. What is remarkable is that the figures within the triangular frames of the pediment are themselves engaged in a figurative dance which is responsive to the frame of the temple roof. The gods are in a very real sense dancing; a fact that harkens back to an earlier archaic period when the temple activities literally happened in the natural landscape and were centered on ritualistic movement. Pediment with its roots *ped*, or foot and *ment*, mind, is thought to imply the idea of the rituals of pacing out a sacred *temenos*, the precinct or perimeter which is actually the temple proper in ancient Greece. The roots might be said to imply something akin to that which is made in the mind through the action of the foot. The act of demarcating *temenos* is a cutting off from the everyday in a ritualistic act of making sacred. The movement implicit in this idea is echoed by the related word *tempo*, the rate, rhythm or pace of a dance or musical performance.

These are ideas that for me immediately struck me upon with my first viewing of Forsythe's piece. My own work and research is not typically antiquarian but there was something in Forsythe's dance which brought these very ancient and primal relationships forward in my mind. It seemed that Forsythe's piece was simultaneously evoking these early visual associations of body and frame to revisit their implications in the contemporary world.

Figure 1: Figure superimposion

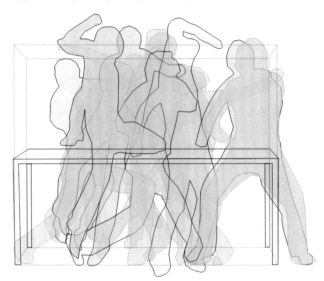

Graphics: Stephen Turk

ENTANGLEMENT

Indeed, Forsythe's work is in my view an attempt to grapple with these issues and present an updated model for the ways in which the knowledge of dance, conventionally understood and associated with a presumed authentic and 'real' nature of bodily reality, can instead be seen as part of a world subject to the probabilistic nature of quantum reality and postmodern theories of the body. Forsythe's choreography and his interest in exploring these ambiguities with the *Synchronous Objects* project might from this point of view be seen as revisiting dance's ancient role as 'physics'.

Given the complexities of the associations outlined here, the idea of entanglement drawn from scientific theories of quantum reality has in our analysis and design project served as a central trope for understanding the implications of the dance. Forsythe's work seems to have a strong scientific and mathematical interest. Visually in the organization of the piece we saw a strong connection to contemporary graphic representations of scientific principles. Scientific illustrations of entangled particles for instance have a curious affinity and resonance with both Forsythe's dance in plan and indeed have strong echoes in the graphic research produced by the *Synchronous Objects* team overall.

So too did it have strong affinities to the ancient precedents we were invoking in our work. The perceptual and conceptual notion of entanglement can be said to occur at many levels in *One Flat Thing, reproduced*. These would include affects produced by the perceptual field of the dance both at the scale of figure to figure as well as figure to frame relationships. In developing our project we began our understanding of entanglement visually and spatially by mobilizing a series of these historical figural precedents that we believed both related to and echoed these ideas.

For instance, Michelangelo's incomplete sculptures known as the prisoners, particularly the example of the figure known as the *Bearded Slave* from the early 1520s, served as a model of the body caught and measured in a defined volume; a body entangled in a material substrate, struggling to escape from these bounds. For us the implied energy and tension embodied in these works and their echo of classical notions of the idealization of the body as the foundation of measurement now uncomfortably bound and entangled in a volume serves as a resonant framework in our study of Forsythe's choreographic work.

Within *One Flat Thing, reproduced*, the visual interconnections between dancers, their apparent and actual physical intertwining, can be said to be a function of kinds of entanglement. These are general motifs which establish mutual dependencies and produce larger chains of contrapuntal effects within the 'field' produced by the work. We metaphorically transferred this idea to one of volumetric enclosure and registration to capture the dynamic unfolding of these relationships. Our project diagrams demonstrate the process of abstraction and interpretation of the figuration implied by composites of individual dancers relative to the frame of the tables within the dance; a process dependent upon our figure/volume metaphor. These diagrams were then used as a kind of tracery which implied a dynamic force relationship acting on the bounds of a material substrate.

The entanglement of the figure emerging from this process was allowed to register on a pair of implied cubic volumes. We saw the tables as demarcating spaces both above and below the tabletop, producing volumes which for us were analogous to a rotated and reduplicated version of the *Prisoner* sculpture. This visually establishes the core spatial translation we undertook. I should stress that this was an interpretive exercise which was in no way understood as a deterministic translation. But rather was seen as echoing certain visual and spatial qualities we were interested in capturing within a newly emergent spatial volume. These visual and tactile motifs however point to a deeper understanding of the implications of the 'collapsed' nature of the figure and frame dichotomy in the work as suggested by the argument of the *chora*. It is my belief that the complex combinatorial relationships between dancers and their mutual dependencies, pairings, alignments and cues are extended out from this figure/ frame system and that the choice of the motif of an array of figures and tables is best reflected in the notion of entanglement.

Entanglement in the sciences is used to describe the quantum states of particles which have become interdependent upon one another to the point that the observation of one causes an instantaneous transformation in the state of the other regardless of the distance of their physical separation. This seemed an apt metaphor for the structure of the dance in our mind. It is important to stress that for us our collection of furniture blocks was intended to be performative and through their use to evoke this entangled interdependency. We thus settled on a process which stressed this conceptual framework by systematically translating thematic components of the dance through a series of what we called block entanglement methods.

The constellation of interdependencies in the piece is structured around a complex set of themes which are triggered by an internal set of cues and signals. The performers are constantly measuring and judging the temporal and spatial behaviors of all other performers in their local area as well as those at a distance who may provide signal 'data' for the initiation of particular sequences. We therefore used the thematic diagram produced by the *Synchronous Objects* team as an essential guide in our investigation.

Given the arguments developed above we explored the potential imaginary collapse between these terms into a third in-between condition. We searched for a way to make a non-literal translation of the table dance by taking into account the effects of the piece and finding parallel architectural phenomena in which they could be re-inscribed. Our goal was not to produce a simple one to one transposition between the notational and contrapuntal analyses and an architectural object but rather to produce a space that was performative and combinatorial in a resonant way with *One Flat Thing, reproduced.*

Our project drawings demonstrate the technique of thematic trace that we used to inscribe discrete themes from the dance into unique volumetric structures; drawings which though produced by the measured rigor of contemporary digital modeling techniques point to the ambiguity inherent in all such processes. In our view Forsythe, by multiplying and extending the focal relationship between body and table foils the idea of simple legibility in acts of measuring. By arraying and making mobile a grid of tables and allowing them to be occupied by a fluid set of occupants he shifts the focus from a possible deterministic reading of measure to one of statistical and probabilistic performance.

FURNISHING PERFORMANCE

Playing upon the close association of the words performance and furnishing the project revisits the question of furniture's secondary relationship to the architectural envelope. The complex contrapuntal structure of Forsythe's work and its field-like distributed phenomena were used as templates to reconsider the possibility of a set of abstract 'entangled' elements which were capable of acting both as furniture-like objects and as architectural frames.

The blocks were produced by computer modeling 18x18x54 and 36 inch cubic 'bench-like' modules. Individual blocks in the system are formed by studying the relationship between different dance themes and finding qualitative aspects of these which are registered in the formal, material and textural qualities of the fabrication cutting process. The blocks thus become resonant 'containers' of thematic variation which can be arrayed and positioned in space interactively over time by the occupants of the installation.

Figure 2: Vray perspective

They were imagined as being the result of the entangled forces of the dancers; the implied volumes both above and below the table surfaces acting as the receptacle of these forces. An entire installation was imagined as a kind of *chora* space in which the thematic combinatorial translations of Forsythe's work could be choreographed by the 'audience' itself. This performative space in our view would provide the same kind of self reflexivity and awareness between viewers and occupants that occur in the original work and play upon notions of dance and architecture's historical roles as symbolic modes of measuring the world. The visitors to this architectural installation could perform the piece themselves by picking up and moving the block furniture elements. The lightness of the material, in this case high density foam, would permit individuals to position or stack blocks into complex ensembles and combinatorial assemblies. The blocks which would exist in a state of constant rearrangement and assembly and would effectively play upon the nature of conventional furniture typology; reconfiguring the ways in which furniture users interact with an architectural envelope to form zones of spatial occupation.

Figure 3: Block diagram 12

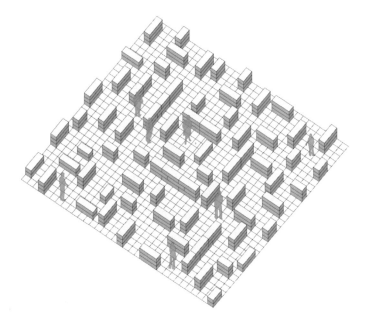

One Flat Thing, reproduced can be seen as ultimately 'environmental' in the sense that it produces an atmospheric perceptual effect through a give and take of dynamic forces in a spatial field and it is this quality which we were most interested in capturing in our installation proposal. The idea of entanglement which served as our operable metaphor can be seen in connection to a greater problematic of 'locality' in contemporary thought which through the interplay of space and temporality reinitiates the archaic link between architecture and dance. So in conclusion our object for the *Synchronous Objects* project was less about the creation of a fixed condition or ideal translated map or thing but rather our goal was to produce an analogous dynamic evolving system responsive to spatial and temporal frames of perception and occupation within an animated local condition.

References

David, A.P. (2006): The Dance of the Muses: Choral Theory and Ancient Greek Poetics, Oxford, NY: Oxford University Press.

Grosz, Elizabeth (1995): Space, Time and Perversion: Essays on the Politics of Bodies, New York: Routledge.

_____ (2008): Chaos, Territory, Art: Deleuze and the Framing of the Earth, New York: Columbia University Press.

Hersey, George (1988): The Lost Meaning of Classical Architecture: Speculations on Ornament from Vitruvius to Venturi, Cambridge, Mass.: MIT Press.

Ley, Graham (2007): The Theatricality of Greek Tragedy: Playing Space and Chorus, Chicago: University Of Chicago Press.

Lonsdale, Steven (1993): Dance and Ritual Play in Greek Religion, Baltimore, Md.: Johns Hopkins University Press.

Manning, Erin (2009): Relationscapes: Movement, Art, Philosophy, Cambridge, Mass.: MIT Press.

Mau, August: (1973): Pompeii; its life and art, trans. by Francis W. Kelsey, Washington: McGrath.

Rehm, Rush (2002): The Play of Space: Spatial Transformation in Greek Tragedy, Princeton, NJ: Princeton University Press.

Ulmer, Gregory (1994): Heuretics: The Logic of Invention, Baltimore: John Hopkins University Press.

Synchronous Objects, Choreographic Objects, and the Translation of Dancing Ideas

NORAH ZUNIGA SHAW

A broad range of new projects are happening today at the intersection of dance research and digital media and concerned with the re-articulation and transmission of bodily knowledge in contemporary dance practices. A few recent examples include The Forsythe Company's *Motion Bank* project focusing on the work of Bruno Beltrão, Jonathan Burrows, and Deborah Hay; Wayne McGregor's work with Scott deLahunta, Philip Barnard and others on choreography and cognition; Emio Greco's interactive installation and DVD *Capturing Intention* created with Bertha Bermudez, Chris Ziegler and other collaborators; Steve Paxton's DVD *Material for the Spine* created by Contredanse; the ambitious online digital archive for Siobhan Davies' work created by Sara Whately and her team in the UK; and my own work in this arena, a web-based collaboration with William Forsythe entitled *Synchronous Objects for One Flat Thing, reproduced* that is the subject of this essay.[1] With very different outcomes, each of these projects is concerned with the idiosyncratic nature of choreographic knowledge and with discovering new possibilities for tracing and transmitting ideas contained within the specific dance practices of each artist. These are in depth creative and analytical endeavors undertaken by teams of re-

---

1   For more information on: *Motion Bank*: http://motionbank.org/en/; Wayne McGregor's work: http://www.eng.cam.ac.uk/teaching/urops/projects-08.html; Emio Greco's *Capturing Intention*: http://insidemovementknowledge.net/context/background/capturing-intention; Steve Paxton's DVD: http://www.contactquarterly.com/ce/ce06.html#dvd-sp; Siobhan Davies' archive: http://www.siobhan-daviesreplay.com.

searchers that integrate empirical curiosities with post-positivist politics of particularity.

Published online, *Synchronous Objects* is a collaborative choreographic visualization project that flows from dance to data to objects. The dance is William Forsythe's *One Flat Thing, reproduced* (Frankfurt, 2000) a contrapuntal ensemble piece exhibiting an exquisite chaos that is tightly structured by its three interlocking systems of organization. The data are numeric translations of the choreographic structures/systems in the dance. And the objects – animations, graphics, computer applications – are visual expressions of those structures. They are communicative (we wanted to share and transmit information and invite responses), investigatory (we wanted to examine Forsythe's choreographic thinking starting from his questions and interests), exploratory (we wanted to find out how to visualize those interpretations as artists and scientists working in close collaboration with Forsythe and his company), and ultimately creative (we wanted to catalyze the creation of new ideas and new works of art using the ideas in the dance).

In *Synchronous Objects* and the other projects mentioned, research is a creative interdisciplinary pursuit. I am one of the creative directors for *Synchronous Objects* along with William Forsythe and Maria Palazzi. We made the project with many international consultants and collaborators including members of the Forsythe Company and a large interdisciplinary team of students, faculty and staff researchers from the Advanced Computing Center for the Arts and Design (ACCAD) who contributed their collective intelligence to the work. These are not objective studies carried out by seemingly detached scholars but instead are subjectively informed endeavors. And they do not attempt to preserve the live moment nor do they attempt to represent all of dance and choreography. This is not dance documentation for repertory or reconstruction although it certainly could contribute to those types of endeavors. But our work begins from a different point. Instead we ask, what else is there? Or as Forsythe said often during our collaboration "What else might this dance look like?" and "What else, besides the body, might physical thinking look like?". We are working with the difficult but also generative problem of making dance knowledge explicit and sharing it not only on stage and in the studio (as dancers are accustomed) but also through media objects.

These artists (Steve Paxton, Emio Greco, Wayne McGregor, Siobhan Davies, William Forsythe …) are participating in (and often initiating) collaborative projects with groups of researchers designed in part to define their own legacies but also with the hope of strengthening the field as a whole. The products of each are particular to the artist and to the team of researchers who come together to create them and are focused on specific aspects of dance knowledge. In our case, *Synchronous Objects* focuses explicitly on choreographic structure in Forsythe's work and on his interest in mobilizing choreographic ideas beyond the body into myriad other interdisciplinary manifestations that he calls 'choreographic objects' (described below). Together these projects and the many others that continue to emerge are the beginnings of what I hope may become a lively discursive space, placing dance at the center of interdisciplinary knowledge exchange about embodiment and physical thinking.

ON CHOREOGRAPHIC OBJECTS

"One could easily assume that the substance of choreographic thought resided exclusively in the body. But is it possible for choreography to generate autonomous expressions of its principles, a choreographic object, without the body?" (Cf. WilliamForsythe.de)

The idea of a choreographic object allows for the transformation of a dance from one manifestation (the performance on stage) into an array of other possibilities (such as information, animation, or installation). Choreographic objects enact a form of translation but not translation only. Like any good literary translation, a choreographic object stays true to the original thinking space of the maker while allowing for new comprehension of the work. And as in all translation, there are gains in communication there are losses as well. One can never fully comprehend German poetry in English and one can never fully comprehend dance without live performance. But we translate the poetry in order to give more people an experience of it; and we translate dances into choreographic objects in order to generate new expressions of the form.

Choreographic objects therefore are never about abandoning live performance. The idea is not to either have live performance *or* have choreographic objects. Just as in the translation of a poem from German to English one does not assume that the German original will be abandoned but that the translation will enable new forms of engagement with the work. The point here is to assert the value of live performance and the kinesthetic communication that is dance by also asserting the possibility of a multiplicity of other manifestations of choreographic thinking. As Forsythe says in his essay on the subject, "a choreographic object is not a substitute for the body, but rather an alternative site for the understanding of potential instigation and organization of action to reside. Ideally, choreographic ideas in this form would draw an attentive, diverse readership that would eventually understand and, hopefully, champion the innumerable manifestations, old and new, of choreographic thinking." (Id.) Choreographic objects are, in part, translations of the instigations, instructions, and methods of organization that choreographers use to create action. They create additional modes of communication and exchange.

At the same time, this work goes beyond the purview of translation. Translation implies a close adherence to the original but in the creation of a choreographic object, ideas are allowed to jump and swerve out of familiar territory into new spaces. There is rigorous analysis and in-depth study of a source in order to bring forth its attributes but then the outcome becomes a new work in its own right. For example, *Synchronous Objects* can be understood as a choreographic object or a collection of 20 choreographic objects that function together to communicate the ideas in the dance via animations, interactive tools, and so on. This act of translation took place not only in the creation of data from the dance but also in the close collaboration between the research team and Forsythe to learn from him how the dance works and its conceptual foundations. Moving beyond translation then, the choreographic objects in *Synchronous Objects* integrate the information learned through the labors of translation into new creative outcomes. They are closely linked to the dance, they issue forth from it (as does any translation) but they also step out into parallel virtual incarnations or transformations.

The concept of choreographic objects is active in *Synchronous Objects* but it can also be illustrated through examples from Forsythe's installation works. For example, in the late 1980s/early 1990s, Forsythe collaborated with architect Daniel Libeskind on a project called *The Books of Groningen N7*.[2] Libeskind was commissioned to mark the city boundaries of Groningen and he collaborated with Forsythe on one of them, *N7*. Forsythe and Libeskind planted a row of trees and then connected wires from concrete posts to different branches of each tree thereby influencing their growth over time. What else might physical thinking look like? In this case, it looks like the life span of a tree. They are choreographing growth. In another example, *Scattered Crowd* (Frankfurt, 2002), Forsythe suspends 4000 white balloons in large architectural spaces. The visitors to the space choreograph the balloons and the environment they encounter influences their actions. What else might physical thinking look like? In this case, it looks like the interactions between balloons and the movement and choices of the visitors to the space.

---

2   My knowledge of this project comes from conversations with William Forsythe at the Ohio State University during the creation of *Synchronous Objects*. More info is available here: http://www.williamforsythe.de/installations.html (March 30, 2011).

Like his stage works, Forsythe's choreographic objects hold his recognizable physical genius but they manifest it through media, inanimate matter, and the experiences of those encountering the work. The torque of the trees branches in *N7* and the organization of their movement (growth) into subtle forms of alignment can be likened to the extended épaulement so characteristic of Forsythe's style and the curious torque of the dancers' limbs. The instigations to action provided by a room full of responsive balloons and the acute, communal attention required of the visitors to *Scattered Crowd* evoke the performance state of dan-cers in his ensemble works and the complex, seemingly chaotic, but carefully crafted visual counterpoint of pieces such as *One Flat Thing, reproduced* (Frankfurt, 2000) and others. In fact, Dana Caspersen (Forsythe's wife and a long time dancer in the Company) describes *Scattered Crowd* as "an air-borne landscape of relationship, of distance, of humans and emptiness, of coalescence and decision"[3], a phrase that could be used to define counterpoint as it is practiced in The Forsythe Company. And in *Synchronous Objects* several of the recurring choreographic principles of the Company are explained in the annotated videos that reveal alignments, cues, and the recombination of movement material as they play out in the piece, in tools that let users experience and create works from the principles themselves, and in our own imaginative reincorporations of the instigations to action that Forsythe used to make the original stage work.

Dance, Data, and Objects

In *Synchronous Objects* we explore the question 'what else might physical thinking look like?' by delving deeply into the systems that organize one dance. We translate those systems into data and conceptual frameworks and then generate new manifestations of the dance in the form of visual objects/screen-based media. The dance is our choreographic resource, the source from which everything else emanates. The objects are re-articulations of the dance via the data and our own research/artistic interests. They are both creative and analytical. Some help reveal patterns and allow the eye to see or 'read' the dance differently, others use the patterns and ideas in the dance to generate new animated forms, and still others are tools that allow for interaction with the same ideas. The three areas of our process flow in and out of each other, at times line-

---

3   Press materials for *Scattered Crowd*. Example available here: http://archive.kfda. be/2005/en/projectdetail.action-projectid=7473&id=331.htm (March 30, 2011).

ar, at times circular and layered. The data are indications of what we (the research team and Forsythe) chose to prioritize. They are numeric translations of the choreographic structures in the piece. The process of decoding the dance was a creative dialog that dilated between insider accounts and outside observation, analytical needs and aesthetic interests. It was a profoundly collective endeavor conducted over several years in close collaboration with William Forsythe and dancers Jill Johnson, Christopher Roman, and Elizabeth Waterhouse. As we came to fully understand the counterpoint that unfolds in the dance we worked to devise methods for quantifying it in the data and expressing it in the objects. This effort produced two key sets of data: spatial data taken from our source video of the dance and attribute data gleaned from dancer accounts.

Our goal in gathering spatial and attribute data was to discover patterns of organization that we could use to create the objects. We were not concerned with documenting or reconstructing the dance for the stage, nor were we concerned with purely scientific questions. Instead we worked with the Forsythe Company to unearth the choreographic building blocks of the piece, quantify them, and repurpose this information visually and qualitatively. As in many forms of inquiry, quantification requires a reductive process that necessarily obscures certain aspects of knowledge (performance quality, and kinesthetic awareness) in order to reveal others (in this case, choreographic structure). Drawing from the methodologies of many disciplines – dance, design, computer graphics, geography, and statistics – we intentionally privileged the inside view of the dance and used this to drive our process.

In many ways I would liken our data gathering process to the ecological research methods I learned as an undergraduate in environmental science. I remember well the way we were taught to analyze the river and estuarine ecosystems we were studying. The first day was always spent in situ, looking, sensing, and trying to discern patterns. Where did the grass end and the trees begin, what trees where on the edge of the grass and which were deeper in the groves? Why were there patterns of certain grasses in clumps and patches of bare earth? What patterns of life could be discerned through more in depth analysis such as testing the acidity of the water, analyzing samples for microbial life, and identifying specific flora and fauna? When did we need to seek out and reference other expert analyses of this particular ecosystem? We treated the dance in much the same way one might encounter an estuary where the salty water mixes with the fresh and the slightest imbalance or lack of attention can have ripple effects through the entire system. The focus of the researcher brings acute attention to the dance as a phenomenon while simultaneously holding a broad focus to the patterns of connection rippling over its surface. This too can be a form of attention one brings to the audience experience. If upon entering the theater one encounters a dance as if encountering a new culture or a cherished landscape, what patterns, details and discoveries will surface? And then the next step is to imagine how those discoveries may be shared.

SEEING, TRANSLATING, AND REPURPOSING COUNTERPOINT IN *ONE FLAT THING, REPRODUCED*

The dance at the core of our research is *One Flat Thing, reproduced (OFTr)* choreographed by William Forsythe and premiered by the Ballet Frankfurt in 2000. Of the hundreds of possibilities to focus on in this 15 minutes 30 seconds piece for seventeen dancers, our emphasis is on its choreographic structures or systems of organization. This emphasis came from Forsythe's interests and the instigating questions he asked at the inception and throughout the collaborative creation of the project.

Upon first viewing the dance, structure is elusive. Viewers watching a video of the dance often report feeling 'a sense of structure' but struggle to name it. They note that there are occasional moments of unison and/or similarity in the movement material and that there seems to be cause and affect relationships among the dancers. They want to know if the piece is choreographed or improvised and they are intrigued by its complexity. Like many contemporary works, the dance is open to multiple interpretations and ways of seeing. This is true even as *Synchronous Objects* seeks to be explicit about particular aspects of the work and ways of seeing patterns as the choreographer devised them and the dancers enact them. While we invite an infinite proliferation of questions and curiosities in relationship to the work we can also answer the questions that most often arise and share insights that we hope will catalyze new inquiry and creative activity. After many years of research and discussion with Forsythe and the Company, the systems of organization in the dance were distilled into three intersecting categories – movement material, cueing, and alignments – which work together to create the visual counterpoint of the work.

Movement Material Recombination System

While the urgency and immediacy of the dance can make it appear improvised, *OFTr* is a carefully choreographed and tightly crafted work. Members of the company most often refer to the different segments of fixed movement as 'themes'. The 25 main themes are repeated and recombined over the course of the dance in their full and partial forms. Online in *Synchronous Objects* they can be explored individually in a *Movement Material Index* that gives a short clip of each theme and they are outlined in the graphic below (figure 1). In the graphic, dancers names are listed on the left and the themes are listed across the bottom. When themes are performed in full a hash mark is made above the line, and one is marked below when a theme is performed in fragment. This graphic shows that many different dancers perform several of the themes over the course of the work such as T1, T3, and T12. Some themes like T2 and T6 are only performed by certain dancers and very few times. It also shows the recombination of patterns of the work where T1 is performed only once in full but a total of 44 times in fragment by 14 different dancers and so on. This graphic can be understood as a translation of the work making the thematic structures legible. But it also can be used to devise a new dance, animation, or artwork. What if the full and fragment patterns were used to make an architectural form that related to the theme occurrences but also allowed users to recombine the elements in an extension of the choreographic principle that the graphic elucidates? This is precisely what the architectural collaborators on *Synchronous Objects* explored as part of their engagement with the work but it also could be re-explored and re-imagined by visitors to the site who take up this information into their own disciplinary contexts.

Figure 1: Theme and theme fragment occurrences by dancer.

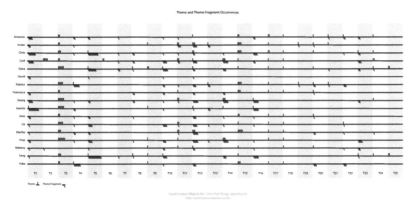

Graphics: Synchronousobjects.osu.edu

In addition to the themes and their interpretation, there are improvisation tasks in *OFTr* that ask dancers to translate specific properties of other performers' motions into their own. The dancers observe each other and make these translations in real time, producing different results in each performance of the work. Improvisations are tightly structured and are most often movements to get from one table to another, tasks in which the dancers wait for a cue and gaze intently at different performers, or alignment improvisations, which are explained later. The *Synchronous Objects* site shows these improvisations in the *Movement Material Index* and in the *Explanatory Video* for the *Index*. The themes and structured improvisations are the building blocks of the work and once the viewer becomes familiar with them, become a visible pattern throughout the work. I personally know them so well now that seeing each theme come and go is like seeing friends surfacing and receding as the dance progresses.

The data for the themes and improvisations is visualized in the manner explained above (diagrams, annotated video and so on) but it is also re-purposed in other ways as in the *Generative Drawing Tool* (figure 2). In this tool, the actions of moving brushes on the screen are organized by the choreographic data (such as the occurrence of themes and their fragments) from the dance.

Figure 2: Generative Drawing Tool within Synchronous Objects. This tool takes data from the dance and allows users to map that data to the actions and attributes of various brushes that move on the screen and create a drawing.

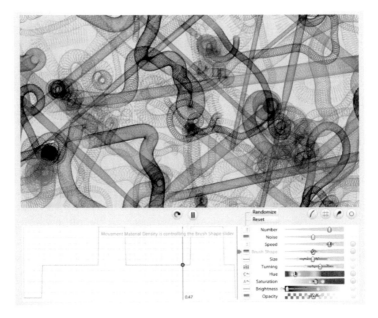

Where the *Movement Material Index* helps reveal structure in the piece, the *Generative Drawing Tool* begins to answer the question: 'what else this dance might look like'. The algorithms for the moving brushes allow them to be directed by the data but also to move based on a broader set of action choices. In this way, like the dancers, they could perhaps be seen to be doing both choreographed movement and structured improvisation. And both objects might inspire new scholarly and creative activity and invite audiences into a closer more attentive readership of choreographic form. For example, rather than looking only for unison as an indicator of structure, viewers might begin to watch this dance and others for the fleeting instances of similarity and the patterns of repetition that build over longer periods of time.

Cueing System

The timing of the dance is influenced by the choices made in the short instances of improvisation and in how the dancers perform the set movement material. But the true internal clock of the dance is the elaborate cueing system that Forsythe and the dancers created over many years. The musical score by Thom Willems does not direct the timing of the dancers' motions. Instead they wait for and give cues in a constantly shifting network of attention. While cues are common in live performance, the volume in this piece, more than 200 total cues in just over 15 minutes, is unusual. The cueing system also gives the feeling of cause and effect that audiences often note. In *Synchronous Objects* the cues became a vital form of information from the dance about time and the networks of attention and responsibility between the dancers.

The *Cue Annotations Object* shows the cues as they play out with the video of the dance. These animated drawings are didactic in that they 'teach' cueing in the dance. But they also demonstrate the mixture of quantitative and qualitative, analytical and creative work that is central to the project. To make the marks, attribute data from the personal accounts of each of the dancers was cross-referenced and cleaned until a precise network of cues given and received could be constructed. The accuracy of the dancers' accounts was remarkable with only a handful of discrepancies between the accounts that can be attributed to the many changes in the dance over the ten years of its development. As that data set was compiled the iterative animation design process evolved until the lines had the right organic feeling, combined with visual clarity that we wanted (the *Synchronous Objects* Process Catalog for this object shows samples from this development). The animated lines have a kinesthetics of their own that translates a hidden structure in the work that could be sensed but not seen before this process was undertaken. The lines seek to communicate the way in which information is flung out into space with precise but qualitatively inflected actions and received because of the acute physical attention of the recipient who then transforms the cue into new action. Forsythe describes these annotations (and the alignment annotations) as a picture of the dancers minds – what they are intending and the quality of their attention. For example, in figure 3 it is noticeable that the cue network is spread across the entire company with many dancers giving cues to many different people. It is immediately clear that Georg and Sang give more cues than the others and to more people. In this way, the graphic is also a map of responsibility in the dance. Unlike a translation, these forms of information revealed by graphics and data were not available in the original source.

Figure 3: All Cues Given graphic from Synchronous Objects. Shows all of the cues given by each dancer and to whom.

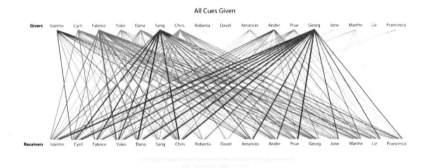

Alignment System

The last system, and the most important for unlocking structure in the dance, is the system of alignments. Alignments are moments of synchronization between the dancers when their actions share some but not all attributes. On a spectrum from unison to difference, alignments are closer to difference. Within the field of complex action that is *One Flat Thing, reproduced*, alignments are those flickering moments of shared directional flows, similar timing, and analogous shapes that the eye catches but can't hold. Alignments are patterns; they are forms of relationship that can be understood as a kind of visual agreement. They occur in every moment of the dance and are constantly shifting throughout the group. The term alignment emerges from the working practices of the Forsythe Company but it is not the only word they use, other terms include hook-ups, agreements, and isometries.

Like the cues, alignments are visualized in *Synchronous Objects* with different degrees of abstraction from the original dance. They can be seen in direct relation to the dance as a form of structural translation (or revelation of hidden information), a step away from dance when the video is subtracted from the annotations, and as an independent set of ideas as in the *3D Alignment Forms Object* (figure 4).

Figure 4: 3D Alignment Forms Object within Synchronous Objects. This object takes a sampling of two dancers' alignments into three-dimensional space and lofts volumes between them creating new spatial configurations.

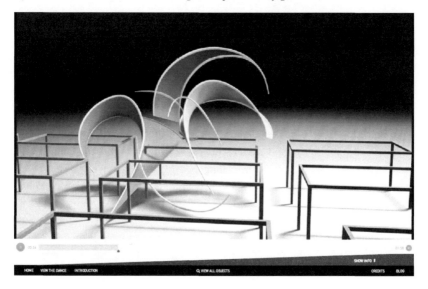

Counterpoint

All three of these systems together – movement material, cueing, alignments – combine to create the tapestry of visual counterpoint that is *One Flat Thing, reproduced*. We define counterpoint in this dance as 'a field of action in which the irregular and intermittent coincidence of attributes produces an ordered interplay'. This definition assumes as a starting point 'a field of action' with a high degree of difference within which 'irregular and intermittent' patterns can be recognized. Imagine the play of light on the water, the intersection of branches in a tree canopy, or the motions of pedestrians on New York City streets. Each of these phenomena presents the eye with complexity but also presents irregular patterns of interaction that can be discerned and highlighted. Those patterns are the ordered interplay. This is not unlike counterpoint in music although it is much more difficult to quantify and that is a subject for another essay.

Another way to understand counterpoint is to imagine it on a spectrum with *One Flat Thing, reproduced* on the left and a marching band on the right. In a marching band structure is obvious, it is clear how they are related, they are all literally marching to the same tune. The primary visual effect is unity. But underneath the surface is a deep structure of difference, diversity and even disagreement. The marchers have different politics, different training, they come from different home lives, and they may or may not get along when they are off the field. Counterpoint is the exact inverse. In counterpoint, difference and dissonance is the primary visual effect. It is at the layer of the deep structure that the relationships, alignments, and forms of agreement are at work. For contemporary society in which there is very little unity and marching to the same tune too often connotes times of violence and repression, counterpoint may be a very necessary metaphor for living.

What if we were to encounter those instances of disagreement or difference in our work lives, in our schools and on our streets with contrapuntal attention? Rather than forcing things into the marching band what if we brought heightened sensitivity to our connections as the cueing system in the dance demonstrates so clearly? What as yet unseen structures of agreement, fleeting instances of relationship and alignment of ideas might be percolating under the surfaces of our lives? Since the publication of *Synchronous Objects* in 2009, the story of counterpoint, has surfaced as one of the most important aspects of the work. We speak about it, we demonstrate it in the dance and our visualization objects, we teach it in workshops using dance improvisation and the interactive tools on the site, and we continue to explore it in our interdisciplinary working methods, in other dances, and in other aspects of our lives. In closing, I suggest that our objects are perhaps most of all manifestations of the exuberant exchange of ideas we experienced in their creation. Our creative process moved in a constant dilation between independent and collective intelligence, between the known and the unknown, chaos and order, focus and an always shifting network attention. In short, our process was is in itself a form of counterpoint.

REFERENCE

Forsythe, William: "Choreographic Objects: Essay", http://www.william-forsythe.de/essay.html (March 30, 2011).

WEBSITES

CUED – UROP Projects, http://www.eng.cam.ac.uk/teaching/urops/projects-08.html (March 30, 2011).

Contact Collaborations – Contact Editions, http://www.contactquarterly.com/ce/ce06.html#dvd-sp (March 30, 2011).

Inside Movement Knowledge » Capturing Intention, http://inside movement-knowledge.net/context/background/capturing-intention (March 30, 2011).

Home | Siobhan Davies RePlay, http://www.siobhandaviesreplay.com (March 30, 2011).

KunstenFestivaldesArts – Projects, http://archive.kfda.be/2005/en/project-detail.action-projectid=7473&id=331.htm (March 30, 2011).

Motion Bank | a context for moving ideas, http://motionbank.org/en (March 30, 2010).

Synchronous Objects, http://synchronousobjects.osu.edu (March 30, 2011).

William Forsythe Choreographic Objects: Works & Projects, http://www williamforsythe.de/installations.html (March 30, 2011).

WORKING PRINCIPLES

Communicating, Distilling, Catalyzing.
On the Creation of Dance Congress Worlds

Sabine Gehm, Katharina von Wilcke

"Taken together, dance supplies a record of where we have been and where we'd like to go, of how we move together and apart, of how we create the environments we inhabit and what we aspire to make of them" (Martin 2009), writes sociologist Randy Martin and makes a plea for concentrating on innovative powers, "those who assemble to create something hitherto unseen and disclose a different basis of incorporation" (id.).

In Martin's utopian thinking, dance reflects our individual and social movements and perspectives. In its concentrated artistic form, it sheds light on the paths taken in the past, present and future. But dance is more than that – sociologists like Martin believe that movement contains social and political potential, even a formative strength that has the capacity to have social effect. He is thus not far from the question of whether 'worldmaking' is possible through art, through dance. Can dance create 'world'? Or rather 'worlds'?

The subject of 'worldmaking'[1] with its possibilities and limitations proved to be essential in thinking about the Dance Congress 2009. It was inspired by a sa-

---

1   The concept of 'worldmaking' refers to Nelson Goodman's "ways of creating worlds". Goodman's philosophy of art and knowledge is based on the idea that the world is not factual, but rather that knowledge of the world is always already 'made': "Furthermore, if worlds are as much made as found, so also knowing is as much remaking as reporting. All the processes of worldmaking I have discussed enter into knowing. Perceiving motion, we have seen, often consists in producing it. Discovering laws involves drafting them. Recognizing patterns is very much a matter of inventing and imposing them. Comprehension and creation go on together." (Goodman 1978:

lon on choreographic modes of work at the Dance Congress 2006 in Berlin hosted by performance theorist André Lepecki and dramaturge Myriam Van Imschoot. At that time, a suggestion by choreographer Thomas Lehmen that art (and other human activity) should be regarded as "making a piece of world" led to a controversy that inspired dramaturge Jeroen Peeters to ask himself in retrospect:

"Are you then adding, transforming, or creating a parallel universe? Who has access to the creation of reality, of the imagination and the representations that shape it? What is the artist's role? What is the ideology behind it? Are we actually the producers of our own life and its conditions?" (Peeters 2007: 117)

The above mentioned relationship of dance and world, creation and worldmaking led in the preparations to the Dance Congress 2009 to questions concerning possible forms of globalized work environments and lifeworlds, the artistic and theoretical approaches to these worlds, the position of choreographers and their methods for creating and depicting worlds. From this perspective, dance becomes a kind of laboratory in which social and political developments can be tracked down and processed, and forms of communication and community reflected on and tested. Dance can absorb, distill, catalyze, analyze, create and, of course, criticize 'worlds', but it is equally dependent on the conditions of the world from which it emerges.[2]

At the same time, the concept of 'worldmaking' brought up questions of how a congress should be organized. How should a congress be constructed in order to facilitate understanding for and reflection of the different working worlds and perspectives of representatives from the fields of choreography, science, pedagogy, journalism and politics? How should it be conceived in terms of content, time and space so that protagonists from various fields of dance can play a part

---

22) This means that both the recognition of worlds, as well as their making is only possible through culturally influenced forms of access and that the processes that are necessary for descriptive worldmaking are always creative ones.

2 These thoughts take their inspiration from the 'world' concept of post-colonial theorist Homi K. Bhabha, according to whom modern, intercultural societies in a globalized world are 'hybrid' and thus subject to constant change. "To me, hybridization doesn't simply mean mixing, but rather the strategic and selective appropriation of meaning, creating space for persons whose freedom and equality are in danger." (Bhabha 2007: n.p.)

with very different motivations and in various forms and so that all participants can move about as freely as possible?

If we define a congress – in keeping with the idea of 'worldmaking' – as a "temporary collective living being that is not yet a state body, but after all already a congress body" (Ploebst 2009/1), or even as a "location where knowledge is not just transmitted, but also transpires" (Roms 2006), then further thoughts bring us to the following concrete realizations: there are no events without the movements of their participants, no worldmaking without (shared) steps. A congress is, truly, above all a temporary microcosm and in itself choreography.

And so, as we directed our attention from the greater/whole to the individual/detail, an easily understandable yet polysemantic congress motto emerged on the basis of the 'worldmaking' idea: "No Step without Movement!" A title, which both contains an implied invitation for all participants to actively help shape their own dance world(s) and which also, as author Helmut Ploebst pointed out, "almost inadvertently [...] sheds light [...] on the fact that no dance step can take place without inherent intellectual, cultural and political movement" (Ploebst 2009/1).

PROGRAM DEVELOPMENT AS A PARTICIPATORY PROCESS

The 'social choreography' of a dance congress with its thematic focuses and bifurcations, "combining threads, tight bundles and diffuse clouds" (id.) is, on the one hand, directly dependent upon the paths and meetings, communications and decisions taken and made beforehand. On the other hand, as a first part of the curatorial process, these preparations are also very much the product of the actual social, as well as political conditions prevalent in culture and education of the particular, specific era that it is taking place in.

While the Dance Congress 2006 sought to establish dance as a culture of knowledge with the programmatic statement of "Knowledge in Movement", as well as raise awareness for a dance scene, which was at the time just beginning to assert itself, the Congress in 2009 was more concerned with the social, political and aesthetic position of dance in theory and practice. The winding path in the search for topics had as its starting point the very different situations that existed in the dance scene in 2006 and 2009: the establishment of strong national and international networks and organizations, which brought together various protagonists in the dance field, had just begun in 2006. Important initiatives such as *Tanzplan Deutschland* or the *Ständige Konferenz Tanz*, who in retrospect have both provided the dance scene with sustainable impulses, already existed – but they did not yet have the years of experience, which three years later contributed to the discussions. The period around 2006 was characterized most of all by the new perspectives afforded by the 12.5 million Euro budget of Tanzplan Deutschland, which sparked hopes, visions and prospects in the dance scene.

Compared to the second Dance Congress, the 2006 event, which was initiated by the German Federal Cultural Foundation and inspired by the dance congresses of the 1920s[3], was more a first inventory of current trends and debates in classical and contemporary dance, dance pedagogy and academia. In numerous individual discussions with dance protagonists, we filtered out positions and ascertained topics that took their bearings, among other things, from the latest fields of research in dance studies. These were then specified in discussions with a work group in order to finally invite appropriate lecturers.

In contrast, the program of the Dance Congress 2009[4] was created with a different, more complex approach, which went through numerous phases. Basically our goal was to develop the most urgent topics of the heterogeneous dance scene as close to the actual reality of them as possible and to open up more appropriate spaces of reflection and action in order to facilitate this dance congress as a "highly dynamic, virtual system" (Ploebst 2009/1).

This other approach was the result of our experiences from the first congress, which Jeroen Peeters describes as follows using the example of one of the salons:

---

3   Patricia Stöckemann on the dance congresses of the 1920s: "In a sustained way, they raised public awareness in Germany for dance [...]. They created the first forums for discussion about dance, demonstrated where dance and dancers stood aesthetically, theoretically and socially; they discussed grievances, developed visions and concrete steps towards qualified training for modern dancers, the establishment of a first dance university and dance as an academic discipline, the promotion of amateur dance or improving the social equality of dancers in society. [...] The dance congresses [...] were meeting places, spaces for debate and exchange between dance protagonists from all fields: dancers, choreographers, dance teachers, as well as those who accompany dance by writing, reflecting and criticizing." (Stöckemann 2006: 10) Despite the different founding histories, the two dance congresses in 2006 and 2009 reflect the enormous charisma of the original congresses.

4   The Dance Congress in 2009 was once again mainly financed by the German Federal Cultural Foundation, as well as supported by the Department for Culture, Sports and Media of the City of Hamburg and the German Research Foundation.

"Throughout the salon, people's eagerness to speak up, make themselves heard and participate in the conversation was striking. It was perhaps symptomatic of the institutionalized
German dance field, in which many artists are invisible, and of a congress that left little
space for audience participation and artists' voices." (Peeters 2007: 114)

As it had been the case in 2006, we also consciously avoided the usual procedures followed for academic congresses in our development of the program for
the Dance Congress 2009. Instead of posting a 'call for papers', topics were
compiled in four Open Think Tanks offered in the context of various festivals in
Hamburg, Berlin, Munich and Düsseldorf. According to the 'Open Space' method developed by Harrison Owen in 1985 in the USA for big conferences, all
participants – in total more that one hundred dancers, choreographers, dance
teachers, scholars, curators and producers – were asked to contribute their ideas,
questions, positions, methods and visions of current art production and work
contexts. These were then discussed in spontaneously formed work groups.[5]

The entire agenda of the Think Tanks grew out of the intentions, suggestions
and self-organization of the participants, who met for the first time in this constellation. In these laboratories, the dance scene took on an initial, highly active
part in designing the program for the Dance Congress 2009.

In the subsequent evaluation of the Think Tanks, thematic catchwords were
formed out of the documentation of the work groups. These were then clustered
into larger topics and finally structured into so-called mind maps. In addition to
this participatory model of finding topics, we were also in active contact with
representatives of the most recent German networks, initiatives and projects (Association of German Dance Archives, Federal Association of Dance in Schools,
Dance Education Conference, and others) as well as the Center for Performance
Studies at the University Hamburg to set the agenda. These diverse proposals
and discussions concerning what contents could be essential were the basis for
the development of ideas for formats and possible lecturers; out of which, in
turn, topics were specified, substantiated or even rejected. The following four
thematic complexes emerged from these processes: Dance and Politics, Creation
and Reflection, Dance (Hi)Stories and Life Stories. Various performances that
experimented with new forms and served as inspiration for unusual congress
formats also played a large role. One such example was *Générique* by the Eve-

---

5   The topics were, among others: writing dance history, the social situation of dancers,
     dance in schools, education, dance politics, trans-disciplinarity, dance and communi-
     cation, curating dance, community dance, financial and work structures, dancers as
     experts, dance and music, the relationship between practice and theory.

rybodys artist collective – a public discussion about a piece that does not exist, in which the collective act of imagination itself becomes the performance. Or the radio performance by the artist group LIGNA, in which the audience explores the space by following instructions given to them via headsets, thereby testing four approaches to utopian movement. In addition, there were a number of work groups who met beforehand by invitation only and whose results were presented as part of the congress, as well as cooperation partners, who had a decisive effect on the development of the program.[6]

For some topics and items on the agenda, we passed on the responsibility to choreographers, theorists, pedagogues, etc. After consulting with us, they chose the speakers and translated the topics into appropriate formats of presentation. This selective delegation of responsibility brought with it new challenges: the struggle to find the 'right' contents – i.e. those oriented towards current debates – and thematic accents, as well as formats that were realistic in terms of time and place, required balancing the odds, a willingness to compromise, as well as the ability to find solutions for all in common dialogue. These were all essential curatorial strategies in this phase.

The four thematic complexes[7], which structured the program at the end of this decision-making process, emerged less as a result of a straightforward objective or the realization of a given concept; it was more the result of participatory and communicative processes with numerous participants. This amounted to arriving at the structure of a congress along winding paths: topics, formats and choice of personnel meander, shift and change; the development process is like a constant see-saw, demanding a incessant willingness to communicate and openness, as well as a precise balance of priorities – especially when one is dealing with such a large array of topics.

---

6   These cooperation partners were curators, artists and academics: Amelie Deuflhard, Anne Kersting, Jochen Roller (Kampnagel Hamburg), Kerstin Evert, Matthias Quabbe (K3-Center for Choreography/Tanzplan Hamburg), Gabriele Klein, Sandra Noeth (University Hamburg, Performance Studies). Other important partners were the German Federal Cultural Foundation, as well as the Tanzplan Deutschland with its experiences gained from its own initiatives: Dance Education Conference, Tanzplan Local, Association of German Dance Archives. Susanne Foellmer also contributed significantly to the development of the program as research associate to the Dance Congress.

7   Dance and Politics, Creation und Reflection, Dance (Hi)Stories, Life Stories, see website http://www.tanzkongress.de.

Given this development, a particular goal of the Dance Congress 2009 was to apply participatory formats. In addition to conventional ways of doing things such as like lectures and podiums, the dominant formats were ones in which the congress participants could actively take part in the discussion and thought processes, or where methods and techniques could be experienced hands-on. We experimented with laboratories, salons, lecture performances, toolboxes and public master classes. Different lecture formats gave impulses from an artistic or theoretical perspective. In the lecture demonstration *Choreographic Thinking Tools*, for example, cognitive scientists, an artist and a dance researcher examined physical and mental processes of creating images. The public could listen in on professional debates such as in *Curating/Producing between Theory and Practice*, where in a 'Q & A' format questions concerning curatorial strategies were discussed together with both curators and artists. Laboratories requested that participants contribute their respective expertise to collaboratively work on results. And after a practical demonstration by school children in the lab *Dance in Schools – Eyes on Quality*, quality criteria for teaching dance in schools was presented and discussed. In master classes, toolboxes and seminars, methods and techniques were tested. The program explicitly aimed at providing events in which theorists and practitioners could enter into dialogue or try out new training methods, choreographic techniques and pedagogical approaches.

It is precisely this difference in formats and the systematic association of theory and practice that distinguishes a dance congress from other, purely academic congresses. A dance congress therefore also requires an accompanying and up-to-date dance program that inspires and expands the contents of debate and is developed in direct relation to the topics of the congress. An event of this size and complexity demands a location that allows for the implementation of a wide array of events and for intense interaction between different formats. As a space in which artistic reflection and production are standard practice, Kampnagel, with its multitude of rehearsal and performance spaces, proved to be an ideal location for spontaneous discussions, in-depth expert debate and interdisciplinary meetings.

HOW WOULD YOU LIKE TO WORK TOMORROW?

In contrast to a dance festival, which asserts a clear curatorial position by presenting 'finished' productions for the audience, critics and programmers to deal with, the preparation of a dance congress is more a question of providing space for topics, propositions, issues and discourse about the art form as such; to facilitate collective thinking about artistic practice, techniques, structures, work processes and forms of production for contemporary and classical dance, as well as its aesthetic perspectives and potential in cultural politics.

Both the interaction of theory and practice, as well as cross-genre work, can trigger ideas and new substantial co-operations, which will ideally maintain a sustainable effect even after the end of the congress.

"Each congress, even the most boring one, creates a highly dynamic virtual system whose overall performance is composed of the individuated experiences of participants and visitors; but not only in the moment of giving or receiving information, but instead first and foremost thanks to the system's influence on the behavior of all participants after the congress and on how their communication 'afterwards' is influenced by the congress's contents." (Ploebst 2009/1)

Dance congress worlds create temporary communities: meetings of individuals from different cultural backgrounds, who – as in any form of artistic production – are brought together by the shared act of searching for new forms and working methods. Ideally, this 'worldmaking' of a dance congress prompts short or long term processes of realization and understanding, which then actively shape dance and its conditions (cf. Goodman 1978).

Evaluating a dance congress also means thinking about omissions and gaps in these temporary worlds. A central thematic focus for the next congress could thus be "an extended, transmedial definition of art, which permits the use of strategies from choreography and dance together with all other all existing and still to-be-developed artistic means [...]" (Ploebst 2009/2). One consideration is to give grants to research projects, as in-depth research and experimentation with form often suffers in artistic processes under the tight time schedule of having to produce. Such research projects could, on the one hand, permit more intensive trans-disciplinary collaboration with other artistic genres and, on the other hand, support advanced theoretical study in cooperation with experts. In addition to an increased interdisciplinary focus that concentrates on neighboring genres as 'accomplices' of dance, cooperation and networking between the various kinds of stage dance and its representatives, as well as the activation of municipal and state theaters and their dance ensembles could be pursued further.

From the current perspective, we also see more emphasis placed on the subject of dance and politics, as well as dance and the economy. How will the context of aesthetic and political, resp. economic issues change in the future? Will the 'crisis', which is not just economic, but also social, influence dance as an art form or the form and content of the next dance congress? And if so, how?

Enough questions and opportunities to therefore mobilize the "innovative powers" as Randy Martin calls them and to concentrate on the role of the curator as described by Hans Ulrich Obrist:

"The curator is an administrator, sensitive lover, author of prefaces, librarian, manager, accountant, animator, conservator, financer, diplomat, watchdog, exhibition guide, press attaché, transporter. [...] He is a catalyst and *passerelle* between art and the world; he opens up complementary paths and develops new possibilities and contexts that would otherwise remain inaccessible." (Obrist 1996: 10-11)

Written in cooperation with the journalist Elisabeth Nehring.

REFERENCES

Bhabha, Homi K. (2000): Die Verortung der Kultur, Tübingen: Stauffenburg.
_____ (2007): Interview with Lukas Wieselberg, ORF, November 9, 2007, http://ecards.orf.at/science/news/1499888 (January 16, 2011).
Goodman, Nelson (1978): Ways of Worldmaking, Hassocks, Sussex: The Harvester Press.
Martin, Randy (2009): "Dancing Through the Crisis", unpublished manuscript.
Obrist, Hans Ulrich (1996): DELTA X – Der Kurator als Katalysator, Regensburg: Schmid + Lindinger.
Peeters, Jeroen (2007): "How do you want to work today?", in: Sabine Gehm/Pirkko Husemann/Katharina von Wilcke (eds.), Knowledge in Motion. Perspektives of Artistic and Scientific Research in Dance, Bielefeld: transcript.
Ploebst, Helmut (2009/1): "Bewegung der Bewegung: Eine Reflexion über den Hamburger Tanzkongress 2009, Teil 1", http://www.corpusweb.net (November, 2009).
_____ (2009/2): "Erregung der Bewegung: Eine Reflexion über den Hamburger Tanzkongress 2009, Teil 2", http://www.corpusweb.net (November, 2009).
Roms, Heike (2006): "Gewusst, wie? – Fußnoten zum Tanzkongress", unpublished congress observations.
Stöckemann, Patricia (2006): "Tanzkongress Deutschland", in: Kulturstiftung des Bundes (ed.), Magazine 7, spring 2006, Halle (Saale).

WEBSITE

Tanzkongress 2009, http://www.tanzkongress.de (January 16, 2011).

Situational Worlds.
Complicity as a Model of Collaboration

GESA ZIEMER

Dance and other stage productions such as music, scenographic arrangements or performances are ephemeral media, whose products cannot be reproduced. Even when a piece is shown over and over again, it is never the same, for it changes from performance to performance, from context to context, from space to space, from audience to audience. Performers act in the now and according to the situation among themselves and with the audience. They work on the level of perception by creating moods and intensities, which cannot be fully explained by the utterly transparent and reproducible blueprints of choreography. These aspects make theatrical work so interesting and at the same time fragile. Dance calls attention to situational potentials, which may be specific, but are also world-generating in other areas of society that are today increasingly characterized by instability rather than stability (cf. Latour 2007: 18ff).[1]

I am thus less interested in the dangers, than in the potentials of instable and temporary environments concerning collective working processes. Dancers possess situational competencies, which enable them to represent something for a moment and create a world. Besides the application of technique, their forms of

---

1 Bruno Latour describes this development as "reassembling the social". His associative sociology diagnoses not only the deterioration of social ties, but also focuses on new – namely associative – connections that do not function according to a stable principle. These are reassemblies, characterized by new links and in which unexpected elements are connected with each other. These links are by no means weak, but cannot be described with traditional categories. They are often transient and lose their strength immediately after articulation.

expression are created by intensely confiding in each other physically and emotionally, although their time together is usually limited. In their specific form of collaboration, they combine such contradictory qualities of contact as intensity and transience, commitment and temporality, the public sphere and intimacy, trust and mistrust, effectivity and fragility. How can such situational forms of collectivity be described? Are such collective dynamics already being similarly practiced in other professional fields due to social transformations or are they unique to dance?

In the following paper, I would like to discuss the concept of complicity as a model of collective work. Complicity is a specific form of collaboration, which emerges in temporary and creative working environments. Complicity cultivates the accessing of twilight zones and permits informal working processes and intimacy. It is precisely the secrecy within the group, which holds its members together and strengthens the collective. In order to deepen our understanding of this term, I will explain how it differs from other social and organizational theoretical terms for group work such as teamwork, the formation of alliances and networking. Friendship also follows a different kind of logic of relationships than complicity. These theoretical thoughts will be combined with statements by the dancer Anna Huber, who I interviewed for our research film (cf. Weber/Ziemer 2007) on her complicity with percussionist Fritz Hauser during the creation of her piece *handundfuss* in 2006. A further research project[2] of mine, in which dancers, musicians, entrepreneurs and academics all equally participated, forms the basis of this analysis.

THE TERM COMPLICITY

What is complicity? In German, complicity is almost exclusively used in a negative way, in order to name collective crimes that are obscure and are committed without a clear perpetrator. The theory of felony as expounded in criminal law offers a concise definition to whose Swiss version I herewith refer. Complicity means accompliceship: "Accompliceship can be distinguished as the collaborative committing of a felony in conscious and purposeful cooperation." (Reh-

---

2   The research project took place from 2006 to 2010 at the Institute for Theory at the Zurich University for the Arts and was financed by the Commission for Technology and innovation Berlin. Project Head: Gesa Ziemer, Research associates: Andrea Notroff, Nina Aemisegger, Film: Barbara Weber, http://www.ith-z.ch/forschung/komplizenschaft/ (January 29, 2011).

berg/Donatsch 2001: 138). The quotation indicates that it is not the responsibility and guilt of a person on which the focus here lies, but the 'co' of accomplice. How is this 'co' practiced? How is it structured? Why is this 'co', which generally is forced to function under adverse circumstances, so effective? These are questions that interest judges, when imposing a sentence. The power of complicity lies in the fact that a group can develop unforeseeable powers in ways that a single person isn't capable of. The specificity of complicity is that the individual can be sentenced on the basis of his or her involvement in the group and not on the grounds of their individual actions.

Complicity is divided into three phases: accomplices mutually make a decision, plan a course of action together and implement it as a joint effort. Classical accomplices pass through these three phases together. The interesting thing about this three-step system is that it includes the entire development from concept to practical implementation. While the decision-making process is still strongly situated in the visionary realm, possible real circumstances are taken into consideration in the planning phase. The implementation then translates the plan into concrete action and is entirely practical. Accomplices thus not only contribute their thoughts, they are also co-perpetrators and in their actions combine theory and practice par excellence. These three steps, which are a succession of idea – feasibility – implementation, therefore brings up questions of whether a transfer of the term to other, legal forms of group work – such as in the framework of art – is possible. The question of 'perpetration' gives rise to possibilities for translation. These exist when, "the party to an offence has reasons to decide on the actual committal of the crime together with others" (id.). The decision-making must refer to the joint realization of the plan. What is clear is that all parties can have a determining influence on the course of the action and thus also bear joint responsibility. A person, who is part of a complicit group, trusts the others, because he knows that the actions of the others will weigh just as heavily as his own. The steering of the collective is thus influenced by the collective itself and not only by an individual. The other person is just as responsible for me as I am responsible for myself. I am just as responsible for the other as for myself.

It is also of some significance for complicity, how accomplices behave towards those, who are not part of the group. Complicity produces exclusion. These are not open integrative groups, who invite as many as possible to take part. Complicity instead aims towards including individuals, who can bring very individual specific abilities into the group. Complicity requires the courage to make one's own strengths relevant for the goal of the group. The forms of expression that complicity can take are therefore also always connected to whether they are behaving towards an evidently or indirectly repressive person or towards a benevolent one.

DEMARCATIONS: TEAMWORK

In order to more clearly define the term, it is helpful to isolate it from other forms of relationships, such as teamwork, the forming of alliances, networking, and friendship. A team is a group of people set on solving a given task. Teams that function well usually consist of people with different abilities, who pursue a certain goal in an efficient manner and reach this goal bar of any incidents and in accordance with a transparent group structure. Teams often adhere to existing structures and do not invent new ones. In management literature, teams are described as result-orientated actors: "They come together to solve problems, exchange information, make decisions, plan strategies and procedures." (Hölscher/Reiber/Pape/Loehnert-Baldermann 2006: 3) Teams act in a planned and structured manner and are composed for longer periods of time. Our society depends on experienced, functioning teams routinely working in given structures in many ways and many places. When we see a fire brigade or a medical team at work, we immediately understand that these teams have to be alert and flexible, but should not constantly question the structures in which they work (cf. Weick/Sutcliffe 2003)[3].

In contrast to teams, who have to avert the unexpected under extreme circumstances, accomplices literally provoke the unexpected to happen. In certain areas of the arts, where unusual aesthetics are a mark of quality, the unexpected is almost expected. In such experimental fields, artistic accomplices do not act purposefully, as they often do not yet know their exact aim. They come together and in this moment of encounter create a direction, a format, a product. Let us apply these thoughts to the production *handundfuss* from 2006, for which Anna Huber and Fritz Hauser collaborated for the first and only time. For both it was also the first experience with interaction between the media of the body and per-

---

3   In such cases, instabilities in the structure would impede a trouble-free and smooth handling of emergencies and may, if worst comes to worst, lead to catastrophes. The organization theorists Karl E. Weick and Kathleen M. Sutcliffe support this observation, having examined so-called High Reliability Organizations, such as teams working in hospitals or nuclear power plants. These are relied upon to avert all unexpected occurrences as early as possible. See: Karl E. Weick/Kathleen M. Sutcliffe: *Das Unerwartbare Managen. Wie Unternehmen aus Extremsituationen lernen* (2003).

cussion. Rehearsals began with movement, percussion, reflection, and improvisation in an empty space. Both are seasoned and experienced artists in their own fields, but working together was new for them. There were no pre-determined structures for their interaction; these were invented in the act of creation. As accomplices, they together developed a form of body percussion, in which the music does not illustrate the dancing and vice versa. The conspiratorial moment, which admitted no outside audience, was crucial in the early rehearsal phase. Making mistakes, overstepping boundaries, senseless and sensible attempts at expression only really become productive under non-public conditions. Especially during the first few rehearsals this intimacy is absolutely necessary.

FORMING ALLIANCES

The term alliance helps to define another useful difference. The term is generally used to describe a strategic form of cooperation between large groups, such as enterprises or nation states, but not between individuals (cf. Todeva/Knoke 2002). Groups form alliances when their power is threatened and it is necessary to have allies in order to secure territory or power. In economics and in politics, alliances are regarded as long-term strategic collaborations aimed at establishing synergies. Usually they serve to increase one's own wealth of knowledge and experience in order to maintain one's market position more effectively and with better target strategies. An alliance comprises coordinated action by a specific group in order to assert their position against competition. The members of an alliance do not necessarily share a common goal. Instead it is more about reaching one's own goal, which under the given circumstances is only possible by entering into an alliance.

Alliances differ from complicity mainly in their strategic procedure. Michel de Certeau's differentiation between tactics and strategy is helpful in this regard, as he defines complicity more as tactics. What distinguishes the tactician from the strategist? The strategist lives in a place "that can be described as his 'own' and that can serve as a basis for the organization of his relationships with a specific outside world (competitors, opponents, a clientele, an 'aim' or 'object' of research)" (de Certeau 1988: 23). Strategists act with purpose from the basis of a specific territory – this may be a company, a nation state, a professionally or socially defined position – and carry out calculated transactions. They intentionally manipulate the balance of power. A subject equipped with willpower and power can gain profit from his advantages, prepare to expand, and remain as independent as possible from external factors. Outside forces can be observed from a safe place, measured up as objects, controlled and incorporated.

In contrast to the strategist, the tactician only has the place of the other. Taktiké literally means the 'art of arrangement and positioning (on a battle field)', which means that the tactician acts in conjunction with others. This etymological difference shows that strategy has a hierarchical, tactics a situational leadership model. A tactician takes the available powers, qualities, and effects, and organizes them quickly and according to the given situation. Accomplices in this case have a relationship to the other, "without being able to fully comprehend and or keep him at a distance" (id.). They constantly juggle with various components that open up opportunities for action. They do not possess an autonomous place that allows them to separate themselves from the others. Tactics run wild and create surprises. They are most likely to occur, where they are not expected.

Complicity, as opposed to alliance, is more a tactical way of acting. It allows partners to utilize opportunities that arise, to combine unlikely elements, and thus create fissures and holes in the fabric of established systems. Tactics, due to their context-orientated ability to react, are highly dynamic and useful for creating new situations. Anna Huber says: "Fritz Hauser came to one of my premieres because somebody said he makes music the way I dance. That's how our collaboration began." (Weber/Ziemer 2007: n.p.) The quote shows that this was not a case of dancer looking for a musician, but of finding one. The interaction is not strategic, mainly because it does not primarily serve to maintain an individual identity as dancer or musician. Instead, this encounter of skills leads to the creation of something else: the result of unpredictable dynamics provoked. This takes place on stage in the very moment, when performers are not exclusively performing their ideal form, but instead using situational arrangement to show how processes develop and effects unfold.

NETWORKING

A network is the form of organization closest to complicity, but there are still differences. Sociologist Manuel Castells describes the social structure of the network, a result of new information and communication technologies, as based on a decentralized flexibilization of work and life, displacement, and less hierarchical organizational structures (cf. Castells 2001: 423). This social transformation is characterized by three essential aspects:

Economy is informational, global, and organized in networks (Castells 2001: 427). These new networks, which Castells describes as a "series of intertwined knots" (Castells 2001: 428), are organized in various ways: Not only do entire companies join networks, but smaller networks are also created within large companies. They form for specific projects, disband upon completion of the project and merge again with other networks. Due to its temporality, complicity could be described as a particular type of networking; especially, where Castells describes networks as not simply reproducing existing dominant networks, but capable of initiating social change. This is the case when "cultural communities" are created that represent values not covered by any other network. Or when networks "are based on alternative projects [...] and build bridges of communication with other networks in society." (Castells 2001: 438) Castells mentions human rights organizations, feminist and ecological movements as examples.

However, he also describes the problems faced by networks. They often find it difficult to coordinate responsibilities, concentrate resources on certain goals, and remain manageable after reaching a certain size. The advantages of dehierarchization thus become a problem, and in this aspect, networks differ from complicity. In contrast to the structure of networks, complicit relationships tend to form much smaller social configurations (cf. Olson 2004: 52f)[4]. It is possible to be part of a network without actually contributing something to it. Complicity, however, requires conscious and active participation. As complicit groups tend to be much smaller, problems in the coordination of responsibilities usually do not occur. Often there is only one representative per function, so conflicts over areas of responsibility are rare. As far as resources are concerned in complicity, the small size of the group usually means that all or most resources are mobilized. So complicity could be defined as an intensification of networking. Undoubtedly Anna Huber and Fritz Hauser and their experimental forms of expression also participate in artistic networks. However, this form of organization is still much too casual. It took complicity to fully solidify the logic of their relationship. And it was the mutual trust, willingness to take risks, the intimacy and

---

4   The economist Mancur Olsen had provided some interesting research. Empirical data support his thesis that small groups are able to develop an ability to act that can weaken much bigger groups. The reason for this seems to be that large groups are often unable to negotiate a strong common interest. Small groups, however, are often interest groups that can act together as one. Based on research by John James, he writes "that in many different institutions – private as well as public, national as well as local – the 'active' groups and subgroups are usually much smaller [...]. A sample test showed that the average size of an 'active' group was 6.5 members, the average of a 'non-active' group was 14 members." (Olson 2004: 52f)

emotionality of the two that led to the microdynamics, which became the nucleus of a singular artistic form of expression. Anna Huber says:

"On stage, we are linked by invisible threads. We hug before and after the performance, but on stage we hardly have any physical contact at all. Still, we know exactly what the other is doing." (Weber/Ziemer 2007: n.p.)

In a network, it is not necessary to know what the others are doing, for its members work very autonomously. Nor is physical presence necessary, as many of the large digital networks have proven. On stage, however, autonomy is linked to physical interaction with the other person. Factors such as rhythm, synchronization, and dynamics are crucial for the success of complicit processes.

FRIENDSHIP

The final social bond, which I will not go into at much length and which differs from complicity, is friendship. Friendship is directed less at temporality, and more towards duration. In its postmodern form, based on difference rather than similarity (cf. Derrida 1997), it does not end, because of long phases of silence and dissonance. Friendship is meant to endure such non-harmonic phases. Gilles Deleuze describes friendship as a "presence that is intrinsic to thought, a condition of possibility of thought itself" (Deleuze 1994: 3). In this concept, which refers back to a fundamental definition of thought, friends primarily articulate themselves as different from one another, they have no shared interests. Their strength lies in the in-between, in the gap, which develops out of their different personalities and behaviors and enables other ways of thinking. Friendship is always unique and it is this very experience of difference, which produces its fascination and a form of sociality beyond institutionalized models of attachment. The power of friendship lies in its purposelessness, which allows for the development of new goals. Friends may accompany us, but rarely do they lead us towards a specific purpose. Friendship does not have to (but can) include compliance. Unlike complicity, it does not have to be practical, as there is nothing to be implemented. Upon beginning their collaboration, Anna Huber and Fritz Hauser did not regard themselves as friends, for they tested everything, which was relevant for them at that point in time in front of an audience. Their complicity does not silence dissonances; these are negotiated productively and lead to a form of expression.

So why can Anna Huber and Fritz Hauser be called accomplices in their production *handundfuss*? The example shows that complicity already begins when an individual form of expression is searched for and hence individual collective working structures established. At the beginning, Anna Huber and Fritz Hauser had no pre-determined goal; they created their own goal and were not able to fall back on already tested group structures. This collaboration was temporary and in its early phase, characterized by intimate, non-public and aimless moments alone in an empty space. It is this conspiratorial moment that distinguishes their complicity from a distanced professional relationship, as we know it from other group formations. The two followed a theatrical principle, which was tactical rather than strategic, although strategic action was not totally negated. Every experienced dancer is also a strategist, who knows, however, when to dance the tactical game in order to create presence. Complicity does not make identity untouchable; it makes it permeable. Once complicity has begun there is no turning back, the shared process of experiencing, learning, and acting is set in motion. Complicity takes place in small group formations, which facilitate active engagement. It is not non-hierarchical, but it plays with hierarchies, which can be altered by the participants in different phases. When complicity is wisely employed, it supports and challenges the idiosyncrasies of the partners where required. Friendship does not necessarily require getting on stage. Complicity, however, includes the presentation of what wants to be presented. Depending on audience participation, complicity is strengthened or loosened. If the reaction is dismissive, complicity usually grows stronger. However, this is not always the case: as in every spy movie, here, too, there are defectors, who may weaken complicity or even end it.

Back to the initial questions: What forms of creating worlds does dance have to offer? Are they special? Or similar in other areas of life? Complicity is a particular form of collective work, which creates specific aesthetic and also social worlds. In dance, the three phases of complicity – decision-making, planning, and realization – are passed through in almost exemplary fashion. Compared to other artistic practices, dance has high situational potential thanks to the element of movement, which requires quick actions and reactions and thus supports situational behavior. This is particularly the case in collectives, who do not simply follow a choreographer's plan, but take on shared responsibility for the outcome. Anna Huber's and Fritz Hauser's unique, temporary and experimental collaboration method is a prime example of complicity. I suspect that the ability to act complicit is also more and more required in other fields of work (cf.

Pongratz/Voß 2004)[5]. Few things can be planned ahead of time and reliably organized, unstable conditions often make it impossible to reproduce team structures, temporary project work makes it necessary to permanently invent new goals, hierarchies are changing, and resources have to be independently obtained. And stepping on a stage is becoming ever more important as a form of presenting results.

REFERENCES

Castells, Mauel (2001): "Bausteine einer Theorie der Netzwerkgesellschaft", in: Berliner Journal für Soziologie, Edition 4, 2001, pp. 423-439.

de Certeau, Michel (1988): Kunst des Handelns, Berlin: Merve.

Deleuze, Gilles (1994): What is Philosophy?, New York: Columbia University Press.

Derrida, Jacques (1997): The Politics of Friendship, New York/London: Verso.

Hölscher, Stefan/Reiber, Wolfgang/Pape, Karin/Loehnert-Baldermann, Elizabeth (2006): Die Kunst gemeinsam zu handeln. Soziale Prozesse professionell steuern, Berlin/Heidelberg: Springer.

Latour, Bruno (2007): Eine neue Soziologie für eine neue Gesellschaft, Frankfurt am Main: Suhrkamp.

Olson, Mancur (2004): Die Logik des kollektiven Handelns, Tübingen: Mohr Siebeck.

Pongratz, Hans J./Voß, G. Günter (2004): Typisch Arbeitskraftunternehmer? Befunde empirischer Arbeitsforschung, Berlin: Edition Sigma.

Rehberg, Jörg/Donatsch, Andreas (2001): Strafrecht I. Verbrechenslehre, Zurich: Schulthess.

Todeva, Emanuela/Knoke, David (2002): "Strategische Allianzen und das Sozialkapital von Unternehmen", in: Jutta Allmendinger/Thomas Hinz (eds.), Organisationssoziologie, (= Sonderheft der Kölner Zeitschrift für Soziologie und Sozialpsychologie 42), Wiesbaden: Westdeutscher Verlag, pp. 345-381.

---

5   Today, instability reveals itself in working lives, whose boundaries are dissolving and which are characterized by self-economization (everyone is an entrepreneur), a high degree of self-discipline (flexible working hours), and growing self-rationalization (everyday life highly determined by technology). This is the conclusion reached by Günter Voß in Hans J. Pongratz/G. Günter Voß: *Typisch Arbeitskraftunternehmer? Befunde empirischer Arbeitsforschung* (2004).

Weick, Karl E./Sutcliffe, Kathleen M. (2003): Das Unerwartbare Managen. Wie Unternehmen aus Extremsituationen lernen, Stuttgart: Klett Cotta.

FILM

Komplizenschaften (2007) (CH, D: Barbara Weber/Gesa Ziemer)

WEBSITE

Institut für Theorie (ith) | Forschung | Komplizenschaft: http://www.ith-z.ch/forschung/komplizenschaft (January 30, 2011).

Protocols of Encounter: On Dance Dramaturgy

SANDRA NOETH

"It's amazing. We all came together at the same time. Because we are all here ... and you're all here ... and so we're all here together", Claire Marshall puts it in a nutshell in *The Thrill Of It All* by Forced Entertainment.[1]

This shared 'being-in-time' and the instantaneousness and immediacy of influences and products, which reveal themselves in it, seems to me one of the fundamental parameters for thinking about dramaturgy in the context of current choreographic work.

Over the last few years, a number of performances, projects and their medial and theoretical extensions have formulated an new understanding of choreography that exceeds the organization of movement in time and space: Mette Ingvartsen's performance *Evaporated Landscapes* can be read as a radical concept of disembodiment, in which neither the choreographer nor other performers set foot on stage, and yet the body is nevertheless, precisely because of its absence, negotiated between the poles of materiality and imagination and constantly created anew in a specific scenario, a machinery of lights, sound, soap bubbles, fog and dry ice. Daniel Aschwanden und Peter Stamer's piece *The Path of Money*, for which they followed the journey of a banknote or rather of its owners during a trip to China, can be interpreted as a choreographic involvement with individual agents of an economy that has escalated into utter confusion. The sound-text performances of Jürgen Berlakovich are experimental set-ups, which

---

1   Forced Entertainment: *The Thrill Of It All*, theater performance, premiere on May 7, 2010 at Kaaitheater, Brussels.

situate the place of choreography in the materiality of language, in what evades speech and speech movements, intention and perception.[2]

Cited here as example and as representative of others, these artists explore in their work the choreographic in other forms or media and in other disciplines, in thinking and writing – thus opening it up to the social and political. Instead of distancing dance from other discursive and artistic practices, this perspective integrates the overflowing and breaking down of barriers by the art form itself.[3] This broadening of the term is not only significant for the practice of those artists, who have already long situated themselves between formats and forms of expression and allowed definitional dividing lines such as the differentiation of 'dance' and 'performance' to become obsolete. It also once more reveals the field of choreography as a historically grown medial hybrid, in mutual manifold exchange with the traditional genres of music, theater, painting or sculpture and moving back and forth between everyday actions and organization, documentation and art work, live event and institutional representation.

At the same time, this version of the choreographic can be read as a conceptual approach and a self-manifesting practice closely connected to various movements of disintegration and interaction, which have shaped the order of the world and its mental environment over the last decades in the form of profound upheavals. Lebanese author Amin Maalouf speaks of a "dérèglement du monde"; an irregularity and absence of rules, which has seized various areas of life individually, but also as a whole: intellectual life, as well as the financial markets, climate development, as well as geopolitical situations and questions of ethics (cf. Maalouf 2009: 11). This environment is marked by an immediacy and acceleration of history, whose events are taking place (in their medialized and fragmented form) before the eyes of the whole of mankind and in real-time, and the simultaneous relativity of individual action, which is shaped by local resour-

---

2 Cf. Mette Ingvartsen: *Evaporated Landscapes* (2009), Daniel Aschwanden and Peter Stamer: *The Path of Money* (2009) and Jürgen Berlakovich: *Sound-Sleeper* (2010).

3 "I believe the worst habit in dance at the moment is to insist on the autonomy of dance as an independent art form or language. I believe that this differentiation could become a disadvantage for dance. While choreographers already take working across genre boundaries with a broadened concept of dance for granted, the battle for the recognition of dance as such is still being fought on other fronts. Either, because we presenters think that our audience needs such thinking in pigeonholes or because funding programs and cultural politics still follow a logic that presupposes separated disciplines," said curator Pirkko Husemann in an analysis of the situation in contemporary dance (Husemann/Wagner 2011: n.p.).

ces and structures. It confronts us with the challenge of having to handle disturbing and disorienting experiences (cf. Maalouf 2009: 89), as well as the 'Unknown'. A situation of concurrent worlds, whose connections and correlations, resonances and counterpoints, paradoxes and ambivalences must continuously be integrated into one's life and actions.

"Parce qu'il ne s'agit pas seulement de mettre en place un nouveau mode de fonctionnement économique et financier, un nouveau système de relations internationales, ni seulement de corriger quelques dérèglements manifestes. Il s'agit aussi de concevoir sans délai, et d'installer dans les esprits, une tout autre vision de la politique, de l'économie, du travail, de la consommation, de la science, de la technologie, du progrès, de l'identité, de la culture, de la religion, de l'Histoire; une vision enfin adulte de ce que nous sommes, de ce que sont les autres, et du sort de la planète qui nous est commune." (Maalouf 2009: 314)

"Shouldn't art, as the traditional authority for the representation of time and as presentation of an era logically be at the center of the crisis?" asks Frédéric Pouillaude (Pouillaude 2009: 354) and points out the extent to which the decomposition of overarching categories of significance and the associated shift from ideological to identitary debates (cf. Maalouf 2009: 23) has also affected the cultural realm and artistic production and creation. With this in mind, a reflection of the status of the choreographic and the performative and their processes of worldmaking seems more relevant today than ever before, especially against the backdrop of the last decade, characterized by a revival of performance art and its extensive museification and historicization. This development has led to a revaluation of photographic, film and written documentation and in recent years of strategies of reenactment. Performances are meanwhile firmly established as equal parts of exhibitions and art fairs, dance festivals and institutional theater programming – and choose this process of institutionalization itself as starting point for their research.[4]

---

4   The Burgtheater Wien has produced – just to name some exemplary situations – the independent New York theater group Nature Theatre of Oklahoma with *Life and Times. Episode I + II* 2009 and 2010 under participation of their own ensemble; performance groups such as Rimini Protokoll or Needcompany are also a regular part of performance season of municipal stages; performative pieces are a integral part of collections, exhibitions, and retrospectives in international art museums such as e.g. *Marina Abramovic: The Artist is Present* at the MoMA (New York 2010), *Move: Choreographing You* at the Southbank Centre/Hayward Gallery (London 2010/2011)

Moments of Transition

Art often takes place in twilight zones, between attempts at framing disciplines, legal definitions of public and private, personal precarity and creative waste. In the flickering and static of the moments of interference generated in these processes, in their lapses and their silence, the human body reveals itself as a place of conflict – it is precisely these moments of exposing-oneself, which artists work on and with. In the process, they do not remain constrained to the level of communication with others on stage or exchange with the audience. Instead, they reject in their artistic approaches the concept of the body as a passive refuge of subjectivity and utilize their bodies as material to participate in the discussion on the social re-negotiation of the conditions and conditionality of human behavior and actions. As directly self-manifesting action rather than agents of communication, they are resistance and simultaneously a venture into defining that what is missing in life today, what is censored, the existing or strived towards premises of life. In these moments, a gulf opens up between the vulnerability and the cultural, economic, ethical or also physical restrictions of the body as carrier of control mechanisms and standardization, of dreams and desires; they overlap and trace the quiet, more brittle borderlines of community beyond the accredited selectivity of our life together. It is precisely in the heterogeneity of its aesthetic forms that performance art can formulate its potential to liberate itself from the constrictions of its traditions and update its topics and motifs in alternate spaces, which are always also social spaces. The in-between spaces and their call for social responsibility open up the body in the constitution of presence not only in regard to the past, but also towards the future. Like a texture, stretched between the regulative and the permeable, art and artists are now more than ever presented with the challenge of affectively dealing with and reacting to the described overall processes of change, of organizing the coexistence of multiple and heterogeneous voices and influences and integrating the 'Outer', the 'Other', the 'Unknown' as possibilities in their work and of finding a place for the dancing body in this shifting environment. In doing so, the bodies present themselves as contemporaries that emphasize their own involvement. They cannot be separated from the life, culture, society that they are constantly reflecting and examining; they are the artistic and personal

---

or the presentation of the *Collection in Motion* at the Museum of Contemporary Art in Zagreb. Choreographers such as Krõõt Juurak (i.e. *Autodomestication*, 2009) or Petra Zanki and Tea Tupajić (*The Curators' Piece,* ongoing) directly refer to the relationship of markets, institutions and artistic production in their work.

negotiations of self-made and foreign experiences. Beyond daydreams and promises, they facilitate encounters in the speechlessness of a communication society that is continuously in the process of differentiation. These bodies make meetings possible that do not exclude emotions, limitations and injuries, but instead integrate the experience of instability and vulnerability and are thus more than a stylization of the everyday. Without negating the experiences of the past or the temptations of the present, they integrate something upcoming in their perspectives.

I am therefore less interested in the shimmering and yet substantially often meaningless phenomenon of the contemporary (and in the knowledge that, strictly speaking, dance only exists as contemporary, cf. Pouillaude 2009), than in moments of transition, in which the paradoxes and inner contradictions of art become visible. For the art of dance and performance, this raises the question of fundamental historical significance for the art form concerning its potential for transcending boundaries: not as a one-dimensional path from the institution into social reality, but as a steady interplay between formalization and its socio-political reappraisal, between everyday experience and aesthetic appearance, between affective immediacy and its distancing discourse.[5] Because choreographic work, for example, functions both as an installation as well as live performance and the formats of presentation and reception mutually influence each other, artists pursue these moments of transition in their artistic research and production and in doing so, also explore implicit ideas of the mobile and mobilization[6] (cf. Noeth 2010). These discursive as well as artistic-practical movements also form the basis for a much-needed new definition of the place of dramaturgy in the context of choreographic-performative processes.

---

5   "I believe that the feelings produced by books are equal to the ideas that they generate. Actually, I don't know how to distinguish between feelings and thoughts. They are made of the same substance", writes Gregg Bordowitz. In the performance-opera *The History of Sexuality Volume One by Michel Foucault: An Opera, 2010* (Premiere October 1, 2010, Tanzquartier Wien), he examined with Paul Chan the epochal theory of Michel Foucault and its inquiry into the mechanisms of ideas and their habitualization, embodiment and transformation into discourse.

6   The moment of transition described here was the subject of the coordinated performance and exhibition project *Push and Pull* by Tanzquartier Wien and MUMOK (October 2010), in collaboration with TATE Modern, London, curated by Barbara Clausen, Achim Hochdörfer, Walter Heun and Sandra Noeth.

WE ALWAYS FALL IN LOVE WITH WORLDS ...

Over the last few years, various events and publications have dealt with the topic of dramaturgy in dance.[7] We are faced with the need to reexamine a practice that originally developed out of theater and drama. In this tradition, dramaturgy functions as a place in which to structure and organize physical as well as intellectual movements in a largely closed, autopoietic construct that constitutes itself in relationship to elements such as time, space, rhythm, movement vocabulary and phrasing, figures and narration or the relationship of music and movement. As an instrument of contexualization and framing, it is usually related to a specific role in the working process designated as a putative 'first viewer' or 'objective observer'. This idea of the dramaturgical as separate from choreographic and discursive processes has been toppled not least of all by a confident and self-reflexive community of dance and performance artists. Both in reaction to and as a consequence of a world 'in search of', they have created room for collaboration in self-organized artistic processes of research and exchange and appropriated spaces that have emerged between definition of roles, division of labor and economic processes of distribution (cf. Ruhsam 2010). I would like to mention as an example the Zagreb based artist collective BADco., who constantly challenge and redefine the function and responsibilities of their members depending on the ongoing projects and issues (cf. BADco.hr); or the method of re-formulation, which the artistwin deufert+plischke use to provide space for different artistic and discursive perspectives and strategies in the development of their work in form of various differentiated principles of imparting material and writing (cf. Deufert/Noeth/Plischke 2009).

As a consequence, even methodological considerations concerning the dramaturgical require adequate further development, which takes into account new perspectives: how can this 'being-with-an-Other' be organized, the relationship to the foreign, the 'Outside' be defined in the artistic process, how can the unexpected, mistakes, dilettantism, or to formulate it more generally, that which evades control, attention, the institution, be grasped as a specific form of knowledge? And how can dance, the body be defined as a space for negotiation

---

7   Cf. i.e. *Performance Research: On Dramaturgy*, Volume 4, Number 3, September 2009 or *Maska: The Dramaturgy of Dance* Number 66-67, 2001. See also the theoretical-artistic conferences Europäische Dramaturgie im 21. Jahrhundert (European Dramaturgy in the 21st Century), 26.-30.09.2007 in Frankfurt am Main or the SDHS Conference Dance Dramaturgy, 23.-26.06.2011 in Toronto.

and as potential[8], which opens itself to the upcoming (cf. Pouillaude 2009: 23)? In this interaction, this texture of mutual, almost non-identifiable, because simultaneous influences, and traces and logics, between crisscrossing, over-lapping, opposing and transforming concepts, ideas and areas of research, it seems helpful to think about dramaturgy not primarily as a form-giving instru-ment, but rather as a shared practice of encounter. The question of how commu-nity is created and whether we can still today say 'we' alongside the 'I' (cf. Pee-ters 2007) is, from this perspective, one of the fundamental questions of dramaturgy; the measuring of the distance to each respective 'Other', which does not remain limited to the relationship of actors and audience and the investigati-on of the protocol of encounters in which artistic, discursive, social worlds are created, according to their central functions. It is about the way that simultaneity is handled e.g. the simultaneity of corporeal, political, ethical and other movements, which develop and negotiate narratives and metaphors of how community is created, how we think about affiliation and preservation, about the old and the new, about classification and availability, about hospitality and territory. Performance art and the parties involved create resonance chambers that are influenced, structured and impregnated by developments. In this regard, they contain and produce complexities and relationships to history, memory, so-ciety on various levels and in different ways – in relation to our bodies, our movements and language. Dramaturgy is exactly the place within a choreo-graphic process that is dedicated to this very nexus of things.

Dramaturgy: Organizing Coexistence

In the course of the described broadening of the definition of choreography, dramaturgy has increasingly given less priority to questions of structure, form or aesthetic. It means more than just binding together the separate elements. And its primary goal cannot be to achieve consensus. Instead it is more about tracing the balance and equilibrium of the individual elements (body, movements, lights, sound, space, etc.), the responsibility of all parties involved, the shifts and changes created in their relationships. Accordingly there is the attempt to think about choreography not necessarily as the creation of a repertory in the sense of a fixed movement or a structured sequence of movements, but as the unknown, the vague, the not-yet-attained, misunderstandings, the monstrosity of all artistic

---

8   Cf. Alain Badiou: "La danse n'est pas un art parce qu'elle est le signe de la possibilité de l'art, telle qu'inscrite au corps" (as cited in Pouillaude 2009: 22).

work, the simultaneity of creating and losing common ground, integrating an shared frame of reference.

In the weaving of the dramaturgical protocol, the focus lies not on the identification of authorship, chronologies or a succession of scenes, images, phrases and ideas, not on the creation of an imitable scheme or the production of a certain form; it is also not primarily about 'right' or 'wrong' and the prevention of mistakes in the process of work and representation. On the contrary, in each process the question arises anew, how the different formative elements are to be handled. Even if they repeat themselves in the artistic process and as a result imply the possibility of defining an identifiable and repeatable corpus, they do not necessarily also permit the definition of more fundamentally valid categories or concepts: they take place in never-ending steps of formulating and reformulating language and movement and generating a choreography of ideas that are the product of being together. In a large number of contemporary artistic productions, form, contents and idea of movement are interconnected, as are likewise various working phases and the tasks involved. The intertwining and the combinatory nature of research, conception, training, production and dissemination in a performance not only has an effect on the shifting positions and demands that artists themselves have to manage, but also reduce the need for a distinction of choreographic discourse from choreographic practice. A dramaturge's material is hence unstable, because he or she is constantly redefining his or her point of departure anew. And it is precisely this moment of insecurity, which sets the body, the voices in motion over and over again. Of course, this is not about formulating a hasty metaphor or images, no false promises of flexibility and hybridity. Instead, I seek to define a dramaturgical mode of thought, which does not focus on efficiency, imitation or well-conducted research. A dramaturgy without a fixed a priori, composed of observations in a constantly transforming texture, within and out of which specifications and decisions must be made; a dramaturgy in which failure is an immanent component and which prevents hasty indulgence in one's own assumptions, preferences and aversions.

To work and think dramaturgically thus covers more than the job description of a single person. It means opening up a divided, usually temporary space of negotiation and the creation and reflection of the evolving act of tracking the diverse traces of what is emerging. It does not mean not making decisions. It is much rather about the shouldering of responsibility with respect to the politics of decision-making. This study affects not only formal definitions and instructions on the level of movement creation, but also questions of proximity and distance, of recognition and responsibility and continues the gesture of inscribing the social. This concept of dramaturgy maintains a strong relationship to the outside. More than the fixing of movement of the development of a specific aesthetic, dramaturgy writes a protocol of encounters, which develop in the shared period of time, in the contributed vocabulary of the situation. Dramaturgy means thinking about these traces of delegating and sharing, about how information is generated, produced, communicated, rejected, reapplied and finally brought onto the stage – in this respect, it is not about communication and not about the representation of a prefabricated status, but about the contemplation of strategies and processes of community and participation.

Dramaturgy is concerned with the emerging and the moment of emergence, with the fluctuation and not the cementing of positions and perspectives, with the clarification of intentions and the formulation of questions and also means to draw closer to each other in this process and in terms of an emancipated friendship, to become vulnerable, but also tangible. Dramaturgy enters another, shared body, organizes processes between intentionality and non-intentionality, between contradicting movements, bodies and relationships. The associated processes and changes of perspective are thus still connected to observation, even when they abandon the position of an accredited 'objective' observer. We are looking here at a practical concept of responsibility for one's own work, but also for the interaction of all participating elements and the temporary community – for a protocol of human and artistic encounters. The dramaturgical accordingly concerns all areas of artistic work and is not located in an outside sphere, mainly occupied with creating contexts and applying knowledge (cf. Peeters 2007).

The relationship between dramaturgy and choreography is friendly one. Dramaturgy is not aimed at suppressing choreography or forcing it into a specific dance-technical or aesthetic or virtuous form. As a consequence, dramaturgy does not "belong" to anyone. It is a monster – phantasmal, an analysis that in its survey of the conditions and conditionality of encounters accepts and addresses the instability and vulnerability of life as given. As an instrument of perspective, the focus lies not on a specific form, but on the question how decisions are felled, how communication is created, as well as the related experiences of manipulation and imitation, of representation and participation. Dramaturgy traces the permeability of the choreographic process in its various forms and articulations and in this very process of revealing the artistic and social strategies of worldmaking, enables a dialog between artists, the audience and an Outside. A concept of the dramaturgical oriented along such lines and the protocols of encounters can reveal the potential of the choreographic to place the body, the dance as active agents in personal and social conflict zones.

REFERENCES

Deufert, Kattrin/Noeth, Sandra/Plischke, Thomas (2009): MONSTRUM. A book on reportable portraits, Norderstedt: Books on Demand.

Husemann, Pirkko/Wagner, Anna (2011): Schlechte Angewohnheiten – Context #8 (= festival programme), Berlin: Hebbel am Ufer.

Maalouf, Amin (2009): Le dérèglement du monde, Paris: Grasset.

Maska: The Dramaturgy of Dance, Number 66-67, Ljubljana: Maska.

Noeth, Sandra (2010): "Dramaturgy. Mobile of ideas", in: Walter Heun/ Krassimira Kruschkova/Sandra Noeth/Martin Obermayr (eds.): SCORES#0. The skin of movement, Wien: Tanzquartier Wien, pp. 36-47.

Peeters, Jeroen (2007): "Living together on stage", in: Christiane Kühl/Florian Malzacher/Andreas R. Peternell (eds.), Herbst: Theorie zur Praxis, Graz: steirischer herbst, pp. 20-23.

Performance Research: On Dramaturgy, Volume 4, Number 3, September 2009, London: Routledge.

Pouillaude, Frédéric (2009): Le désoeuvrement chorégraphique. Etude sur la notion d'œuvre en danse, Paris: VRIN.

Ruhsam, Martina (2010): Kollaborative Praxis: Choreographie, Vienna/Berlin: Turia + Kant.

Notes on Contributors

BEVILACQUA, FRÉDÉRIC
Researcher and coordinator of the Real-Time Musical Interactions Team at IR-CAM (Institute for Music/Acoustic Research and Coordination), Paris. Master in Physics and PhD in Biomedical Optics from the Swiss Federal Institute of Technology in Lausanne. Main areas of research: gesture analysis and gesture-sound interactions. He collaborated with various composers and choreographers, including Myriam Gourfink, Emio Greco | PC and Richard Siegal. Recent publications: *Continuous Realtime Gesture Following and Recognition* (2010, with B. Zamborlin et al., in: *Embodied Communication and Human-Computer Interaction*), *Online Gesture Analysis and Control of Audio Processing* (2011, with N. Schnell et al., in: *Musical Robots and Interactive Multimodal Systems*), *Modular Musical Objects Towards Embodied Control Of Digital Music* (2011, with N. Rasaminmanana et al., in: *Modular Mudical Objects Towards Embodied Control of Digital Music*).
See: http://imtr.ircam.fr

BRANDSTETTER, GABRIELE
Professor for Theater and Dance Studies at the Free University of Berlin. Main areas of research: history and aesthetics of dance and theater, modern advantgarde, contemporary theatre, dance and performance. Recent book publications: *Bild-Sprung. TanzTheaterBewegung im Wechsel der Medien* (*Image-Leap. DanceTheaterMovements in Changing Media*) (2005), *Improvisieren. Paradoxien des Unvorhersehbaren. Kunst – Medien – Praxis* (*Improvisation. Paradoxes of the Unforeseeable. Art – Media – Practice*) (2010, ed. with H.-F. Bormann, A. Matzke), *Notationen und choreographisches Denken* (*Notation and Choreographic Thinking*) (2010, ed. with F. Hofmann, K. Maar), *Theater ohne Fluchtpunkt. Das Erbe Adolphe Appias: Szenographie und Choreographie im zeitgenössischen Theater* (*Theater without Vanishing Points. The Legacy of Adolphe

Appia: Scenography and Choreography in Contemporary Theater) (2010, ed. with B. Wiens).
See: http://www.geisteswissenschaften.fu-berlin.de

DIERS, MICHAEL
Professor for Art History at the University of Fine Arts Hamburg and Extraordinary Professor for Art History at the Humboldt University of Berlin. Main areas of research: renaissance art, modern art, 20th century and contemporary art, photography and new media, political iconography, art and media theory, history of science. Longstanding editor of the paperback series *kunststück*; co-editor of the *Collected Writings of Aby Warburg*. Recent book publications: *Fotografie, Film, Video. Beiträge zu einer kritischen Theorie des Bildes (Photography, Film, Video. On a Critical Theory of the Image)* (2006), *Werkstatt und Wissensform (Workshop and Form of Knowledge)* (2010, ed. with M. Wagner).
See: http://www.hfbk-hamburg.de and http://www.kunstgeschichte.hu-berlin.de

FDILI ALAOUI, SARAH
Master in Engineering and Applied Mathematics; training in contemporary and classical dance. She currently works on her PhD on advanced models for human-computer interaction, co-directed by Christian Jacquemin (LIMSI-CNRS) and Frédéric Bevilacqua (IRCAM). Recent publications: *Gestural Audiotory and Visual Interactive Platform* (2011, with B. Caramiaux et al.), *From Dance to Touch: Movement Qualities for Interaction Design* (2011, with B. Caramiaux and M. Serrano), *Dance Interaction with Physical Model Visualization Based on Movement Qualities* (2011, with F. Bevilacqua et al.).
See: http://sarah.alaoui.free.fr

FOSTER, SUSAN LEIGH
Distinguished Professor at the Department of World Arts and Cultures at the University of California, Los Angeles (UCLA) and choreographer. Main areas of research: history and theory of choreography, gender studies, postcolonial studies, history of theory. Recent book publications: *Dances that Describe Themselves* (2003), *Worlding Dance* (2008), *Choreographing Empathy* (2010).
See: http://www.wac.ucla.edu

GEHM, SABINE
Master in Cultural Studies from Hildesheim University. Dramaturge, independent curator and cultural manager, e.g.: Kampnagel Hamburg (1994-2001), international network for performing arts *Junge Hunde* (2001-2005), *Veronika*

Blumstein – Moving Exiles (2006), *Moving Heads* (2007), International Festival TANZ Bremen (since 2004). Director of the Dance Congress 2006 in Berlin and 2009 in Hamburg; she is currently preparing the Congress in 2013 (with K. von Wilcke). Book publication: *Knowledge in Motion* (2007, ed. with P. Husemann, K. v. Wilcke).
See: http://www.tanzkongress.de

GINTERSDORFER, MONIKA
Studied German Philology and Theater, Film and Television in Cologne and theater directing in Hamburg. From 2000-2004, she worked as a director for the Schauspielhaus Hamburg, Münchner Kammerspiele and Salzburger Festspiele. In 2005, she began collaborating with Knut Klaßen and a German-African team of performers at the Volksbühne im Prater Berlin, Kampnagel Hamburg, FFT Düsseldorf, sophiensaele Berlin, Theater Aachen, Schauspielhaus Köln, Ringlokschuppen Mülheim and Deutsches Theater Berlin. Selected pieces: *Othello, c'est qui* (2008), *Logobi 01-04* (2009), *Betrügen* (2009), *Très très fort* and *Macbeth – très très fort* (2009). Theater festival *Abidjan Mouvement* (2009).
See: http://www.gintersdorferklassen.org

HICKETHIER, KNUT
Professor emeritus for Media Studies at the University of Hamburg. First executive Director of the Research Center for Media and Communication at the University Hamburg. Main areas of research: media theory, media history and analysis, theory and history of television and history and theory of film. Recent book publications: *Die schönen und die nützlichen Künste. Literatur, Technik und Medien seit der Aufklärung* (*The Fine and the Useful Arts. Literature, Technology and Media since the Enlightenment*) (2007, 4. ext. edition, ed. with K. Schumann), *Film- und Fernsehanalyse* (*Film and Television Analysis*) (2010, 4. ext. edition), *Einführung in die Medienwissenschaft* (*Introduction to Media Theory*) (2010, 2nd edition).
See: http://www.slm.uni-hamburg.de

KLEIN, GABRIELE
Professor for Sociology of Movement and Dance at the University of Hamburg and Director of Performance Studies/Hamburg. Main areas of research: contemporary dance and choreography, social choreography, transnationalisation of dance cultures, popular cultures. Recent book publications: *Stadt-Szenen. Künstlerische Produktionen und theoretische Positionen* (*City-Scenes. Artistic Productions and Theoretical Positions*) (2005), *Performance* (2005, with W. Sting),

Methoden der Tanzwissenschaft (*Methods of Dance Studies*) (2007, with G. Brandstetter), *Tango in Translation* (2009).
See: http://www.performance.uni-hamburg.de and http://www1.uni-hamburg.de/gklein

KUNST, BOJANA

PhD in Philosophy from Ljubljana University and dramaturge. Currently DAAD-Visiting Professor at the University of Hamburg, Department for Human Movement *Studies*/Performance Studies. Main areas of research: performance theory, body theory. Book publications: *Impossible Body* (1999), *Dangerous Connections: Body, Philosophy and Relation to the Artificial* (2004) *Processes of Work and Collaboration in Contemporary Performance* (2010).
See: http://kunstbody.wordpress.com

LIGNA

Performance group, founded in Hamburg in 1997 by Ole Frahm, Michael Hüners and Torsten Michaelsen. The group develops pieces which establish new spaces of action, enable unlikely, collective movements and reinvent the role of the audience. With their models of performative radio use, such as the radio ballet, they intervene in the public sphere and question its norms and controls. Selected works: *Radioballett* (*Radio Ballet*) (2002/03), *Übung in unnötigem Aufenthalt* (*Exercise in Unnecessary Residency*) (2009), *Der neue Mensch* (*The New Human*) (2009), *Ödipus, der Tyrann* (*Oedipus, the Tyrant*) (2011). Their works were shown a.o. in Europe, Beirut, Buenos Aires, São Paulo, Shanghai.
See: http://ligna.blogspot.com

MARTIN, RANDY

Professor and Chair of Art and Public Policy and Director of the graduate program in Arts Politics at the Tisch School of the Arts, New York University. Recent book publications: *A Public Voice for the Arts* (2006, with M. Schmidt Campbell), *An Empire of Indifference: American War and the Financial Logic of Risk Management* (2007), *The Returns of Alwin Nikolais: Bodies, Boundaries, and the Dance Canon* (2007, with C. Gitelman), *Under New Management: Universities, Administrative Labor and the Professional Turn* (2011).
See: http://admin.tisch.nyu.edu

NOETH, SANDRA

Head of Dramaturgy and Research at the Tanzquartier Wien. Studied Cultural, Art and Dance Studies at Université Paris 8 – Seine Saint-Denis, LMU München/Theaterakademie München and University of Bremen. From 2006-2009, she was research assistant at the Department for Human Movement Studies/Performance Studies at the University of Hamburg. Recent publications: *MONSTRUM. A Book on Reportable Portraits* (2009, with K. Deufert, Th. Plischke), *Hospitality is Not Equal. Über Choreographie als gastfreundschaftlichen Raum* (*Hospitality is Not Equal. On Choreography as a Space of Hospitality*) (2009, in: *Zwischenspiele*, ed. by S. Tigges et al.), *Dramaturgy, Mobile of Ideas* (2010, in: *SCORES #0: The Skin of Movement*, ed. by Tanzquartier Wien). See: http://www.tqw.at

REIN, ANETTE

PhD in Ethnology, 2000-2008 Director of the Museum of World Cultures in Frankfurt am Main, since 2009 Lecturer and Assessor at e.g.: Reinwardt Academy Amsterdam, Universities of Frankfurt am Main, Bayreuth and Mainz. Main areas of research: the museum, (im)material cultures, anthropology of dance, ritual, gender, anthropology of the body, human rights and Indonesia. Recent publications: *Balinese Temple Dances and Ritual Transformation in the Process of Modernization* (2004, in: *The Dynamics of Changing Rituals*, ed. by J. Kreinath et al.), *One Object – Many Stories: The museum is no 'neutral' place* (2009, in: *MUSEUM AKTUELL*), *What is a museum – a collection of objects or a network of social relationships?* (2010, in: *MUSEUM AKTUELL*).

SCHNELL, NORBERT

Studied Telecommunications and Music in Graz, Austria, holds the degree *Diplom Ingenieur* of the Technical University and the University of Music and Dramatic Arts Graz and worked as studio assistant at the IEM (Institute of Electronic Music and Acoustics, Graz). He is currently researcher and developer at the Real-Time Musical Interactions Team at IRCAM focussing on real-time digital audio processing techniques for interactive music applications and on his dissertation on the development of novel interactive music media. Main areas of research in artistic research projects at IRCAM: sound simulation, music making, and music pedagogy. Recent publications: *MuBu & Friends – Assembling Tools for Content Based Real-Time Interactive Audio Processing in Max/MSP* (2009, with A. Röbel et al., in: *International Computer Music Conference*), *First Steps in Relaxed Real-Time Typo-Morphological Audio Analysis/Synthesis* (2010, with M. A. Suárez Cifuentes, J.-P. Lambert, in: *Sound and Music Compu-*

ting), *Study on Gesture-Sound Similarity* (2010, with B. Caramiaux, F. Bevilacqua, in: *Music and Gesture*).
See: http://imtr.ircam.fr

SHAW, NORAH ZUNIGA
Associate Professor at Ohio State University Department of Dance. Since 2004 Director for Dance & Technology at the ACCAD (Advanced Computing Center for the Arts and Design). Main areas of work: choreographic knowledge as a locus for interdisciplinary and intercultural creativity. *Synchronous Objects*, her most recent collaborative project with choreographer William Forsythe and animator Maria Palazzi, was launched online (Synchronousobjects.osu.edu). She is currently working on a book about *Synchronous Objects* and a project with Brazilian choreographer Bruno Beltrão funded by The Forsythe Company's *Motion Bank* initiative.
See: http://dance.osu.edu

SÖRGEL, SABINE
Lecturer in Drama, Theatre and Performance at the Department of Drama, Theatre and Performance, Aberystwyth University, Wales. PhD in Performance and Media Studies. Main areas of research: postcolonial theory, cross-cultural corporeality and identity construction in contemporary theatre and dance performance. Recent book publication: *Dancing Postcolonialism – The National Dance Theatre Company of Jamaica* (2007).
See: http://www.aber.ac.uk

TOWNSEND, JULIE
Associate Professor at Interdisciplinary Humanities in the Johnston Center for Integrated Studies at the University of Redlands in California, PhD in Comparative Literature. Recent publications: *Staking Salomé: the Literary Forefathers and Choreographic Daughters of Wilde's "hysterical and perverted creature"* (2008, in: *Oscar Wilde and Modern Culture: The Making of a Legend*, ed. by J. Bristow), *Tenuous Arrangements: The Ethics of Rape in Disgrace* (2009, with K. Middleton, in: *Saving Disgrace*), *The Choreography of Modernism in France: La Danseuse, 1830-1930* (2010).
See: http://www.redlands.edu

TURK, STEPHEN
Associate Professor at the Knowlton School of Architecture at Ohio State University. Main areas of research: representation and the instrumental nature of technology, film and postmodern theory, interactive networked environments, performance arts, computer aided fabrication, and furniture design. He is a licensed architect practicing in Ohio. His projects and writings have been published in national and international journals including *Global Architecture, Performance Research, ID Magazine*, and the *Journal of Architectural Education*. Recent publication: *Tabling Ecologies and Furnishing Performance* (2009, in: *Design Ecologies*, ed. by L. Tilder and B. Blostein).
See: http://knowlton.osu.edu

VON WILCKE, KATHARINA
Master in German Philology with a focus on theater and media and Spanish at the University of Hamburg. Manager for individual artistic projects, e.g.: International Summer Theater Festival Hamburg (1985-94), Theater of the World in Dresden (1996), Theater Festival *Junge Hunde* (1997), International Theater Academy Ruhr (1999), German Dance Platform 2000, 5. Festival *Politik im Freien Theater* in Hamburg (2002), *ErsatzStadt* at the Volksbühne am Rosa-Luxemburg-Platz (2003/2004), *HEIMSPIEL* 2011. Director of the Dance Congress 2006 in Berlin and 2009 in Hamburg; she is currently preparing the Congress in 2013 (with S. Gehm). Book publication: *Knowledge in Motion* (2007, ed. with S. Gehm, P. Husemann).
See: http://www.tanzkongress.de

ZIEMER, GESA
Professor for Cultural Theory and Cultural Practice at the HafenCity University Hamburg. Main areas of research: artistic urban research, complicity as a collective form of interaction. Recent publications: *Paradox Festival. Ereignis oder Event? (Paradox Festival. Happening or Event?)* (2010, in: *Kreativität trifft Stadt. Zum Verhältnis von Kunst, Kultur und Stadtentwicklung*, ed. by IBA Hamburg) (*Creativity meets City. On the Relationship of Art, Culture and Urban Development*), *Mit wem arbeiten? Von der Partizipation der Zuschauenden zur Produktion von Publikum (Who do we work with? From Participation of the Viewer to Production of Audience)* (2011, in: *artcollector [3]*).
See: http://www.gesa-ziemer.ch